MW00723742

American Legal Institutions
Recent Scholarship

Edited by Eric Rise

A Series from LFB Scholarly

Law Clerks, Support Personnel, and the Decline of Consensual Norms on the United States Supreme Court, 1935-1995

Bradley J. Best

LFB Scholarly Publishing LLC
New York 2002

KF8742
.B473
2002

Copyright © 2002 by LFB Scholarly Publishing LLC

All rights reserved.

Library of Congress Cataloging-in-Publication Data

Best, Bradley J., 1968-
  Law clerks, support personnel, and the decline of consensual norms on
the United States Supreme Court, 1935-1995 / Bradley J. Best.
      p. cm. -- (American legal institutions)
   ISBN 1-931202-35-4 (alk. paper)
   1. United States. Supreme Court--Officials and employees--History. 2.
Judicial opinions--United States--History. 3. Law clerks--United
States--History. 4. Judicial process--United States--History. I.
Title. II. Series.
   KF8742 .B473 2002
   347.73'2636--dc21
                                        2002010424

ISBN 1-931202-35-4

Printed on acid-free 250-year-life paper.

Manufactured in the United States of America.

Contents

Tables

Illustrations

Acknowledgments

I thank Professors Laura Arnold, Jnan Battacharyya, Thomas Castellano, and David Kimball of Southern Illinois University at Carbondale. Each offered invaluable guidance and proposed numerous substantive changes to the initial drafts of this book.

I am especially indebted to Professor Albert P. Melone of Southern Illinois University at Carbondale. My accomplishments in academic life are each traceable to his role in my professional development. Professor Melone's wise counsel continues to make my life as an academic immeasurably satisfying.

I thank Leo Balk of LFB Scholarly, Inc. During the preparation of this book he accorded me courtesies and deference ordinarily reserved for writers of much greater accomplishment. I deeply appreciate his willingness to include my book in this wonderful series. I am equally grateful to Professor Eric Rise of the University of Delaware for his thoughtful review of the original manuscript. Professor Rise's endorsement is to me an honor of unmatched importance.

I wish to express my profound appreciation for the support provided by many friends and colleagues at Austin Peay State University. Also, I thank the faculty and staff of the Vanderbilt University libraries for allowing me unlimited access to their collections. The mere proximity of this world-class institution civilizes all that I do as a professor.

I wish to thank my wife, Lisa Kesting Best for her boundless good cheer during the preparation of this book. That we share equally in one another's successes has doubled the rewards of this endeavor. Also, I thank my brother, Thomas M. Best, for lending me the wisdom of an experienced educator and the unconditional support that only a good friend can provide.

Last, I thank my parents, Ronald and Jennie Best. I owe to them debts too numerous to mention. To list the kindnesses and accommodations each has afforded me would be, in and of itself, a life's work. The rewards of this project belong as much to them as anyone.

The merits of this book reflect the contributions of these and many other persons. The failures, errors, and shortcomings of this book are, however, my sole responsibility.

CHAPTER 1

Toward a New Theory of the Decline in Consensual Norms on the United States Supreme Court: Institutional Analysis, Small Groups, and Law Clerks

Introduction

In their recent study of dissent behavior in judicial organizations, Scott D. Gerber and Keeok Park argue that the institutional context unique to the United States Supreme Court is closely linked to the large number of nonconsensual opinions authored by the justices in each term.[1] Professors Gerber and Park find that when moving to the U.S. Supreme Court from one of the Circuit Courts of Appeal, justices author increasing numbers of dissenting and concurring opinions. Furthermore, the authors encourage scholars to adopt "neo-institutional" approaches to studies of nonconsensual opinion writing - approaches which integrate in one model the importance of organizational structures and competing explanations of judicial behavior. Interestingly, however, Professors Gerber and Park make no claims about which features of the Court institution may be related to the high frequency of nonconsensual opinion writing. The authors simply argue for the importance of institutional constraints as factors influencing the opinion writing behavior of individual judges and justices.

---

[1]Scott D. Gerber and Keeok Park, "The Quixotic Search for Consensus on the U.S. Supreme Court: A Cross-Judicial Empirical Analysis of the Rehnquist Court Justices," *American Political Science Review* 91 (1997): 390.

Gerber and Park are not unique in their belief that the Court's institutional context is related to patterns of disagreement among justices. Several scholars suggest, but leave untested, an interesting proposition about the structure of the Court organization and patterns of nonconsensual opinion writing. These authors assert that increasing numbers of law clerks on the Court are linked to patterns of nonconsensual opinion writing.[2] Similarly, studies of "small group" behavior on the Court suggest a connection between the opinion writing practices and patterns of interaction among law clerks, support staff, and justices. Further, anecdotal accounts of law clerk behavior on the Court point to an increasingly autonomous and influential law clerk institution, one intimately connected to the production of written opinions.[3] Moreover, at the intersection of studies of dissensus in judicial institutions, studies which depict the Court as a "small group," historical accounts of law clerk behavior on the Court, and scholarly suggestions that institutional processes shape the behavior of individual political actors, I locate the general proposition that increases in the numbers of law clerks and support personnel employed by the Supreme Court are related to historical increases in the frequency of nonconsensual opinion writing.

The New Institutionalism in Public Law Research: Identifying Constraints on Individual Behavior

In the 1950s and 1960s, the methodological individualism that dominated explanations of electoral behavior informed nearly all research questions in the public law field. The watershed studies of Berelson, Lazarsfeld, and McPhee in 1954, and Campbell, Converse, Miller, and Stokes in 1960,

---

[2]For example, see Richard Posner, *The Federal Courts: Challenge and Reform* (Cambridge: Harvard University Press, 1996), p. 357; David M. O'Brien, *Storm Center: The Supreme Court in American Politics* (New York: W.W. Norton Company, 1996), p. 328.

[3]Edward Lazarus, *Closed Chambers: The First Eyewitness Account of the Epic Struggles Inside the Supreme Court* (New York: Times Books, 1998).

confirmed that studies of individual level political behavior would be of central importance to the discipline's research enterprise.[4] Noteworthy explanations of judicial voting behavior presented by Professor's Sidney Ulmer, Harold Spaeth, and Glendon Schubert fulfilled C. Hermann Pritchett's wish that public law scholars use quantitative techniques to explain the voting behavior of individual justices and "let a hundred flowers bloom."[5]

Since that time, the public law field has focused on reductionist models of judicial behavior. From Professor Pritchett's classic study *The Roosevelt Court* to Jeffrey Segal and Harold Spaeth's *The Supreme Court and the Attitudinal Model*, judicial behavior specialists have devoted considerable attention to explaining the voting behavior of individual judges and justices.[6] These studies generally depict judicial behavior as epiphenomena of various micro-level processes. Specifically, these studies explain the behavior of collegial courts as aggregations of individual policy preferences. Parsimonious and strikingly successful at explaining judicial activity, this approach treats individual level values, attitudes, and ideological proclivities as the most useful means of accounting for the behavior of judicial organizations. Most important, the reductionist bias of the last several decades generally ignores the role of institutions as factors that shape individual behavior.

Despite the methodological individualism that defines most political behavior research published in the last several decades, several scholars maintained a focus on institutional processes as factors shaping individual and collective behavior. In 1967, with most public law specialists at a full

---

[4]Bernard R. Berelson, Paul F. Lazarsfeld, and William N. McPhee, *Voting* (Chicago: University of Chicago Press, 1954); Campbell, et al. *The American Voter* (New York: Wiley, 1960).

[5]C. Hermann Pritchett, "The Development of Judicial Research" in *Frontiers of Judicial Research.* ed. Joel B. Grossman and Joseph Tanenhaus. (New York: John Wiley and Sons, Inc., 1969), pp. 27-42.

[6]C. Hermann Pritchett, *The Roosevelt Court* (New York: MacMillan Publishers, 1948); Jeffery A. Segal and Harold J. Spaeth, *The Supreme Court and the Attitudinal Model* (New York: Cambridge University Press, 1993).

reductionist bent, Eugene Rostow counseled that scholars view judicial behavior as a set of multi-causal phenomena. Professor Rostow suggested that the most successful attempts to model judicial decision making would be those that viewed law "in a matrix." He argued that "any attempt to confine it more narrowly would be misleading" and neglectful of ". . . all of the forces which press upon it and demand its arbitraments."[7] What Professor Rostow counseled was that public law scholars not be seduced by the seemingly hegemonic influence of psychometric treatments of judicial decision making. Rather, he seems to suggest that in their efforts to explain the substance of judicial decisions, public law scholars should adopt inclusive models, remembering that institutional and structural features of the legal system necessarily inform the behavior of judges and justices. As Professor Rostow prescribed, the public law research bibliography came to increasingly reflect the importance of institutions as key exogenous variables in models of judicial behavior.

In the following year, Samuel Huntington's important work *Political Order in Changing Societies* provided the theoretical underpinnings for future studies of institutionalization processes in judicial organizations.[8] Huntington's contributions are evident in comparative and single-nation studies of judicial institutions such as Schubert and Danelski's cross-national examination of judicial behavior. Schubert and Danelski's research is, at least implicitly, a recognition of the need to examine how variation in institutional design impacts the form and substance of judicial decision making.[9] Although not aimed at judicial institutions, the theoretical constructs posited by Huntington fueled cross-national

---

[7]Eugene Rostow, "The Supreme Court as a Legal Institution," in *Perspectives on the Court*. ed. Max Freedman, William M. Beaney, and Eugene V. Rostow. (Evanston: Northwestern University Press, 1967), p. 57.

[8]Samuel Huntington, *Political Order in Changing Societies* (New Haven: Yale University Press, 1968).

[9]Glendon Schubert and David Danelski, ed. *Comparative Judicial Behavior: Cross-Cultural Studies in Political Decision-Making in the East and West* (New York: Oxfors University Press, 1969).

examinations of judicial organizations. Prominent research in this genre include Professor's Schmidhauser's comparative treatment of the processes of institutionalization in judiciaries and legislatures and Gadbois's evaluation of the degree of institutionalization in the Supreme Court of India.[10]

In the 1980s, several scholars looked closely at the role of institutional structures in shaping individual behavior. In a widely read article, James L. Gibson lamented what he regarded as the continued balkanization of the public law field, urging models of judicial behavior that integrated a broader range of variable types.[11] Gibson calls for an increased attention to the relationship between the behavior of individual actors and institutional features. Gibson's admonition is observed by those scholars conducting research of the type that came to be called "new institutional" or "neo-institutional" - studies which view policy outcomes as products of interactive process among institutional structures and individual motives.

In 1988, Rogers Smith presented what is perhaps the most cogent call for integrated models of judicial behavior. Professor Smith argues that if public law scholars intend to build a complete picture of judicial behavior, they must focus on the "interrelationships between human 'institutions' and 'structures' and the decisions and actions of political actors."[12] Professor Smith explains: "In these approaches to the study of politics,

---

[10]John R. Schmidhauser, "An Exploratory Analysis of the Institutionalization of Legislatures and Judiciaries," in *Legislatures in Comparative Perspective*. ed. Allan Kornberg. (New York: Oxford University Press, 1973); George H. Gadbois, "The Institutionalization of the Supreme Court of India," in *Comparative Judicial Systems: Challenging Frontiers in Conceptual and Empirical Analysis*. ed. John R. Schmidhauser. (London: Butterworths, 1987).

[11]James L. Gibson, "From Simplicity to Complexity: The Development of Theory in the Study of Judicial behavior," *Political Behavior* 5 (1983): 7-49.

[12]Rogers M. Smith, "Political Jurisprudence, the 'New Institutionalism,' and the Future of Public Law," *American Political Science Review* 82 (1988): 91.

institutions are expected to shape the interests, resources, and ultimately the conduct of political actors, such as judges. . . ."[13]

Although the commentaries of James Gibson and Rogers Smith have not triggered a displacement of the reductionist paradigm in public law research, the "new institutionalism" that has recurred in the political science discipline in the last two decades calls on the discipline's lengthy history of identifying institutions as important independent variables in models of political activity. James G. March and Johan P. Olsen's thoughts are instructive on this point: They state: "Historically, political theory has treated political institutions as determining, ordering, or modifying individual motives, and as acting autonomous in terms of institutional needs."[14] Not surprisingly, then, recent commentaries on the judicial behavior subfield encourage attention to what Peter Hall and C.R. Taylor cogently label the central question of institutional analysis: "How do institutions affect the behavior of individuals?"[15]

In the last two years, commentaries by scholars such as Howard Gillman and Lawrence Baum reaffirm that attention to the importance of institutions will characterize future efforts to identify causal factors in the judicial decision making process.[16] For example, Professor Baum argues that the current debate between economic and psychological explanations of judicial behavior signals the importance of institutional factors in structuring the psychologically driven behavior of judges and justices. Baum's prescriptions for future research include an admonition that public law scholars remain cognizant of the primacy of "institutional situations

---

[13]Ibid., p. 91.

[14] James G. March and Johan P. Olsen, "The New Institutionalism: Organizational in Political Life," *American Political Science Review* 78 (1984): 735.

[15]Peter A. Hall and C.R. Taylor, "Political Science and the Three New Institutionalisms," *Political Studies* 44 (1996): 939.

[16]Howard Gillman, "The New Institutionalism, Part I" *Law and the Courts* Winter (1996): 6-11; Lawrence Baum, *The Puzzle of Judicial Behavior* (Ann Harbor: University of Michigan Press, 1997), p. 134.

in the operative goal orientations of decision makers."[17]

It is important to note, however, that much of the "new" in the "new institutionalism" is passe to sociological theorists. Evidence of this is found in the thought of Herbert Simon and Phillip Selznick. Prior to the work of March and Olsen, Professors Simon and Selznick discussed the importance of "organization" in molding the behavior of individuals. Simon explains that "[o]rganization is important, first, because organizational environments provide much of the force that molds and develops personal qualities and habits."[18] As regards the executive in the public bureaucracy, Simon concludes that "[h]is behavior and its effect on others are functions of his organizational situation."[19] Selznick characterized an organization as "a dynamic conditioning field which effectively shapes the behavior of those who are attempting to remain at the helm."[20] Thus, the "new institutionalism" in the public law field is traceable to principles long-recognized outside the political science discipline.

It is also important that the "new institutionalism" in public law overlaps conceptually with rational choice theory of the type posited by William Riker. Professor Riker argues that rational choice approaches to political behavior must ". . . return to the study of institutions" wherein ". . . we must use the tools of rational choice theory to explore how institutional arrangements, themselves the products of past political choices, act as 'congealed tastes' that influence the kind of values that are

---

[17]Ibid.,, p. 134

[18]Herbert A. Simon, *Administrative Behavior: A Study of Decision Making Processes in Administrative Organization* (New York: The Free Press, 1957), p. xvi.

[19]Ibid., p. xvii

[20]Philip Selznick, *The TVA and the Grass Roots: A Study of Politics and Organizations* (Berkeley: University of California Press, 1949), p. 10.

'feasible and likely' outcomes of decision processes."[21] Moreover, it is important that institutions structure the range of behavioral options available to political actors.

Strategic models of judicial decision making represent the theoretical development most consistent with Professor Baum's admonition. Recent publications such as Epstein and Knight's *The Choices Justices Make* and Maltzman, Spriggs, and Wahlbeck's *Crafting Law on the Supreme Court* reflect that the public law discipline is increasingly focused on the role played by institutional characteristics in shaping case outcomes and opinion writing behaviors.[22] These studies uncover a large volume of evidence supporting the proposition that institutional and strategic variables are casually proximate to final votes on the merits and opinion writing activities. In a related study, Wahlbeck, Spriggs, and Maltzman find that institutional and strategic factors are significantly linked to individual justices' decision to draft dissents and concurrences.[23] Yet, judicial scholars are yet to fully address the question of how changes in institutional resources influence the occurrence of bargaining and accommodation behaviors, activities linked to the justices' decisions to draft individual opinions.

It seems almost axiomatic that resource availability is inextricably linked to the character of an institution. Following this, I submit that those resources which structure judicial institutions are causally prior to the performance of the organizations's principal duties. Moreover, the "new institutionalism" in public law research would dictate that

---

[21] William H. Riker, "Implications from the Disequalibrium of Majority Rule for the Study of Institutions," *American Political Science Review* 74 (1980): 444-5. Quoted in Smith, pp. 93-4.

[22] Lee Epstein and Jack Knight, *The Choices Justices Make* (Washington, D.C.: Congressional Quarterly, Inc., 1998).; Forrest Maltzman, James F. Spriggs, and Paul J. Wahlbeck, *Crafting Law on the Supreme Court: The Collegial Game* (Cambridge, UK: Cambridge University Press, 2000).

[23] Paul J. Wahlbeck, James F. Spriggs, and Forrest Maltzman, "The Politics of Dissents and Concurrences on the U.S. Supreme Court," *American Politics Quarterly* 27 (1999): 488.

institutional resources not only shape a judge or justice's decisions regarding the desired direction of a case outcome but also influence his rational calculations about how to best employ scarce resources in furtherance of desired policy. Assuming the correctness of Walter Murphy's argument that Supreme Court justices encounter a limited stock of resources with which to advance policy goals,[24] changes in resource availability alters the justices' calculus of how to most effectively employ those resources toward substantive policy outcomes. I conclude that the applicability of the "new institutionalism" as an approach to understanding the behavior of courts is predicated on empirical studies which link institutional resources to the decisions of individual judges and justices. Thus, examining linkages between resource availability and individual decisions in judicial institutions is an important means of testing the appropriateness of the "new institutionalism" as an approach to studies of judicial behavior.

Public law scholars' attention to the importance of institutional arrangements in structuring individual behavior are but one dimension of political scientists' recognition of institutions as exogenous variables. Sheldon Wolin, a prominent scholar in the field of political thought, considers the independent influence of institutional structures for individual behavior. Professor Wolin explains that "[w]hat is important for political theory is that these institutionalized practices play a fundamental role in ordering and directing human behavior and in determining the character of events."[25] Further, Nelson Polsby's discussion of institutionalization processes in the U.S. House of Representatives is among political science's most notable examples of

---

[24]Walter F. Murphy, *The Elements of Judicial Strategy* (Chicago: The University of Chicago Press, 1964), p. 199.

[25]Sheldon Wolin, *Politics and Vision* (Boston, Little, Brown Publishers, 1960).

institutional analysis.[26] Polsby examined previously untested criteria of institutionalization, adding substantially to the theoretical basis of institutional research. Most important, Polsby's discussion of "density" as a criteria of institutionalization signals the need to examine processes of institutionalization in judiciaries, particularly with regard to the causes and consequences of increasing support personnel and the routinization of case selection procedures.[27] Later studies by Shepsle and Weingast indicate the importance of institutional rules, norms, and behavioral expectations in shaping policy outcomes in legislative settings.[28]

Studies by Harrison Fox and Susan Webb Hammond and Robert Salisbury and Kenneth Shepsle are of particular importance, revealing that the increasing numbers of staff have profoundly changed the behavior of individual members of Congress.[29] Professors Salisbury and Shepsle find that historical increases in staff assistance are linked to members' ability to rely less on the expertise of colleagues and function as independent "enterprises" within the larger organization.[30]

I conclude that despite the discipline's focus during the last several decades on the connection between individual characteristics and behaviors, institutional analysis is common to the history of political

---

[26]Nelson Polsby, "The Institutionalization of the U.S. House of Representatives," in *Congress: Structure and Policy*. ed. Mathew McCubbins and Terry Sullivan. (Cambridge, Cambridge University Press, 1987).

[27]Polsby, p. 123.

[28]see Kenneth Shepsle and Barry R. Weingast, "Positive Theories of Congressional Institutions," *Legislative Studies Quarterly* 19 (1994): 149-79; Kenneth Shepsle and Barry R. Weingast, "The Institutional Foundations of Committe Power," *American Political Science Review* 81 (1987): 85-104.

[29]Harrison W. Fox and Susan Webb Hammond, *Congressional Staffs: The Invisible Force in American Lawmaking* (New York: The Free Press, 1977); Robert H. Salisbury and Kenneth A. Shepsle, "U.S. Congressmen As Enterprise," *Legislative Studies Quarterly* 6 (1981): 559-76.

[30]Salisbury and Shepsle, pp. 559, 569-70.

science inquiry and studies both during and since the genesis of the behavioral research tradition. Thus, this book is but another installment in a lengthy history of institutional research. This book considers the importance of variation in one institutional resource for the behavior of individual justices. Furthermore, this study considers whether one institutional feature has structured the opinion writing behavior of individual justices. More specifically, this book examines the linkage between the growth of the law clerk institution, increasing numbers of support personnel on the Court, and historical increases in the frequency of nonconsensual opinion writing.

The New Institutionalism and Explanations of Dissent in State Supreme Courts

Despite the political science discipline's lengthy history of institutional research, applications of neo-institutional models are unusual in studies of dissent behavior on both the U.S. Supreme Court[31] and intermediate appellate courts in the federal system.[32] However, the tenets of the "new institutionalism" - the discipline's re-consideration of institutional factors as shapers of individual behavior - have found particular applicability to studies of dissent and dissensus on state courts. Moreover, the "new institutionalism" has profoundly influenced studies of dissent behavior on state courts of last resort. It is of no small consequence that state court systems are an ideal subject for comparative study. The number and variation in institutional arrangements makes state court systems particularly useful for examinations of how variation in organizational structures is related to patterns of dissensus. In their "neo-institutional" model of dissent on state supreme courts, Paul Brace and Melinda Gann Hall explain, ". . . the neo-institutional approach to judicial decision making stresses the independent role of standard operating procedures,

---

[31]Gerber and Park, p. 1, n. 10.

[32]Donald R. Songer, "Consensual and Nonconsensual Decisions in Unanimous Opinions of the U.S. Courts of Appeals," *American Journal of Political Science* 26 (1982): 225-39.

external decision rules, and organizational structures in defining the values, norms, and interests of judicial institutions."[33] Most important, the authors find particular value in a "neo-institutional" model of dissent behavior. They write: "The results indicate that justices' decision to dissent reflect significantly more than attitudinal disagreement, reactions to various types of case facts or responses to contextual forces. Rather, dissents are the product of all of these types of variables interacting with institutional rules and arrangements."[34]

"Neo-institutional" perspectives on dissent behavior are not new to studies of state court behavior. Indeed, scholars examined linkages between dissensus and institutional structure during the 1970s and 1980s.[35] The most prominent "neo-institutional" models of judicial dissent are those written in the late 1980s and 1990s by Paul Brace and Melinda Gann Hall.[36] These studies share the theme of testing variables which theoretically "either inhibit or promote the expression of personal

---

[33]Paul Brace and Melinda Gann Hall, "Integrated Models of Judicial Dissent," *Journal of Politics* 55 (1993): 920.

[34]Ibid., p. 914.

[35]See Bradley C. Canon and Dean Jaros, "External Variables, Institutional Structure, and Dissent in State Supreme Court," *Polity* 4 (1970): 185-200; Edward N. Beiser, "The Rhode Island Supreme Court: A Well-Integrated Political System," *Law and Society Review* 8 (1974): 167-86.; Henry R. Glick, "Dissent in State Supreme Courts: Patterns and Correlates of Conflict," in *Judicial Conflict and Consensus: Behavioral Studies of American Appellate Courts.* ed. Sheldon Goldman and Charles Lamb. (Lexington, KY: The University Press of Kansas, 1986).

[36]Melinda Gann Hall and Paul Brace, "Order in the Courts: A Neo-Institutional Approach to Judicial Consensus," *Western Political Quarterly* 42 (1989): 391-407; Paul Brace and Melinda Gann Hall, "Neo-Institutionalism and Dissent in States Supreme Courts," *The Journal of Politics* 52 (1990): 44-70.; Melinda Gann Hall and Paul Brace, "Toward an Integrated Model of Judicial Voting behavior," *American Politics Quarterly* 20 (1992): 147-68.

preferences in decisions and lead either to greater consensus or dissent."[37]

For studies of state courts, integrated models offer a more complete picture of the determinants of dissensus. That a similar approach has not permeated examinations of the United States Supreme Court speaks to the continued focus on reductionist models of voting behavior and the balkanization of the public law field which is fueled by that approach. Thus, public law scholars are charged with an important task; they must continue to test the precepts of the "new institutionalism" by building and examining models that integrate institutional factors with more proven explanations of judicial behavior. I submit that an important step in this process is to consider basic relationships between institutional variables and broad trends in Supreme Court voting and opinion writing behavior. My pursuit of an integrated model of Supreme Court opinion writing behavior begins with a consideration of the many competing explanations for disagreement on the Court.

Modeling the Decline in the Consensus norm on the U.S. Supreme Court

I discussed above that public law scholars have done little to bring "neo-institutional" or "new institutional" perspectives to models of dissensus on the U.S. Supreme Court. However, public law scholars have produced several explanations of dissent behavior that inform applications of institutional perspectives. David O'Brien's recent scholarship points to the impact of technological innovation and the 1935 move into the Court's current building as important factors in the rise of the individual opinion.[38] Other explanations point to important contextual factors that impact the nature of the organization's opinion writing tasks. Among these factors

---

[37]Melinda Gann Hall and Paul Brace, "Toward and Integrated Model of Judicial Voting Behavior," p. 151.

[38]David M. O'Brien, "Institutional Norms and Supreme Court Opinions: On Reconsidering the Rise of Individual Opinions," in *Supreme Court Decision Making: New Institutionalist Approaches*. ed. Cornell W. Clayton and Howard Gillman. (Chicago: University of Chicago Press, 1999), pp. 101-102.

are changes in the occupant of the chief justice's seat, the frequency of turnover on the Court, the number of inexperienced justices serving in each term, the size of the Court's workload, changes in the substantive composition of the Court's docket, and the degree of ideological differences among the justices. A review of these approaches, however, begins with judicial scholars' earliest efforts to come to terms with disagreement on the Court.

Judicial scholars' attention to the importance of nonconsensual opinions is traceable to Charles Evans Hughes's 1928 commentary on the propriety of written dissents. Hughes implied that dissents reflect both the judiciary's willingness to give important questions of law a full airing and its tendency to re-evaluate previous decisions. In short, Hughes implied that the nonconsensual opinion is a key referent of the health of the Court's deliberative processes.[39]   Thus, the nonconsensual opinion deserves the attention of judicial scholars because it is patent evidence that the Supreme Court, at least in terms of its internal procedures, is a political institution - one in which policy decisions often reflect the clashes of competing views rather than the enunciation of self-evident, unanimously-agreed-to principles. Moreover, the frequency with which the Court produces nonconsensual opinions is an indicator of the extent to which the Court is engaged in political conflict. Knowing how political the Court is and identifying those factors that make the Court behave like a political institution brings us closer to understanding the Court's role in the American polity.

To be surprised that conflict is the defining characteristic of Supreme Court behavior is to be seduced by what Walter Murphy and Joseph Tanenhaus identify as the "judicial myth."[40] Moreover, unless it is accepted that a proper judicial decision awaits discovery on the shelves of the Court library, disagreement among justices regarding case outcomes seems almost a truism; if Justice Holmes is correct that "[t]he

---

[39]Charles Evans Hughes, *The Supreme Court of the United States* (New York: Columbia University Press, 1928), pp. 67-68.

[40]Walter F. Murphy and Joseph Tanenhaus, *The Study of Public Law* (New York: Random House, 1972), p. 10.

life of the law has not been logic: it has been experience" and is at least in part a creature of "... the prejudices which judges share with their fellow men ...,"[41] then it should be expected that different justices will come to different conclusions simply because they are, as individuals, different.

Paul Freund's discussion is particularly instructive on this point. Professor Freund recalls that Justice Holmes remarked:

> How amazing it is that, in the midst of controversies on every conceivable subject, one should expect unanimity of opinion upon difficult legal questions! In the highest range of thought, in theology, philosophy, and science, we find differences of view on the part of the most distinguished experts - theologians, philosophers, and scientists. The history of scholarship is a record of disagreements. And when we deal with questions relating to principles of law and their application, we do not suddenly rise into a stratosphere of icy certainty.[42]

Moreover, it seems reasonably settled among judicial scholars that disagreement on the Court is inevitable. Indeed, dissenting votes and opinions were issued on even the highly consensual Marshall Court of the early 1800s.[43] However, a brief look at early Supreme Court history reveals that high frequencies of written expressions of dissent and disagreement are unique to the 1940-1998 period.

Scholars seeking to explain instances of dissensus among justices become immediately aware of several facts about Supreme Court

---

[41]Oliver Wendell Holmes, Jr., *The Common Law* (New York: Dover Publications, Inc., 1991), p. 1.

[42]Oliver Wendell Holmes, Jr. address, *Proceedings of the American Legal Institute* 13 (1936): 61. Quoted in Paul A. Freund, *The Supreme Court of the United States: Its Business, Purposes, and Performance* (Gloucester, MA: World Publishing Co., 1972), p. 31.

[43]Meredith Kolsky, "Justice William Johnson and the History of Supreme Court Dissent," *Georgetown Law Journal* 83 (1995): 2074.

behavior. With the exception of the brief period of seriatim opinion writing during the 1790s, the first 140 years of Supreme Court history is characterized by modest rates of nonconsensual opinion writing. During the 1790 to 1800 period, the justices authored a total of 4 concurring and dissenting opinions. During the 1800 to 1829 period the justices authored the same number of dissenting opinions as the Court produced during the 1941 term. Further, the 36 concurring opinions written by the justices during the 1945 term equals the total number of concurrences drafted during entire span of the Court's first fifty terms.[44] Moreover, prior to 1940, in arriving at a final disposition in cases granted plenary review, the justices of the United States Supreme Court typically authored fewer than 20 separate opinions for every 100 majority opinions written in each term.[45] In recognition of the fact that during the first 140 years of our constitutional history Supreme Court justices authored relatively few dissenting and concurring opinions,[46] several judicial scholars have sought to identify determinants of the notably different opinion writing practices during the twentieth century.

Public law scholars generally attribute the abrupt change in opinion writing practices to alterations in expectations about consensual opinion writing behaviors. Bowen argues that this abrupt change in opinion writing behaviors signaled a radical transformation "in the consensual norms which had marked the previous 140 years of the Court."[47]

---

[44]Figures are calculated from data presented in Albert P. Blaustein and Roy M. Mersky's *The First One-Hundred Justices: Statistical Studies on the United States Supreme Court* (Hamden, CT: Archon Books, 1978), pp. 137-41.

[45]Stacia Haynie, "Leadership and Consensus on the U.S. Supreme Court," *Journal of Politics* 54 (1992): 1159.

[46]Ibid., p. 1158.

[47]Terry Bowen, "Consensual Norms and the Freshman Effect on the United States Supreme Court," *Social Science Quarterly* 76 (1995): 223; The historical presence of a long since discarded consensus norm is supported by the research of Epstein, Segal, and Spaeth. See Lee Epstein, Jeffrey A. Segal, and Harold J. Spaeth, "The Norm of Consensus on the U.S. Supreme Court,"

Moreover, the increase in the numbers of dissenting and concurring opinions being written was not only ". . . dramatic in magnitude, but represented an apparently permanent alteration in the Court's decision-making regime."[48] Data presented by David O'Brien in his book *Storm Center*[49] reveals that during the period of rapidly increasing numbers of concurring and dissenting opinions, the justices authored decreasing numbers of opinions for the Court and increasing numbers of plurality opinions. Thus, since the 1940 term, Supreme Court justices have demonstrated a persistent and historically remarkable change in their observance of consensual norms, expressing disagreement in the writing of increasing numbers of nonconsensual opinions.[50]

Recent efforts to explain the changes in opinion writing behaviors employ the concepts of traditional behavioral studies of judicial decision making. Explanations such as changes in the personnel comprising the Court, changes in docket composition, changes in the size of the Court's workload, and changes in leadership styles of chief justices are typical of recent examinations of dissent behavior. However, recent studies of dissensus on the Court also suggest the need to consider linkages between opinion writing behaviors and what are perhaps more subtle, complex interactions among Supreme Court personnel. In fact, several Court observers assert that historical increases in the frequency of nonconsensual opinion writing are related to the increasing numbers of law clerks employed by the justices. Moreover, current studies of nonconsensual opinion writing behaviors imply a need to reconsider the lessons of research on "small group" theory, law clerk participation on the Court, and dissent behavior among Supreme Court justices.

The most common explanation for the decline in the consensus norm,

---

American Journal of Political Science 46 (2001): 376.

[48]Thomas G. Walker, Lee Epstein, and William Dixon, "On the Mysterious Demise of Consensual Norms in the United States Supreme Court," *Journal of Politics* 50 (1988): 362.

[49]O'Brien, pp 318-20.

[50]Bowen, p. 223.

however, is differences in the leadership style of chief justices. Caldeira and Zorn adopt a monocausal explanation for the historical increase in dissensus on the Court, arguing that the justices' observance of a consensus norm varies with different chief justices.[51] The authors state that "[n]o other external event or institutional change, from the Judge's Bill of 1925 to changes in caseload, accounts for the explosion of conflict under Stone and its persistence from 1941 to the present."[52] Thus, the authors apparently suspect no important relationship between changes in the size of the Court organization and opinion writing practices. Caldeira and Zorn acknowledge that "writing dissents takes time and energy,"[53] but do not test the proposition that changes in factors that increase the justices' "time" and "energy" are linked to the frequency of nonconsensual opinion writing.

Walker, Epstein, and Dixon also attribute the change in opinion writing behaviors to alterations in the behavioral expectations of Chief Justice Harlan Fiske Stone.[54] The authors argue that as opposed to his predecessor, Chief Justice Charles Evans Hughes, Chief Justice Stone employed a leadership style that encouraged disagreement among the associate justices.[55] The authors consider only dissenting opinions as referents of nonconsensual opinion writing.

In her examination of historical changes in opinion writing behaviors, Stacia Haynie also finds that differences in leadership styles on the Court are related to dissent behavior. However, Professor Haynie argues that future studies of dissent behavior should be broadened to include the

---

[51]Gregory A. Caldeira and Christopher J.W. Zorn, "Of Time and Consensual Norms in the Supreme Court," *American Journal of Political Science* 42 (1998): 900.

[52]Caldeira and Zorn, p. 875.

[53] Ibid., p. 877.

[54]Walker, Epstein, and Dixon, p. 384.

[55]Ibid., p. 384.

importance of concurring opinions as indicators of dissensus.[56] By Caldeira and Zorn's definition, the authoring of dissenting and concurring opinions are closely linked to the intensity of the justices' satisfaction with the content of a majority opinion. The authors state that a dissenting opinion results from ". . . deeply-held convictions about the law and thus should be published; concurrences may not. . . ."[57] It follows that because a concurrence reflects a basic policy agreement between the author and the Court majority (or plurality), the justice's calculus of whether to write a concurrence may be more sensitive to the availability of the "time and energy" referred to by Caldeira and Zorn. In short, it is important to examine dissenting and concurring opinions as discrete phenomena. In the chapters that follow, I treat dissenting and concurring opinions as distinct but related modes of dissensus.

Inasmuch as studies of the declining consensus norm point to the importance of leadership style as a factor related to disagreement among justices, more detailed studies of leadership also speak to the relevance of interpersonal interactions on the Court as determinants of dissent behavior. Furthermore, it is in studies of leadership on the Court that a clear theoretical linkage is drawn between "small group" models and studies seeking explanations for the historical decline in the consensus norm on the Court.

Arguing that Chief Justice Burger exacerbated conflict on the Court, Bernard Schwartz explains that Burger's conference leadership techniques, opinion assignment practices, opinion writing behaviors, and informal relations with his colleagues is indicative of a Chief Justice " . . . miscast in the role of leader of the Court" and ill-equipped to suppress conflict.[58] Professor Schwartz indicates that Chief Justice Burger's

---

[56]Haynie, p. 1160.

[57]Caldeira and Zorn, p. 877.

[58]Bernard Schwartz, *The Ascent of Pragmatism: The Burger Court in Action* (Reading, MA: Addison-Wesley Publishing Co., Inc., 1990), p. 8.

diminished legal acumen,[59] departures from established tenets of opinion assignment procedures,[60] and manipulative vote switching practices[61] constituted a portrait of a most infuriating leader. Indeed, the record of Warren Burger's service as Chief Justice reveals instances of abdication of his leadership role and a general failure to fulfill his stated goal of modifying the libertarian bent of Warren Court jurisprudence.[62]

In Schwartz's discussions of Earl Warren's leadership abilities, additional evidence is found for the importance of the chief justice in attenuating conflict. Here Schwartz relates the "Super Chief's" ability to at conference relate the critical issues of cases being discussed in such a way as to appeal to the associate justice's practical sensibilities. As Professor Schwartz notes "Chief Justice Warren brought more authority to the Chief Justiceship than had been the case for years."[63] He also states that Chief Justice Rehnquist similarly recognized the importance of mitigating conflict on the Court. Schwartz explains that Chief Justice Rehnquist was acutely aware that plurality decisions represented a failure on the part of the Chief to marshal his brethren.[64]

It is indisputable that the judicial behavior bibliography is replete

---

[59]Ibid., p. 9.

[60]Ibid., pp. 13-14.

[61]Ibid., pp. 13-14.

[62]Bernard Schwartz relates several instances in which Chief Justice Burger abdicated his role as opinion leader in decisions of particular moment. Schwartz states that in the important *Buckley v. Valeo* and *U.S. v. Nixon* cases, Chief Justice Burger allowed the Court's opinion to be written "by committee" rather than by the institution's recognized leader. See Bernard Schwartz, *Decision: How the Supreme Court Decides Cases* (New York: Oxford University Press, 1996), see particularly pp. 142-48.   For a more detailed discussion of Earl Warren's leadership abilities see Bernard Schwartz, *Super Chief: Earl Warren and His Supreme Court* (New York: New York University Press, 1983).

[63]Schwartz, *Decision*, p. 89.

[64]Ibid., p. 20.

with examinations of the specific relationship between leadership on the Court and dissension among the justices. Several studies of former chief justices indicate that a shift in leadership styles in the early 1940's is related to changes in the functioning of the Court. Studies by Mason,[65] Murphy,[66] and Pritchett[67] reveal that changes in the behavioral expectations of chief justices influenced the Court's collective observance of the consensus norm. In the most detailed examination of the relationship between leadership on the Court and opinion writing, Danelski identified the importance of the Chief Justice's social and task leadership skills as factors in the maintenance of consensus.[68]

Is there evidence suggesting that nonconsensual opinion is a multi-causal phenomenon driven by factors other than changes in the occupant of the chief justice's seat? Although arguing for the primacy of leadership styles in models of dissent behavior, research on the declining consensual norm reveals several other variables that may be connected to patterns of nonconsensual opinion writing. For example, Haynie's research is exploratory with respect to several competing determinants of dissensus. However, like Walker, Epstein, and Dixon, Haynie finds that docket composition, partisan composition, and workload variables are unrelated

---

[65]Alpheus T. Mason, *Harlan Fiske Stone: Pillar of the Law* (New York: Viking Press, 1956), pp. 601-3.

[66]See Murphy, *The Elements of Judicial Strategy*

[67]C. Hermann Pritchett, *The Roosevelt Court: A Study in Judicial Politics and Values*, 1937-1947 (Chicago: Quadrangle Books, 1948).

[68]David Danelski, "The Influence of the Chief Justice in the Decision Process," in *Courts Judges,and Politics.* ed. C. Hermann Pritchett. (New York: Random House, 1960); *A Supreme Court Justice is Appointed* (New York: MacMillan Publishers, 1964); "Causes and Consequences of Conflict and its Resolution in the Supreme Court," in *Judicial Conflict and Consensus.* ed. Sheldon Goldman and Charles Lamb. (Lexington: University of Kentucky Press, 1986).

to historical changes in nonconsensual opinion writing.[69] These findings do not preclude examination of these or other factors in models of nonconsensual opinion writing.

Other studies present additional competing explanations of dissent and dissensus. In their 1993 study, Segal and Spaeth find that the presence of civil liberties issues is associated with dissensus.[70] Furthermore, Segal and Spaeth find much support for the proposition that attitudinal considerations are principle causes of voting and subsequent opinion writing behaviors on the Court. In addition, Wahlbeck, Spriggs, and Maltzman examined the importance of ideological heterogeneity among majority coalition members for the opinion drafting process.[71] Although the authors found no relationship between ideological heterogeneity and the number of opinion drafts circulated among coalition members prior to the announcement of a majority opinion, the authors use of an ideological heterogeneity score may have application to explanations of nonconsensual opinion writing among the Court as a whole.[72] I suspect that a similar measure of ideological heterogeneity may be an appropriate method of building into a model of dissent and dissensus a variable that approximates the attitudinal factor suggested by Segal and Spaeth. In sum, the literature on dissent and dissensus is yet to resolve the importance of docket composition and ideological heterogeneity on the Court as determinants of nonconsensual opinion writing behavior.

To date, there is no empirical evidence to support the proposition that increases in the total number of case filings are related to changes

---

[69]Ibid., pp. 1165-1166.

[70]Jeffrey A. Segal and Harold Spaeth, *The Supreme Court and the Attitudinal Model* (New York: Cambbridge University Press, 1993), p. 291.

[71]Paul J. Wahlbeck, James F. Spriggs, and Forest Maltzman, "Marshalling the Court: Bargaining and Accommodation on the U.S. Supreme Court" (paper presented at the Annual Meeting of the Western Political Science Association, San Francisco, March 14-16, 1996), p. 13.

[72]Ibid., p. 20.

in opinion writing behaviors. However, if caseload is viewed from the perspective of the number of cases disposed of by signed opinion per term, sound theoretical reasons exist to suspect that changes in workload may influence the frequency of dissent behavior. The number of cases disposed of by signed opinion in each term represents the frequency with which the justices are confronted with the opportunity to express independent views through the writing of dissents and concurrences.

Several studies suggest that workload considerations may, however, structure the incentives encountered by the justices in the decision making environment. In his recent survey of judicial behavior research, Professor Baum explains that some empirical evidence supports the notion that non-policy considerations, such as workload management concerns, describe the range of motives exemplified by Supreme Court justices.[73] Maltzman and Wahlbeck argue that workload concerns inform opinion assignment practices on the Supreme Court.[74] Wahlbeck, Spriggs, and Maltzman's earlier study of strategic behavior on the Court reveals that the magnitude of a justice's workload is inversely related to the number of opinion drafts the justice is either willing or able to circulate in the decision making process.[75] The authors' finding indicates that the magnitude of a justice's workload structures his ability or willingness to produce formal, written expressions of the majority coalition's policy views.[76] Wasby also argues that workload considerations influence a justice's decision to author dissenting and concurring opinions.[77] In his detailed examination of the

---

[73]Baum, p. 28.

[74]Forrest Maltzman and Paul J. Wahlbeck, "May it Please the Chief? Opinion Assignments in the Rehnquist Court," *American Journal of Political Science* 40 (1996): 438.

[75]Wahlbeck, Spriggs, and Maltzman, pp. 17, 22.

[76]Ibid., p. 25.

[77]Stephen L. Wasby, *The Supreme Court in the Federal Judicial System* (Chicago: Nelson-Hall Publishers. 1988), p. 234.

workload of the Supreme Court, Posner suggests that changes in the workload demands on the institution are inextricably linked to the Court's handling of the principle task of opinion writing.[78]

In addition, increases in caseload may influence the justices' willingness and ability to engage in the consensus seeking behavior that results in fewer nonconsensual opinions. Professor O'Brien explains that Justices White and Powell found the size of the Court's caseload encouraged the justices to work independent of on another. He writes:

> Today, justices "stay at arms length," in Byron White's view and rely on formal printed communications party because the workload discourages justices "from going from chamber to chamber to work things out." Powell also remarked that "collegiality diminishes as the caseload increases."[79]

From these discussions I infer that caseload concerns may be closely related to the collective opinion writing behavior of justices. Specifically, I infer that caseload concerns may be related to the justices' collective ability to author concurring and dissenting opinions. Thus, a study of collective opinion writing behaviors should carefully consider the importance of changes in the Court's caseload for changing patterns of consensus.

Finally, I find that recent studies of the decline of consensual norms on the Court are, in a theoretical sense, implicitly linked to studies of a "small group" effect. Haynie argues against a monocausal approach to explanations of historical increases in the numbers of dissenting and concurring opinions authored by the justices.[80] In her discussion of the importance of the Chief Justice's leadership style, Haynie comments that future studies of nonconsensual opinion writing must consider a broader

---

[78]Posner, *Federal Courts: Challenge and Reform*, p. 141.

[79]O'Brien, p. 156. See also Powell's quote in "Inside the High Court," *Time*, December 5, 1979, 60, 64. Quoted in O'Brien, p. 156.

[80]Haynie, p. 1168

range of interactions within the Court institution.[81] Haynie suggests that it is in these subtle, more complex forms of interaction that public law scholars will uncover additional determinants of dissensus. Thus, recent studies of the decline in the consensus norm implicitly demand a reexamination of "small group" explanations of judicial behavior. In the next section I consider an alternative definition of the "small group" concept that includes the role of law clerks on the Supreme Court.

Small Group Theory and Studies of Dissensus: A Theoretical Linkage

If it is necessary to explore the connections between a broader range of interpersonal interactions on the Supreme Court and patterns of dissensus among justices, it is imperative to conduct a careful review of studies treating the Court as a "small group." A close examination of the literature considering a "small group" effect on Supreme Court behavior suggests that previous specifications of the "small group" may have failed to consider all patterns of interpersonal interactions on the Court.[82] Moreover, previous specifications of the "small group" do not consider the importance of interactions between justices, law clerks, and other support personnel. Thus, it is possible that an alternative formulation of the "small

---

[81]Ibid., 1168.

[82]"Small group" behavior on the Court generally refers to the linkages between patterns of interaction among the justices and subsequent votes or opinion writing practices. For example a "small group" effect on opinion writing practices is one that results from either the social or task leadership abilities of the chief justice (this might include the chief justice's methodology in conference discussions), opinion assignment decisions, the persuasive abilities of associate justices and related patterns of voting inter-agreement and voting fluidity, or the presence of freshmen justices. In short, the "small group" effect on Supreme Court behavior is a broad, theoretical construct which refers to any pattern of voting or opinion writing behavior traceable to interactions among the nine justices. While the presence of a general "small group" effect is not directly testable, the presence of various types of interaction or alternative formulations of interaction are testable.

group" effect may reveal the importance of interactions among the justices, law clerks, and support personnel for ultimate opinion writing behaviors. I submit that this alternative formulation is founded on both the tradition of "small group" research in the public law field and the lessons of late nineteenth and early twentieth century sociological thought.

The early behavioral treatments of Supreme Court decision making imply that group factors strongly influence the justices' voting activities both individually and collectively. More specifically, early studies of the small group effect turn on an interest in the group context of individual behavior that is reminiscent of late nineteenth and early twentieth century microsociological theory. A brief consideration of the microsociological foundations of early examinations of the small group effect on Supreme Court behavior is instructive to the general theme of this chapter.

In the earliest examinations of a "small group effect"on Supreme Court behavior are remnants of the theoretical propositions of Emile Durkheim, Charles Horton Cooley, George Herbert Mead, and Georg Simmel. Each of these sociological theorists considered the importance of small group interactions for individual and collective behavior.[83] From Durkheim, social scientists have inherited perspectives on the importance of role differentiation within small groups. Cooley studied the impact of memberships in what he termed primary groups, or families, on adult notions of social unity and behavioral norms within communities. Mead was primarily interested in communication within groups, particularly the importance of communication for collective behavior. Simmel's thought is of such moment that it requires a more detailed treatment.

The microsociological theory of Georg Simmel is particularly instructive to this examination of the small group literature. In fact, Simmel made what is perhaps the most significant nineteenth century contribution to the study of small groups. Ritzer reports that Simmel identified as the sociologist's most important task that of explaining social interaction, particularly that which encouraged or resulted from

---

[83]see Paul A. Hare, Edgar F. Borgatta, and Robert F. Bales, *Small Groups: Studies in Social Interaction* (New York: Alfred Knopf, 1965).

small group formations.[84] Moreover, Simmel explored linkages between human interaction and the behavior of institutions. Simmel's thought, then, provides justification for examinations of subgroup formation in collegial organizations. Perhaps most important, in Simmel's thought are genuflections at the more subtle, perhaps complex relationships among persons that at the time of his writing other sociologists and political scientists had left under-treated. Robert Nisbet explains:

> [I]t is the microsociological character of Simmel's work that may always give him an edge in timeliness over the other pioneers. He did not disdain the small and the intimate elements of human association, nor did he ever lose sight of the primacy of human beings, or concrete individuals, in his analysis of institutions.[85]

The connections between Simmel's thought and the research questions posed by early studies of the "small group effect" as well as this book become increasingly apparent. Simmel was acutely aware that social interactions are at least in part responses to the demands of life in complex organizations. Simmel recognized that one strategy used by individuals to cope with group size is to form and become immersed in subgroups. Simmel hypothesized that subgroup formation is an effective means of quieting the noise of interpersonal conflict.[86] That is, membership in subgroups comprised of like-minded individuals soothes confusion and, it may be inferred, provides a sense of legitimacy to ideals otherwise treated as aberrant. The connection is obvious between Simmel's investigations and the mid-twentieth century treatments of clique and bloc formation among Supreme Court justices. Specifically, Simmel's work

---

[84]George Ritzer, *Sociological Theory* (New York: McGraw-Hill, Inc, 1992), p.31, 157.

[85]See Robert Nisbit, "Comment," *American Sociological Review* 24 (1959): 1139-53. Quoted in Ritzer, p. 158.

[86]Ritzer, p. 167.

anticipates Snyder's discussions of clique formation and the elementary bloc analysis undertaken by C. Hermann Pritchett.[87]

C. Hermann Pritchett's 1948 study of voting interagreement among Supreme Court justices revealed that in deciding cases justices align in small groups.[88] Eloise Snyder extended Pritchett's use of bloc membership in positing what has been called the "freshman effect" hypothesis.[89] Snyder argued that the small group environment explained the unique voting and opinion writing behaviors of newly appointed justices. In his examination of the strategic environment of Supreme Court decision making, Walter Murphy broadened the theoretical foundations of small group theory.[90] Murphy argues that interpersonal interactions occur in the context of self-interested, strategic behavior among justices, explaining voting and opinion writing activities.

With regard to long term policy goals, Ulmer reconsidered the strategic foundations of small group formation.[91] Ulmer argues that subgroup formation on the Court is less a consequence of strategic behavior and more a function of the value consensus among justices.[92] Further, Ulmer suggests that subgroup formation is an artifact of shared policy goals among justices, thus accounting for the enduring quality of intra-group relationships and the inability of strategic choices explanations of judicial behavior to elucidate the underlying dynamic of subgroup formation. Most important, Ulmer maintains that attitudinal factors inform

---

[87]C. Hermann Pritchett, *The Roosevelt Court* (New York: MacMillan Publishers, 1948).

[88]Ibid.

[89]Eloise Snyder, "The Supreme Court as a Small Group," *Social Forces* 36 (1958): 232-238.

[90]See Murphy, *The Elements of Judicial Strategy*

[91]S. Sidney Ulmer, "Toward a Theory of Subgroup Formation in the United States Supreme Court," *Journal of Politics* 27 (1965): 133-54.

[92]Ibid., pp. 151-2.

small group formation and that small group explanations of Supreme Court behavior must be reformulated to include the complexities of justices' value orientations.

Additional research by Sprague[93] and Howard[94] supports the notion that voting and opinion writing behaviors are influenced by the institutional context in which Supreme Court justices function, including the small group context of decision making and the behavioral expectations imposed on junior associate justices by senior justices. Sprague found that bloc membership and voting behavior within voting blocs is influenced by changes in bloc membership that occur with turnover on the Court. Thus, Sprague's study reminds scholars that the norm of bloc formation, an artifact of the Court's rules and procedures regarding voting and opinion writing, is itself an institutionally driven phenomenon.

Inasmuch as Ulmer finds that role expectations form much of the substance of small groups interactions, Howard finds support for the "freshman effect" hypothesis in particular and "small group" theory in general. Howard's examination of voting fluidity - the occurrence of justices altering the direction of their votes between the time of the initial conference vote and the final vote on the merits - reveals that interactions between newly appointed justices and their more senior colleagues influence decisions about bloc membership. Howard finds that the small group, i.e., institutional, context in which newly appointed justices find themselves intervenes between attitudes and final votes, moderating their sincere policy preferences and molding subsequent voting behavior in ways predicted by Snyder.

Later studies in the small group genre present findings anomalous to the early notions of the "small group" effect. These studies challenge the veracity of previous conceptualizations of an independent, "small group" effect on Supreme Court behavior. Furthermore, these studies indicate the

---

[93]John Sprague, "Voting Patterns of the United States Supreme Court," *Social Forces* 36 (1968): 43-56.

[94]J. Woodford Howard, "On the Fluidity of Judicial Choice," *American Political Science Review* 62 (1968): 43-56.

primacy of attitudes and ideological dispositions in shaping judicial behavior. The result is a significant weakening of the case for small group models as previously constructed. None of these studies, however, question the viability of alternative formulations of the small group effect or alternative operational definitions of the Court's work group.

Studies by Heck and Hall[95] along with Sheb and Ailshie[96] questioned the veracity of the "freshman effect" hypothesis. Rubin and Melone's examination of Antonin Scalia's first term on the Court also questioned the validity of Snyder's propositions concerning freshman justice behavior.[97] Here, the authors present evidence that Justice Scalia exhibited none of characteristics of the freshman justice. In addition, Melone's 1990 study of Anthony Kennedy's first two terms on the Court shook the theoretical foundations upon which rested all previous studies of the "freshman effect" hypothesis.[98]   Again, Professor Melone reveals that Justice Kennedy's behavior during his initial terms on the Court were entirely inconsistent with Snyder's hypotheses. Reacting to the accumulation of findings anomolous to Snyder's hypotheses, Melone states that the "freshman effect hypothesis is either incorrect or time bound."[99] Grambihler's longitudinal study of freshman justice behavior affirmed Melone's suspicions, stating that, in fact, the "freshman effect" hypothesis

---

[95]Edward V. Heck and Melinda Gann Hall, "Bloc Voting and the Freshman Justice Revisited," *Journal of Politics* 43 (1981): 853-60.

[96]John A. Sheb and Lee W. Ailshie, "Justice Sandra Day O'Connor and the Frehsman Effiect," *Judicature* 69 (1985): 9-12.

[97]Thea F. Rubin and Albert P. Melone, "Justice Antonin Scalia: A First Year Freshman Effect?" *Judicature* 72 (1988): 98-102.

[98]Albert P. Melone, "Revisiting the Freshman Effect Hypothesis: The First Two Terms of Justice Anthony Kennedy," *Judicature* 74 (1990): 6-13.

[99]Ibid., p. 12

is incorrect.[100] Thus, recent studies testing specific operationalizations of "small group" influences question the viability of extant formulations of the "small group" effect.

These findings do not fully negate the importance of small group theory as instructive to judicial scholars' understanding of Supreme Court behavior. In fact, the scholarly community continues to seek a reformulation of the "small group" effect that captures the ways in which justices orient themselves to one another. Studies by Brenner and Hagle[101] and Wood, et.al.,[102] are evidence of the continuing effort to model "small group" processes on the Supreme Court.

Further, the importance of studies of voting fluidity create a lingering suspicion that "small group" and institutionally-based influences on judicial behavior deserve reconsideration. These studies indicate that decision making structures influence opinion writing behaviors. Howard's early study of voting fluidity reveals that vote switching is common to the Court's decision making processes.[103] One implication of Howard's research is that small group processes influence vote choice between the times of the initial and final votes on the merits. A later study by Brenner reveals that vote switching occurs only infrequently, implying that small

---

[100]Kenneth Lee Grambihler, "A Longitudinal Analysis of the Freshman Effect Hypothesis of United States Supreme Court Justices (1953-1988 Terms)" (Ph.D. diss., Southern Illinois University, 1993). For a related study of freshman justice behavior see Kenneth Lee Grambihler and Albert P. Melone, "Initial Behavior of Newly Appointed Supreme Court Justices," *Illinois Political Science Review* 4 (1998):63-71.

[101]Saul Brenner and Timothy Hagle, "Opinion Writing and the Acclimation Effect," *Political Behavior* 18 (1996): 235-61

[102]Sandra Wood, Linda Camp Keith, Drew Lanier, and Ayo Ogundele "'Acclimation Effect' on the U.S. Supreme Court: A Replication," *American Journal of Political Science* 42 (1998): 690-97.

[103]Howard, pp. 44-9.

group processes do not significantly influence vote choice.[104]

Law Clerks and Support Staff: Expanding the Size of the Court's Work Group

Jeremy Bentham noted in the eighteenth century that "the law is not made by judge alone, but by judge and company."[105] Bentham's observation, though made long prior to the genesis of the law clerk tradition, could have easily been made by any contemporary observer of the Supreme Court's internal procedures. In fact, Bentham's observation is even more profound considering that he accurately characterized the culmination of more than a 100 year course of change in the internal operations of the Supreme Court. A review of the judicial process literature indicates that this change has occurred in the form of increased participation by the law clerks in several of the Court's most important tasks. Moreover, scholars have come to recognize law clerks as important actors in the business of Supreme Court, directly assisting the justices in the core tasks of case selection and opinion writing. Initially relegated to exclusively ministerial or clerical duties, law clerks now perform decision making and opinion writing tasks not wholly unlike those of the justices themselves. Indeed, as Bernard Schwartz explains, the expanding role of law clerks has changed "the very nature of the Supreme Court."[106] I submit that the changing nature of the law clerks' participation on the Court has produced significant changes in the task environment encountered by the justices. I find that the judicial process literature indicates that the increasing presence of law clerks on the Court accounts, in part, for historical changes in the individual and collective opinion writing activities of the justices.

---

[104]Saul Brenner, "Fluidity on the Supreme Court, 1956-1967," *American Journal of Political Science* 26 (1982): 388.

[105]Quoted in Baier, Paul R. "Law Clerks: Profile of an Institution." *Vanderbilt Law Review* 26 (1973): 1125.

[106]Schwartz, Bernard, *A History of the Supreme Court*, p. 369.

The judicial behavior literature implies that the increasing presence of law clerks on the Court has altered the task environment encountered by the justices. Further, it follows that this change in the task environment has had the operational effect of altering the set of incentives encountered by justices in the opinion writing process. The research literature implies that increasing participation of law clerks on the Supreme Court may have eliminated institutional disincentives to the authoring of dissenting and concurring opinions. Thus, I argue that expanding the operational definition of the "small group" environment to include the contributions of law clerks may account for changes in the opinion writing behaviors of the justices. I infer from the judicial process literature that justice-law clerk interactions constitute a form of small group behavior that may account for the increasing numbers of separate opinions drafted by the justices.

Like exponential increases in the magnitude of the Court's workload, law clerk participation on the Court is predominantly a twentieth century phenomenon. Baier remarks that "from the data it appears the introduction of the law clerks in the early 1880s was no historical accident; rather it sprang up as the Court's protective response to its burgeoning docket."[107] Inasmuch as scholars agree that exponential growth in the size of the Court's docket accounts for the genesis of the law clerks tradition, the consequences of the institutionalization of the law clerk are not fully understood. However, a brief consideration of the early development of the law clerk tradition reveals an important question that warrants empirical examination.

Much as the adoption of law clerk assistance was no historical accident, the expansion of the Court's docket is not without identifiable causes. From the ratification of the Constitution in 1789 until 1802, justices performed extensive supervisory and decision making duties in the lower federal courts. This "circuit-riding," as the justices called it, was significantly curtailed with the passage of the Judiciary Acts of 1801 and

---

[107]Baier, pp. 1132-33. Quoted in David Weiden, "Conflicts and Cues: The Institutionalization of the Supreme Court Law Clerk and the Court's Agenda" (paper presented at the 1998 Annual Meeting of the Midwest Political Science Association, Chicago, April 23-26, 1998), p. 5.

1802. Per the Congress's edict, the Acts called for increased staffing in the lower federal courts such that the justices would be relieved of most decision making responsibilities outside of Washington. The Judiciary Acts also limited the Court's original jurisdiction, leaving the justices with increased control over the Court's docket. Such changes might have effectively circumscribed the outer boundaries of the Court's docket. However, these early Judiciary Acts also expanded the jurisdiction of the federal district courts, precipitating increased numbers of appeals to the Supreme Court. Thus, while the Court gained via federal statutes the luxury of a shrinking mandatory docket, increases in the number of certiorari petitions permanently expanded the workload of the Supreme Court. As Blaustein and Mersky relate, during the last 65 years of the nineteenth century, the Court decided an ever-increasing number of cases per term. The authors explain:

> In the period which ended with the death of Chief Justice John Marshall in 1835 the Court decided an average of 31 cases per term. The figure more than doubled to 64 in the period 1835 to 1868. Then it nearly quadrupled to 232 decisions per term in the period 1868 to 1900.[108]

During this period of increasing caseloads and prior to 1886, law clerks were employed only in the state and lower federal court settings. Thus, during periods of rapidly expanding caseloads, the justices of the Supreme Court were essentially without clerical assistance. The Supreme Court of the early and middle 1800s was an organization that functioned largely without the benefit of any type of support personnel. This pattern of unassisted labor on the part of the justices would not endure.

During the 1850s and 1860s, the justices became increasingly aware that a burgeoning workload had made a once surmountable docket beyond the capacities of the Court. Newland explains that by 1875, the Court was

---

[108]Blaustein and Mersky, p. 94.

pressuring Congress for relief.[109] Congress addressed the problem of the expanding docket and allocated funds to expand the stock of logistical and technical support available to the justices. In 1886, Congress passed the Sundry Civil Act, allocating to each justice one "stenographic clerk." As Weiden explains, "[b]y 1888 each justice employed a law clerk and the institution of the law clerks was firmly established."[110]

It was not until the early twentieth century, however, that it became evident that law clerks were to be constant elements in the Court's organizational framework. As Oakley and Thompson explain, in 1919 the Court was allowed to expand its staff to include one law clerk for each justice.[111] Yet, many years would pass before law clerks became a part of each justice's chambers. Oakley and Thompson note that the process of placing a law clerk in each chamber occurred over a period of two decades.[112]

The station of law clerks in the nineteenth century is dissimilar to that of Supreme Court law clerks today. In the late 1800s, the role of the law clerk was to assist the justices in preparing for oral arguments and to perform research tasks that would support the justices' formal duties. Although considerably larger than in the early decades of the nineteenth century, the size of the Court's docket apparently allowed the justices complete dominion over the core tasks of case selection, decision making, and opinion writing. Moreover, the substance of opinions was entirely the province of the justices. As the Court's first clerk Samuel Williston explained, "Justice Gray employed clerks exclusively as sources of inspiration and criticism. . . . contributing ideas but not documents to

---

[109]Chester A. Newland, "Personal Assistants to Supreme Court Justices: The Law Clerks," *Oregon Law Review* 40 (1961): 301.

[110]Weiden, p. 5.

[111]John Bilyeu Oakley and Robert S. Thomson, *Law Clerks and the Judicial Process: Perceptions of the Qualities and Functions of Law Clerks in American Courts* (Berkeley: University of California Press, 1980), pp. 16-7.

[112]Ibid., p. 17.

Gray's work as a judge."[113]   No scholar states definitively the period during which the law clerks begun routinely making contributions to the substance of final opinion drafts. Of the first half of the twentieth century, Frank merely indicates that "the function of the clerks in relation to the writing of opinions also varies widely."[114]

Though an enduring fixture in the Court organization, law clerks were not until the twentieth century permanently affixed to each justice's chambers.   Oakley and Thompson explain that law clerks were sporadically employed by the justices during the period of burgeoning dockets in the late 1890s and that it was not until 1919 that Congress permanently authorized expenditures for each justice to employ one full time law clerk.[115]   By this time the number of case filings had increased dramatically and the justices were writing upwards of 300 opinions per term.[116]   Moreover, studies by Baier,[117] and Oakley and Thompson[118] suggest that rapid increases in case filings in the late nineteenth and early twentieth century required that law clerks become an increasingly important element in the opinion drafting process.   Other accounts also trace the increasing importance of law clerks to dramatic increases in workload.[119]

The relationship between the Court's workload and the role of law clerks on the Court is undoubtedly linked to the passage of the Judiciary

---

[113]Quoted in Oakley and Thompson, p. 14.

[114]Frank, p. 116.

[115]Oakley and Thompson, p. 14.

[116]Blaustein and Mersky, pp. 139-40.

[117]Baier, p. 1125.

[118]See Oakley and Thompson

[119]See J. Harvie Wilkinson, *Serving Justice: A Supreme Court Clerk's View* (New York: Charterhouse Publishers, 1974), p. 18.

Act of 1925.[120] Often referred to as the "Judges Bill," Congress, per the urging of Chief Justice William Howard Taft and Justice Willis Van Devanter,[121] passed this legislation in apparent reaction to the Court's burgeoning caseload.[122] The practical effect of the legislation was to increase the Court's discretionary jurisdiction, eliminating what had since 1789 been a docket consisting primarily of mandatory appeals. Further, passage of the 1925 Act meant that the majority of cases granted plenary review by the justices would come to the Court via issuance of the writ of certiorari. As Abraham explains, law clerks came to occupy a central position in the process of selecting those cases deserving of issuance of this discretionary writ.[123] This transformation in the role of the law clerks was ultimately realized in 1972 with the creation of the "cert pool," a Burger Court innovation in which ". . . the petitions [for certiorari] would be divided equally among all the clerks in the pool, and the cert memos prepared by them would be circulated to each of the justices participating."[124] Presumably a reaction to Chief Justice Burger and Justice Lewis Powell's belief that the Court was increasingly unable to manage its workload, the creation of the "cert pool" and the justices' reliance on the recommendations of the "cert pool" is, according to Bernard Schwartz, a product of the "sheer volume" of work which now confronts the Court organization.[125]

---

[120]43 Stat. 936.

[121]Henry J. Abraham, *The Judicial Process: An Introductory Analysis of the Courts of the United States, England, and France*, 6th ed. (New York: Oxford University Press, 1993), p. 177.

[122]See H.W. Perry, "Certiorari, Writ of" in *The Oxford Companion to the Supreme Court of the United States*. ed. Kermit. L. Hall. (New York, Oxford University Press, 1992), p. 130.

[123]Abraham, p. 243.

[124]Schwartz, *The Ascent of Pragmatism*, p. 37.

[125]Ibid., p. 37.

By 1946, the Court's docket of case filings had grown to 1150.[126] Frank reports that in that year, two clerks were authorized for each justice.[127] Furthermore, during the 1941-1947 terms the justices produced concurring and dissenting opinions at a rate unprecedented in the previous 159 years of Court history.[128] Thus, because the size of Supreme Court work group had grown during the first one-half of the twentieth century, the Court had, in a behavioral sense, become a much different organization. Fragmentation in the opinion writing process had, itself, become an institution within an institution.

During the second half of the twentieth century, the number of case filings has continued a steep, upward trend. Former Supreme Court clerk Harvie Wilkinson argues that the magnitude of both the Court's docket and caseload management problems resulted from a marked increase in case filings during the period 1951 to 1971.[129] Wilkinson reports that the number of case filings would triple during the 1950s and 1960s. This, he suggests, triggered Congress's decision in 1974 to authorize the employment of three clerks for every sitting justice. Today, each of the justices is allowed to employ four law clerks. Both Justice's Rehnquist and Stevens, however, typically employ three law clerks.[130]

---

[126]Data provided by the Administrative Office of the United States Courts, Washington, D.C. *Cases Filed, Disposed Of, and Remaining on the Dockets in the Supreme Court of the United States During the October Terms, 1945-1954.*

[127]Frank, p. 116.

[128]See data provided by Blaustein and Mersky, p. 140.

[129]J. Harvie Wilkinson, p. 18.

[130]Data available from the Public Information Office of the United States Supreme Court. It is important that the Court routinely employs several law clerks which are assigned to the retired justices. As Edward Lazarus explains, the clerks assigned to work for the retired justices often assist the active justices. See Edward Lazarus, *Closed Chambers: The First Eyewitness Account of the Epic Struggles Inside the Supreme Court*, p. 19.

The factual depiction above is similar to a large portion of the research on law clerks. Albeit an interesting set of reflections on the historically commensurate increases in workload and the number of clerks employed by the Court, these observations reveal little about the evolving character of the Supreme Court's task environment and the law clerks' role in that evolutionary process. This literature does little to elucidate the underlying dynamic or consequences of what Bernard Schwartz described as the role of law clerks in changing "the very nature of the Supreme Court."[131] Additionally, the research on law clerks makes no attempt to approximate the moment at which the presence of law clerks altered the nature of the Court's task environment in a manner that produced quantitative effects on the justice's output of written opinions.

Other impressionistic interpretations in the research literature permit a tentative hypothesis regarding the period in which the clerks began to exert a significant influence on the opinion writing output of Supreme Court justices. Although on the periphery of the opinion production process, law clerk contributions to the substance of final opinions are arguably phenomena of the past fifty years. Oakley and Thompson explain that in the 1880s Justice Gray required law clerks to compose draft opinions.[132] However, the authors explain that these opinions were used primarily for discussion and argument purposes and were not a part of the substance of final drafts. Not until the late 1950s did scholars produce discussions of law clerks as proximate to the opinion writing process. In his 1958 book *The Marble Palace*, John P. Frank suggested that by the 1940s, at least, the law clerks were making substantive contributions to the justices' opinions.[133] In fact, Frank argues that during this period "sometimes clerks are allowed to do the bulk of the

---

[131]Ibid., p. 369.

[132]Oakley and Thompson, p. 13.

[133]Frank, pp. 118.

serious writing for the Justice."[134] Moreover, prior to the late 1950s, several scholarly descriptions of the work of law clerks still indicated that clerks performed only research and ministerial tasks. In the first half of the twentieth century Justice Louis D. Brandeis commented that "the reason the public thinks so much of the Justices of the Supreme Court is that they are almost the only people in Washington who do their own work."[135] In 1958, Alexander Bickel, former clerk to Justice Frankfurter, explained that law clerks read, evaluate, and suggest changes to draft opinions but do not make substantive contributions to final drafts.[136]

It remains, however, that by the late 1950s scholarly treatments of the opinion writing process were giving unqualified credence to the view that the presence of law clerks had significantly altered the nature of the Court's task environment. Alexander Bickel's widely read discussion of Justice Brandeis's work on the court contains several references to the justice - law clerk nexus. Characterizing government institutions generally, Frank noted in 1958 that "we live in the age of the staff researcher, the first-draft man; most important public officials make use of them."[137] In the same year, former law clerk Alexander Bickel observed that the work of law clerks is inextricably tied to the production of Supreme Court opinions. Bickel went so far as to suggest that law clerks participation in the opinion writing process has altered the nature of the Court's collective conscience. Bickel argues that "the law clerkship is in its modest way one of the influences that keep judicial law rationally responsive to the needs of the day."[138]

---

[134]Ibid., p. 117.

[135]Quoted in Bernard Schwartz, *A History of the Supreme Court*, p. 369

[136]*New York. Times*, April 17, 1958, p. A16.

[137]Frank, pp. 118-119.

[138]Bickel, Alexander, "The Court: An Independent Analysis." *New York Times*, April 27, 1958, section 6 (Magazine). Quoted in Baier, p.1126.

Justice William Rehnquist posited a more definitive characterization of the role of law clerks vis-a-vis the opinion writing process. Modifying an earlier statement,[139] Rehnquist announced that law clerks were, in fact, so proximate to the opinion writing process as to exert some influence over the substantive content of final drafts.[140] Other accounts of the work of clerks corroborated early descriptions of the role of clerks in the case selection process but were less clear on the role of clerks in the production of written opinions. Justice Tom Clark , quoting Justice Robert Jackson, explained that "a suspicion has grown at the bar that the law clerks. . . constitute a kind of junior court which decides the fate of certiorari petitions. This idea of the law clerks' influence gave rise to a lawyer's waggish statement that the Senate no longer need bother about confirmation of justices but ought to confirm the appointment of law clerks."[141]

Recent accounts of the Supreme Court's operations indicate that clerks continue to be prominent figures in the opinion drafting process. Lazarus' controversial book *Closed Chambers* portrays the Court as essentially "clerk driven" with the justices functioning primarily as

---

[139]In December of 1957 Rehnquist allowed that clerks exercised significant influence over the case selection process. He stated that clerks were given broad authority over the process of handling petitions for certiorari and making recommendations to the justices about those petitions. Yet, Rehnquist was reticent to suggest that the law clerks were instrumental in influencing the substantive content of opinion. As I indicate above, he later recanted this characterization. See Rehnquist, William H. "Who Writes the Opinions of the Supreme Court?" *U.S. News and World Report,* Dec 13, 1957, pp. 74-5.

[140]Rehnquist, William H. 1958. "Another View: Clerks Might 'influence' Some Actions." *U.S. News and World Report* (February 21, 1958), p. 116.

[141]Justice Robert H. Jackson as quoted by Tom Clark, "Internal Operation of the United States Supreme Court." *Journal of the American Judicature Society* 43 (1959): 45-8.

editors of the clerks' written work.[142] Posner's depiction of law clerks in the federal judiciary is also illuminating. He writes:

> What are these able, intelligent, mostly young people doing?
> Surely not merely running citations in Shepard's and shelving the
> judges' law books. They are, in many situations, "para judges."
> In some instances, it is to be feared, they are indeed invisible
> judges, for there are appellate judges whose literary
> style appears to change annually.[143]

Further, Chief Justice William Rehnquist explains that his clerks are responsible for preparing the first draft of nearly all opinions.[144] Sean Donahue, former Clerk to Justice Stevens, corroborates the Chief Justice's account of the opinion writing process. Donahue explains that clerks are intimately involved in the process of writing and producing opinions.[145] Donahue reports that Justice Stevens allowed clerks a large amount of autonomy and influence in the opinion writing process. Most important, Donahue argues that the law clerks are, in general, key actors in the Court's opinion writing process. Donahue states explains:

> As has been widely reported, clerks do a great deal of the Court's
> opinion drafting. I estimate that well over half of the text the
> Court now produces was generated by law clerks. The most

---

[142]Edward Lazarus, *Closed Chambers: The Justices, Clerks and Political Agendas that Control the Supreme Court* (New York: Times Books, 1998).

[143]Richard A. Posner, *The Federal Courts: Crisis and Reform* (Cambridge: Harvard University Press,1985), p. 106. Quoted in Schwartz, *History of the United States Supreme Court*, p. 38.

[144]Rehnquist, William. 1987. *The Supreme Court: How it Was, How is Is* (New York, William Morrow and Company, 1987), pp. 299-300.

[145]Donahue, Sean, "Behind the Pillars: Remarks on Law Clerks." *The Long Term View: Massachusetts School of Law* 3 (1995): 77-84.

common practice is to have a law clerk write the first draft of an opinion, followed by editing, rewriting and perhaps reorganization by the Justice. This process varies enormously from case to case; it may result in a near total rewrite or in only minor changes.[146]

Perhaps most important for this book is Posner's observation that the current role of law clerks on the Court is the culmination of a process of change. In 1996, Posner argued that during the last thirty-five years, the role of law clerks in the opinion writing process has increased.[147] Bernard Schwartz characterized the historical transformation in the role of the clerks in the following way: "In the Supreme Court, as in most institutions, the balance of power has shifted increasingly to the bureaucrats and away from the nominal heads. Law clerks now have tremendous influence."[148] This finding is corroborated by Corey and Baum who found significant relationships between ideological positions of Supreme Court justices and those of the lower court judges from whom they recruited law clerks. The authors observe that this result confirms the justices' awareness that law clerks are able to notably influence the content of written opinions.[149]

Thus, the research literature on law clerks decidedly supports the proposition that law clerks are inextricably linked to the process of producing Supreme Court opinions. Furthermore, the research literature supports the proposition that the work of the law clerks is intimately tied to the character of the Court's task environment. Most important, the research on law clerks reveals the presence of historical transformations in both the role of law clerks and character of the Supreme Court as an

---

[146]Ibid, p. 80

[147]Posner, *Federal Courts: Challenge and Reform*, p. 143.

[148]Schwartz, *The Ascent of Pragmatism*, p. 39

[149]Corey Distlear and Lawrence Baum. 2000. "Selection of Law Clerks and Polarization in the U.S. Supreme Court," *The Journal of Politics* 63 (2000): 871-2.

institution. The purpose of this book is to investigate the linkage between the two processes.

Research Implications: Law Clerks, Support Personnel, and the Decline of the Consensus Norm

From the existing literature I infer two points: First, the increasing presence of law clerks has altered the Court's task environment in a matter that diminishes the frequency of interaction among the justices, encouraging each justice to act individually and conduct his or her business on the Court as but one of "nine small, independent little law firms."[150] My inference is similar in content to Posner's suggestions about the causes of the decline in the consensus norm. Posner writes:

> The standard explanation is that the greater difficulty of the average Supreme Court case, ... and the Court's increasing involvement in areas of the law where there is no value consensus....makes greater disagreement inevitable. No doubt. But I suspect that the number of law clerks is also a factor. The decision to write a dissenting or concurring opinion is always discretionary, since the judge who does not want to join the decision of the majority can simply note his dissent from or his concurrence in the result. The less help a judge has, the less likely he is to write an opinion when he doesn't have to.[151]

In addition to the importance of clerks in remedying workload crises, several studies mention the importance of law clerks as factors influencing the number of dissenting and concurring opinions written by the justices. I infer from Posner's discussions a linkage between the ratio of the number of law clerks to the number of majority opinions written by the Supreme

---

[150]Lewis F. Powell, Jr., Report to the Labor Law Section of the American Bar Association., Atlanta, GA, August 11, 1976. Quoted in Segal and Spaeth, p. 297, n. 63.

[151]Posner, *The Federal Courts: Challenge and Reform*, p. 357.

Court justices and the Court's production of more dissenting and concurring opinions. In discussing differences in opinion writing practices between Supreme Court justices and the judges in the U.S. Courts of Appeals, Posner notes a higher law clerks to majority opinion ratio on the Supreme Court. Posner then explains that Supreme Court justices write more dissenting and concurring opinions than lower federal court judges.[152] A clear implication of Posner's discussion is that because of the number of law clerks assigned to the Court, justices enjoy the slack personal and institutional resources necessary to draft large numbers of noninstitutional opinions. Posner does not subject this assertion to empirical examination.

Stewart and Heck purport to test the type of assertion made by Posner. They report that historical increases in the numbers of law clerks assigned to the Court are associated with the net loss of opinion writing productivity.[153] Stewart and Heck's findings are, rather ironically and indirectly, supportive of the proposition that increases in the numbers of law clerks is directly related to increases in the numbers of dissenting and concurring opinions authored by the justices. Stewart and Heck operationally define productivity as the number of majority and per curiam opinions as a percentage of the Court's plenary docket. Thus, writing fewer majority and per curiam opinions allows the justices the time to author a greater number of dissenting and concurring opinions. Finding a negative relationship between the presence of law clerks and this operational definition, it is implicit to Stewart and Heck's findings that increases in the numbers of law clerks is associated with increases in the frequency of nonconsensual opinion writing (i.e., plurality, dissenting, and concurring opinions).

Posner's study provides yet another clue that the increasing presence of law clerks is associated with an increasing frequency of nonconsensual opinion writing. Posner points out that while the justices have not

---

[152]Ibid., p. 141.

[153]Joseph Stewart and Edward Heck, "Caseloads and Controversies: A Different Perspective on the Overburdened U.S. Supreme Court," *Justice System Journal* 12 (1985): 370-83.

increased the number of cases granted plenary review,[154] the justices have authored increasing numbers of concurring and dissenting opinions.[155] Posner also notes that this change has occurred in the context of historically exponential increases in the total number of case filings per term.[156] I infer from Posner's observation that law clerks may be responsible for creating the slack resources necessary for the authoring of increasing numbers of separate opinions. Specifically, it may be that law clerks manage the Court's workload and provide research and opinion writing support in a manner that permits the justices to behave independently, and in an increasing fashion, nonconsensually for the purposes of opinion writing.

A related piece of research encourages my suspicions about the linkage between law clerks and independent behavior on the part of the justices. Sandra Wood's examination of the determinants of inter-chamber memorandum writing supports the proposition that increased law clerks participation on the Court facilitates entrepreneurial, if not atomistic, behavior by the justices. Professor Wood argues that changes in the number of law clerks assigned to the justices is linked to the frequency of memo writing among justices prior to final votes on the merits.[157]

The judicial behavior genre offers no direct suggestion that increases in the number of support staff are linked to changing patterns of nonconsensual opinion writing. However, a cursory glance at historical data on the growth of the Court's budget appropriations,[158] the justice's

---

[154]Posner, *The Federal Courts, Challenge and Reform*, p. 53-56.

[155]Ibid., p. 357.

[156]Ibid., p. 55-56.

[157]Sandra L. Wood, "Bargaining on the Burger Court: Of Memos, Changes and Endorsements" (paper presented at the 1998 Annual Meeting of the Midwest Political Science Association Conference, Chicago, IL. May 23-25), p. 11.

[158]Segal, et. al., pp. 39-40.

requests to Congress for additional staff support,[159] and the number of support personnel employed by the Court reveals notable, and often abrupt, expansions in the size of the Court organization.[160] Further, Jeremy Bentham's observation that "law is not made by judge alone, but by judge and company"[161] deepens my suspicions that significant expansions in the size of the Court's work group, whether in the form of increasing numbers of law clerks or increasing numbers of support staff, are related to changes in the Court's formal expressions of the law. Moreover, I detect no in-principle reasons why the theoretical assertions of studies on the law clerks are not equally applicable to the work of support personnel. Thus, inferences about the relationship between the increasing presence of law clerks and nonconsensual opinion writing behaviors are easily expanded to include propositions about the influence of support personnel on collective opinion writing behaviors.

A second implication of the extant literature involves the role of support staff on the Court. I surmise that if increases in the law clerk resource are linked to alterations in the Court's task environment which is in turn related to changes in the behavior of the justices, other changes in the size of the Court's work group may have similar consequences. Two studies point directly to the impact of support personnel on the behavior of state courts. Mary Lou Stow and Harold J. Spaeth report a significant level of agreement between the policy recommendations of central research staff and the decisions of judges on the Michigan Courts of Appeals. In a related study, Professors Lesinski and Stockmeyer argue that use of central research staff is closely linked to the productivity of the

---

[159]U.S. Senate, Senate Hearings Before the Committee on Appropriations, State, Justice, Commerce, the Judiciary, and Related Agencies, 90th Cong., 2d sess., FY 1969, p. 159. [Government Document Y4.Ap6/2:St2/976 pt. 1.]; U.S. House of Representative, Hearings before a Subcommittee of the Committee on Appropriations, 94th Cong., 1st sess., p. 433. [Government Document y4.Ap6/1:St2/976/ pt.1].

[160] Ibid., pp. 51-52.

[161] Quoted in Baier, p. 1125.

Michigan Courts of Appeals.[162]   It is surprising, then, that public law scholars have devoted little attention to the connections between support staff and the Supreme Court's policy making functions.   Moreover, increases in the number of support staff assigned to the Court may have, in a manner much like that of the law clerks, altered the Court's working environment and influenced the justice's collective behaviors.

Studies of staff influence are common to research on legislative institutions.   Several studies on the Congress note the impact of staff personnel on organizational culture and decision making processes.[163] Furthermore, in his classic 1968 study *Democracy in the Public Service*, Frederick Mosher observes that the public agencies are to be manned by professionally socialized staff trained to adapt their expertise to the task of achieving public goals.[164]   Other studies warrant special consideration. In their recent examination of staff roles in Congress, Barbara Romzek and Jennifer Utter explain that "staff occupy positions of substantial influence in our national policymaking process and their numbers and roles have increased over time."[165]   Similarly, Paul Rundquist, Judy Schneider, and Frederick Pauls argue that "the impact of staff is so pervasive as to make their influence felt in sectors of the decision making and policy making

---

[162]Lesinski and Stockmeyer, "Prehearing Research and Screening in the Michigan Court of Appeals: One Court's Method for Increasing Judicial Productivity," *Vanderbilt Law Review* 26 (1973): 1239-40.

[163]See Richard H. Hall, " Professionalization and Bureaucratization," *American Sociological Review* 33 (1968):92-104; Kenneth Kofmehls, *Professional Staff in Congress* (West Lafayette, IN: Purdue University Press, 1977); Kenneth J. Meier, *Politics and the Bureaucracy: Politics and Policymaking in the Fourth Branch of Government* (Pacific Grove, CA: Brookes-Cole Publishers, 1993).

[164]Frederick Mosher, *Democracy and the Public Service* (New York: Oxford Universirt Press, 1968).

[165]Barabara S. Romzek and Jennifer Utter, "Congressional Legislative Staff: Political Professionals or Clerks," *American Journal of Political Science* 41 (1997): 1252.

processes."[166]

In his study of congressional staff, Michael Malbin attributes the influence of staff to both exponential growth in their numbers and historical transformation in their roles, bringing these individuals ever-more proximate to the policy making process.[167] Harrison Fox and Susan Webb Hammond note that the proliferation of congressional staff has meant that support personnel are at the center of the inter-office communications network, controlling the flow of information among representative's offices, and exerting significant influence over the course of policy making.[168] Salisbury and Shepsle explain that historical increases in staff have "constrain[ed] and shape[d] the behavior of members. . ." bringing expertise and independence to each representative's chambers.[169]

Thus, I argue that the proposition which links law clerks and support personnel to the Supreme Court's opinion writing activities is founded not just in research on judicial institutions, but is also grounded in studies of staff professionals in legislative bodies. I submit that the alternative formulation of the "small group" hypothesis linking law clerks, support personnel, and justices is consistent with scholars' general understanding of the behavior of political institutions. Much like studies of Congress which link unelected staff and professionals to the policymaking process, I suggest that changes in one important institutional feature of the Supreme Court - the number of law clerks and support personnel employed by the

---

[166]Paul S. Rundquist, Judy Schneider, and Frederick Pauls, *Congressional Staff: An Analysis of Their Roles, Functions, and Impacts, CRS Report to Congress.* Library of Congress, Washington, D.C.

[167]Michael W. Malbin, *Unelected Representatives: Congressional Staff and the Future of Representative Government* (New York: Basic Books, Inc., 1979).

[168]See generally Harrison W. Fox and Susan Webb Hammond, *Congressional Staffs: The Invisible Force in American Lawmaking* (New York: The Free Press, 1977).

[169]Salisbury and Shepsle, pp. 559, 570.

Court - may be causally linked to changes in patterns of nonconsensual opinion writing. Moreover, inasmuch as I propose to test an alternative formulation of the "small group" hypothesis, I suggest that an institutional analysis may be useful in explaining the decline in consensual norms on the United States Supreme Court. This is an approach to explaining individual level behavior deeply rooted in the history of the political science discipline.

Conclusions

Judicial scholars have found the perspectives of the "new institutionalism" useful in modeling patterns of dissent and dissensus on state courts. Professors Gerber and Park demonstrate that models founded on "neo-institutional" or "new-institutionalism" perspectives hold promise for explanations of dissent behavior on the United States Supreme Court. However, public law scholars have not tested models of dissensus on the Court which account for one of the most important structural changes in the institution's history - the rise of the law clerk as a key factor in the Court's principal tasks.

Inasmuch as it is derivative of "neo-institutional" studies such as that presented by Gerber and Park, this important, yet untested, proposition is implicated by the theoretical union between studies of dissent and dissensus on the Supreme Court, studies which analyze the behavior of the Court as a "small group," and historical accounts of the work of law clerks on the Court. Moreover, in studies of dissent and dissensus are implications that more subtle forms of small group interaction on the Court are linked to the historical trend toward increasing fragmentation of the opinion writing process. This signals that a reformulation of the "small group" effect may help explain the behaviors of Supreme Court justices. From this, I infer that along with the importance of law clerks, support personnel may be an important organizational resource which structures the ultimate opinion writing behaviors of the justices. Most important, this proposition is at once a test of a reformulated "small group" explanation of judicial behavior and a test of the principle teachings of the "new institutionalism" perspective. For studies of the decline of consensual norms, testing this proposition is essential to a complete explanation of the behavior of the modern Supreme Court.

In chapter 2, I offer a procedure for testing the appropriateness of these inferences. I identify several hypotheses, operational definitions of key variables, methods of data collection, and data analysis techniques designed to test the validity of the general propositions set forth in the discussion above.

Research Design: Testing an Alternative Formulation of the Small Group Hypothesis as an Explanation of the Historical Decline in Consensual Norms

Introduction

In Chapter 1, I reviewed the literature addressing the "new institutionalism" in public law research, studies which approach judicial behavior from the perspective of "small group" theory, historical accounts of the changing role of law clerks on the Court, and empirical studies aimed at modeling the changing patterns of nonconsensual opinion writing on the Court. Also in Chapter 1, I indicate the connection between these lines of research and the basic law clerk/support staff and opinion writing relationship. Related to this basic relationship, I recognize two possible conclusions regarding historical changes in the opinion writing behavior of Supreme Court justices.

It is possible that there is no detectable "small group" effect on the frequency of nonconsensual opinion writing on the Supreme Court; it may be that as elements of the Court's institutional structure, law clerks and support personnel exert no significant influence on patterns of nonconsensual opinion writing. Research by Albert Melone indicates that at least one type of "small group" hypothesis, namely the "freshman effect" hypothesis, is either time bound or simply an incorrect model of interpersonal interaction on the Court.[1] Kenneth Grambihler affirms Melone's proposition, arguing that the "freshman effect" hypothesis is simply incorrect.[2] Thus, it may be that explanations of Supreme Court behavior that rely on the principles of "small group" interaction are similarly incorrect and the hypothesized law clerk/support personnel - opinion writing hypothesis will fail to prove otherwise.

An alternative possibility is that "small group" interactions on the Court do influence opinion writing activities, but demonstrating this empirically requires a reformulation of previous notions of the "small group" effect. This proposition follows from my Chapter 1 discussion of research on law clerks, an extension of the theoretical propositions offered by this literature that includes suspicions about the importance of support personnel, and studies of changing patterns of opinion writing on the Court. More specifically, Stacia Haynie encourages judicial scholars to search for complex patterns of interaction among factors that may account for historical changes in opinion writing among the justices.[3] David O'Brien's unsubstantiated assertion is more overt. O'Brien suggests that increases in the numbers of clerks and their delegated responsibilities contributes to the steady increase in the number of concurring and

---

[1]Albert P. Melone, "Revisiting the Freshman Effect Hypothesis: The First Two Terms of Justice Anthony Kennedy," *Judicature* 74 (1990): 12. The "freshman effect" hypothesis indicates that newly appointed justices demonstrate three qualities: (1) bewilderment concerning their duties; (2) writing fewer opinions than their more senior colleagues; and (3) voting with a centrist or pivotal bloc of justices while joining a conservative or liberal bloc after three years of service. See Eloise Snyder, "The Supreme Court as a Small Group," *Social Forces* 36 (1958): 232-8.

[2]Kenneth Lee Grambihler, "A Longitudinal Analysis of the Freshman Effect Hypothesis of United States Supreme Court Justices (1953-1988 Terms)," (Ph.D. diss., Southern Illinois University, 1993). p. 203.

[3]Stacia Haynie, "Leadership and Consensus on the U.S. Supreme Court," *Journal of Politics* 54 (1992): 1159-69.

dissenting opinions written each year.[4] Judge Patricia Wald makes a similar, albeit untested assertion. She writes: "Indeed a judge sometimes decides whether to file a separate opinion or to dissent in a case based at least in part upon the support she can anticipate from her clerks."[5] Edward Lazarus's observation supports Wald's assertion.[6] Moreover, if these assertions are true, there are reasons to suspect that the increasing presence of other support personnel has also contributed to changes in opinion writing behaviors.

Thus, I infer from the judicial behavior literature that an alternative specification of the small group effect that considers the increasing prominence of law clerks and support personnel may account for changes in the opinion writing behaviors of Supreme Court justices. The principle that underlies the assertions of Wald and O'Brien is that increasing numbers of Court staff are linked to the justice's decisions to draft separate, dissenting, and concurring opinions. Moreover, whether increasing numbers of law clerks and support personnel are related to the number of opinions produced by the Court, particularly those opinion writing behavior associated with dissensus, is an important research question from which I derive the several hypotheses identified below.

General Hypothesis, H1

As the numbers of law clerks and support personnel assigned to the United States Supreme Court during the period 1935 to 1995 has increased, the justices' opinion writing behaviors have become increasingly nonconsensual.

---

[4]David O'Brien, *Storm Center: The Supreme Court in American Politics* (New York: W.W. Norton and Company, 1990), p. 170.

[5]Patricia M. Wald, "Selecting Law Clerks," *Michigan Law Review* 89 (1990): 153.

[6]Edward Lazarus, *Closed Chambers: The First Eyewitness Account of the Epic Struggles Inside the Supreme Court* (New York: Times Books, 1998), p. 271.

Specific Hypotheses of H1

H1a. As the number of law clerks and support personnel assigned to the justices on the United States Supreme Court has increased, the *total number of opinions* written by the justices has also increased.

H1b. As the number of law clerks and support personnel assigned to the justices on the United States Supreme Court has increased, the number of *opinions for the Court* written by the justices has not increased.

H1c. As the number of law clerks and support personnel assigned to the justices of the United States Supreme Court has increased, the number of *separate opinions* written by the justices has also increased.

H1d. As the number of law clerks and support personnel assigned to the justices of the United States Supreme court has increased, the number of *dissenting opinions* written by the justices has also increased.

H1e. As the number of law clerks and support personnel assigned to the justices of the United States Supreme Court has increased, the number of *concurring opinions* written by the justices has also increased.

General Hypothesis, H2

Increases in the number of nonconsensual opinions written by the justices during the period 1935 to 1995 is related to the increasing presence of law clerks and support personnel on the Court when controlling for changes in the ideological composition of the Court, changes in the composition of the Court's docket of cases granted plenary review, changes in the degree of inexperience on the Court, the frequency of turnover in the Court's membership, changes in the leadership style of Chief Justices, and changes in the size of the Court's caseload.

Specific Hypotheses of H2

H2a. Increases in the numbers of separate, dissenting, and concurring opinions written by the justices of the United States Supreme Court is related to a statistically significant degree to the increasing presence of law clerks and support personnel when controlling for changes in the ideological composition of the Court.

H2b. Increases in the numbers of separate, dissenting, and concurring opinions written by the justices of the United States Supreme Court is related to a statistically significant degree to the increasing presence of law clerks and support personnel when controlling for the relative turnover on the Court per term.

H2c. Increases in the numbers of separate, dissenting, and concurring opinions written by the justices of the United States Supreme Court is related to a statistically significant degree to the number of law clerks and support personnel on the court when controlling for the relative inexperience of justices on the Court in each term.

H2d. Increases in the number of separate, dissenting, and concurring opinions written by the justices of the United States Supreme Court is related to a statistically significant degree to the increasing presence of law clerks and support personnel when controlling for changes in the composition of the docket of cases granted plenary review.

H2e. Increases in the number of separate, dissenting, and concurring opinions written by the justices of the Untied States Supreme Court is related to a statistically significant degree to the increasing presence of law clerks and support personnel when controlling for changes in the occupant of the chief justice's seat on the Court.

H2f. Increases in the numbers of separate, dissenting, and concurring opinions written of the justices of the United States Supreme Court is related to a statistically significant degree to the increasing presence of law clerks and support personnel when controlling for changes in the Court's workload.

Conceptualization of Tests for General Hypothesis H1

In the discussion that follows, I identify the sequential steps used in testing the hypotheses identified above. In explicating each step I identify the hypothesis being tested, the operational definitions of the concepts being examined, the specific variables being examined, the sources of data used in testing the hypotheses, and the methods of data analysis used to test the hypotheses.

Testing the first general hypothesis regarding the linear relationship between increases in the number of clerks and support personnel and the trend toward nonconsensual opinions writing by the justices of the

Supreme Court requires a five process. Since the first general hypothesis is merely a guide to specific empirical referents of nonconsensual opinion writing, I begin by testing each of the five specific hypotheses associated with H1. Doing so requires that Pearson correlation coefficients are calculated for each of the five *dependent* and the two *independent* variables identified in H1. In short, I use Pearson correlation coefficients to determine the strength of the linear association between the total number of opinions, the number of opinions for the Court, the number of separate opinions, the number of dissenting opinions, the number of concurring opinions, and the number of law clerks and support personnel employed by the Court in each term. In this book, I examine the importance of increases in the number of law clerks and support personnel assigned to the Court as explanatory factors [independent variables] in the specific opinion writing behaviors of the justices [dependent variables]. In addition to verifying the presence of linear relationships between the independent and dependent variables, Pearson correlation coefficients are calculated to justify the use of linear regression techniques to estimate what proportion of the variability in nonconsensual opinion writing is linked to changes in the numbers of law clerks and support personnel employed by the Court. Thus, each of the five dependent variables is an empirical referent of dissensus among the justices and the willingness and ability of the justices to formally articulate views independent of the opinion that controls the Court's decision. In short, each of the dependent variables is a measure of both the willingness and ability to express a view independent of that prepared by the Court's majority or plurality voting coalition.

Similar to the first general hypothesis, the second general hypothesis suggests a basic relationship between law clerks, support personnel, and the writing of nonconsensual opinions. However, in testing the second general hypothesis I examine the basic relationship between law clerks / support personnel and nonconsensual writing when controlling for the various competing explanations of dissensus on the Court. Here, I limit the range of dependent variables to measures of dissenting, concurring, and separate opinions. Doing so allows a direct comparison of my findings to those presented by Professors Haynie[7], Walker, Epstein, and Dixon[8], Gerber and Park[9] and Caldeira and Zorn.[10] Thus, testing the second general hypothesis, H2, requires that I construct several multiple regression models that include as independent variables the numbers of law clerks, support personnel, and each of the competing explanations of dissensus associated with H2.

The universe of cases used in testing each hypothesis is each term of the United States Supreme Court during the period 1935 to 1995.[11] Furthermore, I collected data on the number of dissenting, concurring and separate opinions produced by the Court, as well as the number of law clerks and the number of support personnel assigned to the Court in each term during the 1935 to 1995 period. This particular period of Supreme Court history is selected for the following reasons: First, including in the analysis data on opinion writing behaviors prior to the 1940 term allows for consideration of the episodic change in consensus norms suggested by Walker, Epstein, and Dixon, and Haynie and

------

[7]Stacia Haynie, pp. 1158-69.

[8]Walker, Thomas G., Lee Epstein, and William Dixon, "On the Mysterious demise of Consensual Norms on the United States Supreme Court," *Journal of Politics* 50 (1988): 361-89.

[9]Scott D. Gerber and Keeok Park, " The Quixotic Search for Consensus on the U.S. Supreme Court: A Cross-Judicial Empirical Analysis of the Rehnquist Court Justices," *American Political Science Review* 91 (1997): 390-408.

[10]Gregory Caldeira and Christopher J.W. Zorn, "Of Time and Consensual Norms on the United States Supreme Court," *American Journal of Political Science* 42 (1998): 874-902.

[11]Use of the ideological heterogeneity score to test H2a limits the universe of cases to the 1946-1995 terms.

Bowen.[12] Second, consideration of opinion writing data since the 1935 term allows for consideration of Haynie's argument that increases in one referent of dissensus, namely the number of concurring opinions, is traceable to the Hughes Court and not the later Stone Court as argued by Walker, Epstein, and Dixon.[13] Moreover, including data from Supreme Court terms prior to the Stone Court is consistent with the need to examine determinants of nonconsensual opinion writing in years prior to the supposed revolution in consensus norms in the 1940s.

The first general hypothesis proposes a relationship between the nonconsensual qualities of the justices' opinion writing activities in each term and the number of law clerks and support personnel assigned to the Court in each term. Further, H1 is examined by testing each of the specific hypotheses associated with H1. Below, I indicate the operational definitions observed and the procedures for testing each of the specific hypotheses associated with H1. However, a few operational definitions warrant immediate explanation.

The dependent variable, the total number of opinions written by the justices in each term is defined as the sum of all opinions for the Court, and the separate, dissenting, and concurring opinions written by the justices. Excluded from this analysis are per curiam opinions and opinions announcing the judgment of the Court. Each of the latter two types of opinions do not contain substantial legal reasoning or substantial legal arguments. I assume that the need to write such opinions does not significantly deplete the stock of institutional resources available for the production of signed opinions. Thus, I contend that changes in the numbers of per curiam opinions and opinions announcing judgement do not reveal the importance of clerks and support staff as factors which create the slack institutional resources necessary for drafting the optional

---

[12]Walker, Epstein, and Dixon, p. 362.; Stacia Haynie, p. 1159; Terry Bowen, "Consensual Norms and the Freshman Effect on the United States Supreme Court," *Social Science Quarterly* 76 (1995): 223.

[13]Walker, Epstein, and Dixon, p. 362.

concurring and dissenting opinions.[14] Moreover, as Justice Stevens explains, the use of per curiam decisions does not preclude the authoring of individual opinions.[15] Thus, exclusion of per curiam opinions from this analysis does not exclude from the study any of the lengthy, written expressions of dissensus that follow orally argued cases.

The total number of law clerks assigned to the Court during a given term is defined as the total number of law clerks assigned to the active and retired justices on the Supreme Court.[16] The total number of support personnel is defined as the total number of full-time employees providing

---

[14]John Paul Stevens states that "the Court is deciding more cases on the merits without the benefit of full briefing and oral argument, using the currently fashionable technique of explaining its reasons in a 'per curiam' opinion - a document written for the Court by an anonymous member of its ever increasing administrative staff. see John Paul Stevens, "Some Thoughts on Judicial Restraint," in *Judicial Politics: Readings from Judicature*. ed. Elliot Slotnick. (Washington, D.C.: The American Judicature Society, 1992), p. 405. Not including in my analysis those per curiam opinions and opinions announcing judgement may suppress some of the influence of law clerks and support personnel on the primary tasks of the Court. However, if dispensing of cases via per curiam opnion is increasingly descriptive of the Court's work, the use of clerks and support personnel to write these opinions may have the effect of reserving the justice's resources for the drafting of the more lengthy signed opinions. Thus, whether or not per curiam opinions are included in the analysis, one can infer the influence of law clerks and support personnel on the frequency with which the justices produce the formal, written expressions of dissensus found in concurring and dissenting opinions. In recent terms, the Court has issued per curiam opinions in 12 or fewer orally argued cases per term. However, in 1976 the Court issued per curiam opinions in 22 orally argued cases.

[15]Ibid., p. 409, n. 3. Data for the number of law clerks assigned to the Court in each term were provided by the Public Information Office of the United States Supreme Court.

[16]Edward Lazarus explains that retired clerks often provide assistance to the active justices. See Lazarus, p. 19.

administrative support services to the Court.[17] Support personnel include the administrative assistant to the chief justice, members of the secretarial pool, employees of the Clerk of Court's office, the Marshal, the Supreme Court police officers working under the supervision of the Marshal, the Reporter of Decisions and the Reporter's assistants, the Court Librarian's staff, the Court Curator, the additional personal staff (excluding the law clerks) assigned to each justice, and the employees of the Court's Legal Office.

Data for all dependent variables is gathered from one source. Data for the total number of opinions, the number of opinions for the Court, the number of separate opinions, the number of dissenting opinions, and the number of concurring opinions during the period 1935 to 1995 are taken from the *Annual Statement of the Number of Printed Opinions, Office of the Clerk of the United States Supreme Court.*[18]   I have carefully corroborated the accuracy of these data using several alternative sources of opinion writing statistics, each of which deserves particular mention. The accuracy of data during the period 1953-1993 are confirmed by reference to the *United States Supreme Court Judicial Data Base 1953-1995 Terms*[19] (hereafter referred to as the Spaeth data set) and the

---

[17]Data for the number of support personnel employed by the Court are taken from Walker, et. al., *The Supreme Court Compendium*, p. 51-52. These data are also found in the *Budget of the United States Government* (Washington, D.C.: Government Printing Office, 1932-1962) and *Appendix to the Budget* (Washington, D.C.: Government Printing Office, 1963-1995).

[18]These data were collected and provided by David M. O'Brien, Department of Government and Politics, University of Virginia. See O'Brien, p. 431, n.146.

[19]Harold J. Spaeth, United States Supreme Court Judicial data Base, 1953-1995 Terms [Computer File]. 7th ICPSR Version. East Lansing, MI: Michigan State University, Department of Political Science [producer], 1996. Ann Arbor, MI: Inter-University Consortium for Political and Social Research [distributor], 1997.

Supreme Court Compendium.[20] The accuracy of opinion writing data for Supreme Court terms during the period 1935 to 1972 are confirmed using Blaustein and Mersky's compilation of opinion writing data on the first 100 Supreme Court justices.[21] Also, the Harvard Law Review's Annual Survey (November issues) was used to corroborate the accuracy of opinion writing data for the period 1946-1995.

The Supreme Court Compendium contains tables of important decisions in Supreme Court history, a brief rendition of the Court's institutional development, a comprehensive statement of the Supreme Court Rules, and a large number of tabular presentations of opinion writing and voting data on the justices serving from the 1953 through the 1997 term. Opinion writing and voting behavior data are reproduced from the Spaeth data set.

The Spaeth data set, formally known as the *United States Supreme Court Judicial Database*, is a compilation of data on all Supreme Court decisions in cases granted plenary review during the 1953-1995 terms. Data on the decisions are grouped into six broad categories, with multiple variables comprising each category. These categories include case identification variables, case background variables, chronological variables indicating the natural Court and chief justice, substantive variables indicating the jurisprudential and factual characteristics of each case, case outcome variables, and voting and opinion writing variables measuring the specific behaviors of each justice. The Inter-University Consortium for Political and Social Research (ICPSR) makes the data set available free of charge to all member institutions. Previously accessible only to mainframe users, the Spaeth Data set is now available from the ICPSR on floppy disks as an SPSS or SAS portable file. Furthermore, James L. Gibson is the author of the *United States Supreme Court*

---

[20]Lee Epstein, Jeffrey Segal, Harold J. Spaeth, and Thomas G. Walker, *The Supreme Court Compendium* (Washington, D.C.: Congressional Quarterly, Inc., 1994).

[21]Albert P. Blaustein and Roy M. Mersky, *The First One-Hundred Justices: Statistical Studies of the Supreme Court of the United States* (Hamden, CT: Archon Books, 1978).

Judicial Data Base Phase II User's Guide.[22] He discusses each category of variables, explains data collection techniques and the Spaeth coding system, and suggests various strategies for aggregating and processing the data for social science research.

The Blaustein and Mersky volume contains a biographical treatment of the first one hundred justices of the Supreme Court, beginning with John Jay in 1789 and ending with William Rehnquist in 1971. Also, eleven tables reveal data on opinion writing practices, prior judicial experience of the justices, and turnover in seat assignments on the Court. In chapters two through five, several authors present analyses of opinion writing practices, a proposed scheme for rating the performance of the justices, criteria for selecting qualified justices, and historical discussions of Supreme Court nominees who never served on the Court. This edited volume is a particularly useful source of disaggregated data on the justices' opinion writing activities.

The data for the independent variable the total number of clerks assigned to the Court in each term is provided by the Public Information Office of the United States Supreme Court. Data provided by the Public Information Office is reported in Appendix A. The Public Information Office of the Supreme Court maintains yearly data on the law clerks and support personnel assigned to the Court. Data for the total number of support personnel assigned to the Court in each term is taken from the *Budget of the United States Government* for the 1935-1962 terms and the Appendix to the Budget for the 1963-1995 terms. These data are also available in the *Supreme Court Compendium.*[23]

Testing the first general hypothesis and the specific hypotheses associated with H1 involves consideration of the basic law clerk/support staff - opinion writing relationship. As I discussed in the previous chapter,

---

[22]James L. Gibson, *United States Supreme Court Judicial Data Base, Phase II User's Guide* (New York: Peter Lang, 1997).

[23]*Budget of the United States Government* (Washington, D.C.: Government Printing Office, successive years, 1935-1962); *Appendix to the Budget* (Washington, D.C.: Government Printing Office, successive years, 1963-1995)

the existence of a direct law clerk - opinion writing relationship presumes that the increasing presence of law clerks has altered the fundamental nature of the Court's task environment. The law clerk-support personnel-opinion writing hypothesis presumes that the increasing presence of law clerks encourages the justices to produce written opinions distinct from those prepared by the Court majority or plurality. Also, this general proposition presumes that the increasing numbers of law clerks are linked to the justices' willingness to issue opinions reflecting the views of only a fragmented majority coalition. In short, this general proposition indicates that the increasing presence of law clerks lowers the threshold point at which the justices discontinue the search for consensus and decide to draft additional opinions or opinions that reflect disagreement on the Court. I infer from the extant literature the existence of a similar relationship between the number of support personnel and the Court's task environment.[24]

Before presenting a quantitative approach to examining the importance of law clerks and support personnel for subsequent opinion writing behaviors, I fully explore and evaluate in light of prevailing knowledge in the field of organizational theory the merits of my central proposition that these professional staff shape the justices' ultimate opinion writing activities. Moreover, I examine the professionalization of the law clerk role, the law clerks' drive for autonomy and influence in the Court organization, and present an original theory that links nonconsensual opinion writing to the increasing numbers of law clerks employed by the Court. This discussion appears in Chapter 3.

Prior to statistically testing a relationship between law clerks, support personnel, and patterns of nonconsensual opinion writing behavior, I present tables of data and graphs that indicate historical

---

[24]I explained in Chapter 1 that several studies of Congress encourage the view that historical increase in staff resources has allowed individual members to decrease the frequency with which they seek the counsel of colleagues on matters of public policy. I include the support personnel variable to test a similar trend in Supreme Court justices' opinion writing behavior. For example, see Robert H. Salisbury and Kenneth A. Shepsle, "U.S. Congressmen as Enterprise," *Legislative Studies Quarterly* 6 (1981):559-76.

changes in the frequency of nonconsensual opinion writing. Also, I present bar graphs that indicate the historical increases in the numbers of law clerks and support personnel employed by the Court during the 1935-1995 period. A graphical representation of the data reveals basic, upward trends in the number of law clerks and support personnel assigned to the Court per term. Also, a graphical representation of the data allows identification of instances of notable increases in the number of law clerks and support personnel as well as periods characterized by little or no change in the number of law clerks and support personnel assigned to the Court.

Graphical and tabular representations of the data will also assist in qualitatively evaluating the linkages between increased law clerks and support staff on the Court and changes in opinion writing behaviors. Throughout the dissertation, I evaluate the persistent changes in nonconsensual opinion writing practices since the 1930s. Further, to supplement an examination of broad trends in the opinion writing data, I relate the justices' commentaries on opinion writing behaviors and law clerk participation on the Court. These scholarly commentaries on the role of law clerks provide an analytical and theoretical context in which to discuss the implications of the data presented in Chapter 4. In short, I begin testing H1 and its associated specific hypotheses by analyzing descriptive data. This process provides a substantive context for the use of more rigorous quantitative techniques in testing for the presence of the same covariational relationships.

I employ one key inferential method to quantitatively test H1 and its associated specific hypotheses. Pearson correlation coefficients are calculated to verify the presence of linear relationships between each of the measures of nonconsensual opinion writing and the total numbers of law clerks and support staff employed by the Court in each term. Calculating correlation coefficients reveals the direction and strength of the linear association between these key variables. Although an elementary inferential technique, these correlation coefficients inform the use of each variable in multiple regression models. Multiple regression models are used to test H2 and its specific hypotheses.

Thus, modeling the presence of a basic law clerk / support personnel - opinion writing relationship involves: (1) examining graphical and tabular presentations of opinion data and historical increases in the numbers of law clerks and support personnel employed by the Court; and (2) calculating Pearson correlation coefficients for each of the five measures of opinion writing and the number of clerks and support personnel assigned to the court in each term.

In a later section, I describe a procedure for testing Hypothesis H2. Testing Hypothesis H2 and its associated hypotheses involves constructing multiple regression models of nonconsensual opinion writing wherein each of the competing measures of nonconsensual opinion writing are included in one model along with measures of the number of law clerks and support personnel employed by the Court. Regression equations are presented to identify and estimate linear relationships between the independent variables, number of law clerks and support personnel assigned to the Court per term, and each of the various indicators of non-consensual opinion writing. Thus, regression equations are used in an effort to identify an independent relationship between the increasing presence of law clerks and support personnel on the Court and changing patterns of nonconsensual opinion writing.

Testing H1a, H1b, H1c, H1d, and H1e

Each of the five types of opinion writing is treated in one of the specific hypotheses of H1. I test H1a by calculating a Pearson correlation coefficient for the total number of opinions written in each term and the total number of clerks assigned to the Court in each corresponding term and the total number of support personnel assigned to the Court in each term. The total number of opinions written by the justices in each term is defined as the sum of the number of opinions for the Court, separate opinions, dissenting opinions, and concurring opinions written by the justices in each term. Because each plenary reviewed case produces a maximum of one opinion for the Court, and the size of the Court's plenary docket has not significantly increased, increases in the total numbers of opinions written in each term is an unambiguous indication of change in the composition of the Court's yearly opinion output; increased numbers of opinions is a signal that the justices are drafting more opinions that do not reflect an institutional position. A direct relationship between the numbers of law clerks, support staff, and the total numbers of opinions written by the Court in each term will imply the importance of law clerks in the justices' willingness to draft opinions apart from that representing an institutional view.

I test H1b by calculating a Pearson correlation coefficient for the total number of opinions for the Court written in each term and the total number of law clerks and support personnel assigned to the Court in each corresponding term. An opinion for the Court is defined as a written opinion, containing substantial legal reasoning, which announces the rationale for the decision of a majority of the Court's justices. Opinions for the Court reflect the justices' ability to attain at least minimal consensus vis-a-vis a particular case. Thus, I argue that an inverse relationship between the numbers of law clerks, support staff, and the numbers of opinions for the Court must be interpreted to mean that expansions in the size of the Court work group are related to the justices' willingness to depart from a norm of writing consensual, institutional opinions.

I test H1c by calculating a Pearson correlation coefficient for the total number of separate opinions written in each term and the total number of law clerks and support personnel assigned to the Court in each corresponding term. David O'Brien defines a separate opinion as a written expression of the Court's ruling in which only a plurality of justices agree to the entire opinion. Increases in the numbers of separate opinions is evidence of a failure or unwillingness to achieve consensus among at least the same five members of the Court with regard to all parts of a single opinion. Thus, I suggest that a direct relationship between the numbers of law clerks, support staff, and the numbers of plurality opinions written per term is an indication that expansions in the size of the Court work group are related to tendencies toward nonconsensual behavior.

I test H1d by calculating a Pearson correlation coefficient for the total number of dissenting opinion written in each term and the total number of law clerks and support personnel assigned to the Court in each corresponding term. A dissenting opinion is defined as a written opinion expressing the rationale for the voting decision of one or more justices who did not vote with the majority or plurality of justices. This definition excludes simple dissents or mere announcements of dissent absent a reasoned statement for the dissent.

Finally, I test H1e by calculating a Pearson correlation coefficient for the total number of concurring opinions written in each term and the total number of law clerks and support personnel assigned to the Court in each corresponding term. A concurring opinion is defined as a written opinion announcing a vote with the Court majority or plurality yet articulating a substantively different rationale for the majority or plurality decision. Not included in this definition are general concurrences or those which merely announce a vote with the majority yet do not contain a reasoned, substantial legal justification for departure from the content of the majority opinion. I do, however, recognize the importance of dissenting votes absent an accompanying written dissent. In Chapter 3, I examine the tendency among twentieth century justices to author a written dissent whenever casting a dissenting vote on the merits.

Although valuable in testing H1 and its associated hypotheses, the Pearson correlation coefficient does not fully reveal the nature of law clerks / support personnel - opinion writing relationship proposed in H1. The Pearson correlation coefficients reflect only the extent of linear relationships between the independent and dependent variables identified in H1. The Pearson correlation coefficients do not reveal the proportion of the variability in the opinion writing variables explained by the presence of the independent variables. Doing so requires the use of regression equations. Further, it is important to estimate the independent relationship between increases in the numbers of law clerks and support personnel employed by the Court and the frequency of nonconsensual opinion writing. I use multivariate regression equations in an attempt to achieve this important goal. In sum, regression analysis is used to test H2 and its associated hypotheses.

Testing H2a, H2b, H2c, H2d, H2e, and H2f

After determining the presence of linear relationships between the two independent variables and each of the dependent variables, I assess the explanatory power of the independent variables when controlling for measures of each competing explanation of dissent and dissensus.

Moreover, testing the second general hypothesis requires an assessment of the correctness of the basic law clerk / support personnel - opinion writing proposition while controlling for competing explanations of dissent and dissensus. To test H2, I utilize multiple regression analysis methods. To test the second general hypothesis I examine the independent effect of increases in the numbers of law clerks and support personnel assigned to the Court on changes in three dependent variables: the total number of separate opinions written per term, the total number of dissenting opinions written per term, and the total number of concurring opinions written per term. When regressing each of these dependent variables on the independent variables, the total number of law clerks and support personnel assigned to the Court in each term, I control for several competing explanations of dissent behavior. I control for changes in the ideological division on the Court, changes in turnover rate on the Court, changes in the level of inexperience among the justices, changes in the substantive composition of the Court's plenary docket, changes in the occupant of the chief justice's seat on the Court, and changes in the Court's workload.

In Chapters 6 and 7, I test the specific hypotheses associated with H2. I present several multivariate regression models for each of the three dependent variables identified above. Each model includes measures on either the law clerk or support personnel variables and each of the control variables associated with H2.[25] The following are approximate mathematical representations of the models presented in Chapter 7.[26]

$$SepOp = a + b1(clerks) + b2(ID) + b3(CJ) + b4(turn) + b5(inexp) + b6(dckt\ comp) + b7(caseload)$$

---

[25]In Chapter 6, I note that the degree of inter-correlation between the law clerk and support personnel variables precludes use of both variables in the same equation.

[26]In the interests of brevity, I include here only one chief justice variable. In the regression models presented in Chapters 6 and 7, several chief justice dummy variables are included in each equation.

SepOp $=a + b1(supp.\ pers.) + b2(ID) + b3(CJ) + b4(turn) +$
$\quad\quad b5(inexp) + b6(dckt\ comp) + b7(caseload)$

DissentOp $= a + b1(clerks) + b2(ID) + b3(CJ) + b4(turn) + b5(inexp)$
$\quad\quad + b6(dckt\ comp) + b7(caseload)$
DissentOp $= a + b1(supp.\ pers.) + b2(ID) + b3(CJ) + b4(turn) +$
$\quad\quad b5(inexp) + b6(dckt\ comp) + b7(caseload)$

ConcurrOp$= a + b1(clerks) + b2(ID) + b3(CJ) + b4(turn) + b5(inexp)$
$\quad\quad + b6(dckt\ comp) + b7(caseload)$
ConcurrOp $= a + b1(supp.\ pers.) + b2(ID) + b3(CJ) + b4(turn) +$
$\quad\quad b5(inexp) + b6(dckt\ comp) + b7(caseload)$

The source of data on the dependent variables for Court terms during the period 1953 to 1995 is identical to that used in testing H1. Sources of data on the control variables are indicated in each of the following descriptions of tests of specific hypotheses.

When testing H2a, i.e., controlling for ideological division on the Court, the universe of study is limited by aggregate data availability when using the ideological heterogeneity score identified in Chapter 1. Tests for H2a involving the use of ideology scores use data prepared by Segal and Cover and Segal, Epstein, Cameron and Spaeth.[27] Data from these two

---

[27]Ideology scores are taken from the following sources: For justices serving during the period 1953-1988 see Jeffrey A. Segal and Albert D. Cover "Ideological values and the Votes of U.S. Supreme Court Justices," *American Political Science Review* 83 (1989): 560. Quoted in Walker, et. al., *The Supreme Court Compendium.* For justices serving during the period 1989-1995 see Jeffrey Segal, Lee Epstein, Charles Cameron, and Harold Spaeth, "Ideological Values and the Votes of U.S. Supreme Court Justices Revisited," *Journal of Politics* 57 (1995): 816. Note: In addition to extending the initial study to include scores for justices Souter and Thomas, Segal, et. al. added to their analysis ideological scores for justices Black, Reed, Frankfurter, Douglas, Murphy, Jackson, Rutledge, Burton, Clark, Vinson, and Minton. Ideological scores for justices Ginsburg and Breyer have been calculated by Jeffrey Segal and appear in the 1997 Edition of the *Supreme Court Compendium.*

sources cover Court terms during the period 1946-1995. Thus, not included in the analysis are ideological heterogeneity scores for the period 1935 to 1945. Moreover, in controlling for changes in the ideological heterogeneity among the justices I examine a truncated version of the universe of study identified in H1 and H2. The smaller number of observations utilized in testing H2a somewhat limits the generalizability of the conclusions about the importance of ideological heterogeneity as a factor in the decline of the consensus norm during the period 1935 - 1995. However, in tests for H2a, I utilize a time series of sufficient length and characterized by considerable variation on the dependent variable. Thus, I believe that despite the use of somewhat truncated samples, tests for H2a allow (at least theoretically) valid conclusions as to the importance of the ideological heterogeneity score variable in the presence of the identified control variables.

Testing H2a. I regress each of the three dependent variables identified in the previous paragraph on the independent variables, the number of law clerks and support personnel assigned to the Court in each term, while controlling for changes in the ideological division on the Court.

I suspect that higher degrees of ideological division on the Court are associated with increasingly frequent nonconsensual opinion writing. The operational definitions of the dependent and independent variables are identical to those indicated in the discussion of procedures for testing the first general hypothesis. I utilize an ideological heterogeneity score to measure change in the ideological division on the Court. Ideological heterogeneity is defined as the standard deviation of ideological scores on the Court for each term of the Vinson, Warren, Burger, and Rehnquist Courts. I use SPSS to determine the standard deviation of the ideological scores of individual justices as determined by Segal and Cover and Segal, Epstein, Cameron, and Spaeth and reported in the *Supreme Court Compendium*.[28] Thus, I calculate an ideological heterogeneity score for each term. This number appearing in the model as continuous data is used as the measure on the control variable when the total number of separate opinions, dissenting opinions, and concurring opinions are sequentially

---

[28]Ibid., p. 45.

regressed on the independent variables, the total number of law clerks and support personnel serving on the Court during each term.

To test H2a, I also use a partisan composition variable as a surrogate measure of the ideological composition of the Court. In an approach similar to that employed by Haynie, I determined the size of the majority party coalition on the Court in each term during the 1935-1995 period. Thus, for a term in which seven of the nine justices were Republican identifiers, a value of "7" is recorded for the observation on the partisan composition variable. In Chapter 6, I present a Pearson correlation coefficient indicating that the partisan composition variable is a viable surrogate for the ideological heterogeneity score. Inasmuch as I expect increases in the ideological heterogeneity score to be associated with increasing numbers of nonconsensual opinions, I expect an inverse relationship between the size of the majority party coalition and the numbers of dissenting, concurring, and separate opinions produced by the Court.

Testing H2b. I regress each of the dependent variables identified in H2 on the total number of clerks and support personnel assigned to the Court in each term, 1935-1995, while controlling for changes in turnover rate among the justices. I calculate turnover rate in a manner identical to that of Walker, Epstein, and Dixon. The authors define turnover as the number of new associate justices per term.[29] *The Oxford Companion to the Supreme Court of the United States* was consulted to determine the dates on which each justice's services commenced.[30] Similar to Walker, Epstein, and Dixon, I expect a direct correlation between turnover rate in each term and the number of nonconsensual opinions written by the justices.[31]

Testing H2c. Recent tests of the "freshman effect" hypothesis indicate

---

[29]Ibid., p. 372. Note that I include all newly appointed justices, including newly appointed chief justices, in tabulating turnover.

[30]Kermit Hall, ed., *The Oxford Companion to the Supreme Court of the United States* (New York: Oxford University Press, 1992), pp. 969-71, 981-982.

[31]Walker, Epstein, and Dixon, pp. 372-4.

no relationship between inexperience on the Court and opinion writing and voting behaviors. Yet, tests of the "freshman effect" hypothesis do not consider the effect on the consensus norm of varying degrees of collective inexperience among the justices. H2c considers whether changes in collective inexperience on the Court conditions the relationship between increases in the numbers of law clerks and the justices' observations of the consensus norm.

To test H2c, I regress each of the three dependent variables identified in H2 on the total number of law clerks and support personnel assigned to the Court in each term, 1935-1995, while controlling for the changes in the level of inexperience on the Court. I define the extent of inexperience on the Court in each term as the number of justices having served less than three full terms on the Court. The *Oxford Companion to the Supreme Court of the United States* was consulted to determine the number of justices during each term whose services has not exceeded three years on the Court. Similar to Walker, Epstein, and Dixon, I expect a direct correlation between the number of inexperienced justices on the Court in each term and the number of nonconsensual opinions written by the justices.[32]

Testing H2d. I regress each of the dependent variables identified in H2 on the independent variable, total number of law clerks and support personnel assigned to the Court in each term, 1953-1995, while controlling for changes in the substantive composition of the Court's docket. I define docket composition according to the analysis conducted by Stacia Haynie and the findings of Segal and Spaeth. As I discussed in Chapter 1, Haynie and Segal and Spaeth propose that the number of civil liberties issues is directly related to instances of dissent behavior. Therefore, I define changes in docket composition as changes in the occurrence of the most dissensus prone issues, those involving civil liberties questions. However, because Walker, Epstein, and Dixon find no significant relationships between the number of civil liberties cases on the Court's plenary docket and instances of nonconsensual opinion writing, I employ an alternative

---

[32]Ibid., pp. 373-374.

measure of docket composition.[33]   Docket composition, then, is operationally defined as the between-terms change in the percentage of the Court's plenary docket allocated to civil liberties cases. Thus, H2d tests the significance of the law clerk and support personnel variables when controlling for increases or decreases in the term-to-term percentage of docket space allocated to civil liberties issues.

Data on the docket composition variable is provided by Richard Pacelle and are identical to that used in his 1991 book, *The Transformation of the Supreme Court's Agenda.*[34] Pacelle defines civil liberties cases as involving due process, substantive rights, or equality issues. Due process cases include issues of criminal procedure and due process issues in administrative hearings. Substantive rights cases involve First Amendment issues and individual rights to abortion, privacy, the rights of conscientious objectors, and the rights of alleged Communists. Equality cases include issues of discrimination based on race, gender, age, or disability.[35]

Testing H2e. H2e examines the relationship between increases in the numbers of law clerks and support personnel assigned to the Court during each term and each of the dependent variables identified in H2 while controlling for changes in the occupant of the chief justice's seat on the Court. Change in chief justices is operationally defined as the end of one chief justice's service on the Court and the first term during which the succeeding justice occupies the chief justice's seat. Consistent with the data presented in previous studies of the decline in consensus norms, I anticipate the chief justiceship of Charles Evans Hughes and Harlan Fiske

---

[33]Haynie, p. 1166; Walker, Epstein, and Dixon, pp. 368-70.

[34]Richard L. Pacelle, *The Transformation of the Supreme Court's Agenda,* (Boulder, CO: Westview Press, 1991), p. 138. Pacelle added to these data measures of the number of civil liberties cases for the 1989-1995 terms.

[35]For a complete explanation of case typologies used in Pacelle'e study see Pacelle, pp. 208-9

Stone to be an important contextual factor that must be controlled.[36]

To test H2e, I employ dummy variables for each chief justice in the multiple regression models. Regression coefficients on each dummy variable are interpreted and inferences made about the importance of the occupant of the chief justice's seat vis-a-vis the frequency of nonconsensual opinion writing. In the regression models, I control for the presence of one chief justice versus another by coding "1" for each term in which a particular chief justice sat on the Court and a "0" for that chief justice variable in all other terms in the universe of cases. Thus, I control for the presence of each chief justice by isolating the terms in which each chief justice served on the Court and examining regression coefficients associated with each chief justice variable. A more complete explanation of the use of these dummy variables appears in Chapter 6.

It is obvious that a thorough testing of H2e also requires a more elementary methodology. However, estimating separate regression models for the period of each Chief Justice's tenure would engender severe methodological difficulties. Doing so would constitute performing separate regressions for the terms under each chief justice's leadership.[37] The small number of observations for three of the chief justices would make tests for statistical significance impossible. In fact, interpretation of coefficients of determination and parameter estimates would be entirely dubious in models examining only the small number of observations available during the tenure of each chief justice.

In addition to the use of dummy variables in the regression models, I test H2e by examining the mean number of dissenting, concurring, and separate opinions written by the justices during the tenure of each chief justice. I present data tables that include average numbers of dissenting, concurring, and separate opinions written by the justices in each term as

---

[36]Walker, Epstein, and Dixon, p. 378-84; Haynie 1162-4; Caldeira and Zorn, pp. 874-902.

[37]Separate regressions would have to be performed for each of the time periods: Chief Justice Hughes (1935-1940 terms), Stone (1941-1946 terms), Vinson (1946-1952 terms), Warren (1953-1968 terms), Burger (1969-1985 terms), and Rehnquist (1986-1995 terms).

well as the mean number of nonconsensual opinions written per case disposed of by signed opinion in each term. Also, I examine linkages between the presence of each chief justice and the frequency of nonconsensual opinion writing by constructing a line graph of the total number of nonconsensual opinions written in each term, noting on the graph the time period of each chief justice's tenure. These procedures facilitate comparison of nonconsensual opinion writing across the tenures of Chief Justices Hughes, Stone, Vinson, Warren, Burger, and Rehnquist.

Testing H2f. I regress each of the three dependant variables identified in H2 on the total number of clerks and support personnel assigned to the Court in each term, 1935-1995, while controlling for changes in the Court's workload. Consistent with Casper and Posner's approach,[38] the concept of workload can be defined in a way other than the total number of case filings in each term. In short, caseload is operationally defined as the number of cases treated by signed opinion in each term. This procedure allows for estimation of how changes in the number of cases treated by signed opinions in each term impacts the frequency with which the justices choose to forgo the time-consuming search for consensus and draft additional opinions reflecting an independent view. Data for the caseload variable are provided by the Administrative Office of the United States Courts.[39]

Thus, to test H2f, I regress each of the three dependent variables identified in H2 on the number of clerks and support personnel assigned to the Court in each term while controlling for changes in the number of cases disposed of by signed opinion per term. I expect that the size of the Court's caseload is directly related to the frequency of nonconsensual opinion writing.

---

[38]Gerhard Casper and Richard A. Posner, *The Workload of the Supreme Court* (Chicago: American Bar Foundation, 1976), pp. 1-2.

[39]See *Cases Filed, Disposed of, and Remaining on the Docket in the Supreme Court of the United States During the October Term* for the successive years 1935-1995.

Autocorrelation and Model Interpretation

Use of multiple regression equations requires confirmation that none of the assumptions of the classic linear regression model are violated.[40] Although in using a regression model I treat the data in a cross-sectional manner, the data collection in this study fits a time-series description. Ostrom points out that time series data analysis is typically characterized by serial correlation in the disturbance terms, a violation of the non-autoregressive assumption of time-series models.[41] Ostrom explains that "virtually all work in time series regression analysis assumes that a first order autoregressive process is generating the disturbances." [42] In some of the multiple regression models presented in Chapters 6 and 7, serial correlation poses significant problems for interpretation, requiring remedial methods.

Before interpreting the regression models, I test for the presence of autocorrelated error terms. I test for the presence of serial correlation in the error terms by calculating Durbin-Watson d test statistics to determine the presence of autocorrelation in the time-series process. The significance of the Durbin-Watson d test statistic is determined by comparing the test statistic against two critical values. Critical values for the Durbin d test statistic at the 0.01 level of significance are found in Gujarati's *Basic Econometrics*.[43]

In the presence of serial correlation, parameter estimates and correlation coefficients are inefficient, often inflated, and fail to reveal the

---

[40]Charles W. Ostrum, *Time Series Analysis: Regression Techniques* (Beverly Hills: Sage Publications, Inc., 1978), p. 18.

[41]Ibid., p. 24. Here, Ostrom explains that "virtually all work in time series regression analysis assumes a first order autoregressive process is generating the disturbance."

[42]Ibid., p. 24.

[43]Gujarati, *Basic Econometrics*, 3rd ed. (New York: McGraw-Hill, Inc., 1995), pp. 820-1.

actual degree of covariance between the independent and dependent variables. Consequently, in the presence of autocorrelated disturbance terms, hypothesis testing may incorrectly indicate the significance of explanatory variables. As Ostrom explains, in the presence of serial correlation in the disturbance terms, "error variance is seriously underestimated and the regression line appears to fit the data much more accurately than it actually does."[44] The practical consequence of this condition is incorrect rejection of the null hypotheses or what is otherwise know as a Type I error. Thus, autocorrelated error terms frustrate interpretation of time-series regression models and compromise the model's usefulness as a tool for testing hypotheses and explaining behavior.

Remedial measures to correct for serial correlation are required in order that the parameter estimates and correlation coefficients reflect the actual impact of the independent variable on the dependent variable absent an inflation in the parameter estimate caused by upward trends in the data. The process of correcting for autocorrelation in a time series is complete when the series exhibits "white noise" or absence of correlation in the disturbance terms.[45]

In instances where the Durbin-Watson d test statistics reveal the presence of serial correlation, I first employed the remedial technique of differencing the data. Differencing the data involves subtracting from the value of each observation on the dependent variable the value of the prior observation on the dependent variable. The result is a new set of values on the dependent variable, values that reflect the "difference" between values in the adjacent observation. This procedure removes one observation and one degree of freedom from the analysis.

Differencing the data produced unsatisfying results. In those models in which the Durbin-Watson d test indicated the presence of autocorrelation, the differencing procedure produced regression coefficients that were not statistically significant on any of the independent variables. This finding precluded the reliable testing of the hypotheses

---

[44]Ostrom, p. 26.

[45]Gujarati, p. 717.

associated with H2 in models compromised by autocorrelation. Thus, in instances of models with autocorrelated error terms, I chose to either enter into the model a lagged version of the dependent variable or cautiously interpret the results of the regression analysis.[46] When the latter option is taken, I adopt an approach similar to that of Caldeira and Zorn; I report the regression coefficients in models compromised by autocorrelation, noting the importance of tentative acceptance of the substantive results inferred from the regression coefficients and adjusted R squared statistics.[47] Cautious acceptance of the results of these models is justified considering that the data set is comprised of the entire universe of cases during the 1935-1995 period, and not a sample of the universe.

Although a necessary procedure in one set of regression models, use of the lagged version of a dependent variable is not a preferred method of correcting for the presence of autocorrelation. While the use of autoregressive terms produced Durbin-Watson d test statistics indicating no serial correlation in the error terms, this type of variable accounts for nearly all of the explained variance in the dependent variable. Also, parameter estimates on autoregressive terms are biased. Additionally, autoregressive term are typically correlated with error terms. If an error term is correlated with a predictor variable, the error term is no longer serially independent and a basic assumption of least squares estimation is violated. In short, use of a lagged version of the dependent variable as one of the predictors does not produce reliable parameter estimates. Moreover, the regression models that include an autoregressive term have few significant independent variables and therefore do not facilitate meaningful tests of hypotheses. Thus, caution is warranted in interpreting the set of regression equations that include an autoregressive term.

Interpretation of regression models not compromised by autocorrelation is straightforward. In regressing each of the dependent variables on the independent variable, coefficients of determination are

---

[47]Caldeira and Zorn, p. 884.

interpreted to ascertain the degree of variance in the dependent variables explained by the independent variables. Parameter estimates are interpreted in an effort to determine the effect of each variable on each of the various dependent variables. Further, because all cases granted plenary review during the period 1935 to 1995 are included in the analysis, no test of significance is required. Further, because all cases granted oral argument and treated with signed opinions are utilized, the data set may be considered a complete population and indications about the nature of statistical relationships are not matters of inference. However, for those readers who prefer that these data be treated as a sample, I identify in the data tables statistically significant regression coefficients and report F test statistics indicating the statistical significance of regression models.

Summary and Implications

In this book, I propose to expand the operational definition of the "small group" environment in which the justices function to include the importance of law clerks and support staff as institutional factors influencing the Court's behavior. Thus, I propose to test a principal tenet of the "new institutionalism" in public law - that institutional structures and resources shape the behavior of individual political actors. Additionally, this test holds particular importance for studies examining the decline in consensual norms on the Supreme Court. I propose that the increasing presence of law clerks and support personnel is linked to changes in the frequency of nonconsensual opinion writing. Moreover, I examine the significance of interactions between Supreme Court justices, law clerks, and support staff as factors contributing to the historical decline in the consensus norm.

I consider factors contributing to long-term changes in the collective opinion writing behaviors of Supreme Court justices. Thus, unlike other studies in the "small group" genre, I do not seek to explain the opinion writing practices of individual justices. Unlike studies of strategic bargaining, persuasion, opinion assignment, and the "freshman effect," I do not seek to specify the nature of the behavior of any individual justice or the interactions peculiar to any specific set of justices. Rather, each observation in this study is comprised of the total instances of nonconsensual opinion writing in each term and measures on the various independent and control variables. Therefore, I seek to contribute to explanations of one of the most striking features of twentieth century Supreme Court behavior: the persistent willingness of the justices to resort to formal expressions of their individual policy perspectives.

In the following chapters, I find support for the hypotheses identified above. These findings contribute to explanations of the historic decline in the consensus norm. These findings also support "small group" explanations of Supreme Court behavior. Moreover, this book contributes to the expanding body of literature that reconsiders the importance of interpersonal interactions on the Court for the ultimate opinion writing behaviors of this important policymaking institution. I conclude that there exists an empirically recognizable "small group" explanation for historical changes in the frequency of nonconsensual opinion writing.

Finally, it is important that I do not quantitatively test variations in the kind or quality of interactions between law clerks, support personnel, and the justices. Rather, I simply examine propositions which link expansion in the size of the Court's work group to increased fragmentation in the opinion drafting process. From these measures of expansion in the size of the work group, I infer the existence among actors of a type of interaction which facilitates the increasing frequency of justices expressing their own views in controversial cases.

CHAPTER 3

The Law Clerks: Informal Organization on the United States Supreme Court

Introduction

In his stirring 1998 book *Closed Chambers: The First Eyewitness Account of the Epic Struggles Inside the Supreme Court,* Edward Lazarus states ". . . the fact that each Justice now runs a separate law firm with four eager associates. . . has made it much easier for each Justice to give in to ego and put out separate concurring and dissenting opinions in a multitude of cases."[1] Bernard Schwartz states that "the clerks are no longer merely 'staff of assistants.' Instead they have evolved into what Justice Douglas called a 'Junior Supreme Court,' which performs a major part of the judicial role delegated by the Constitution to the Justices themselves."[2] Professor Schwartz goes on to argue that "[t]he greatest deficiency in the Supreme Court's decision process has been the increasing delegation - if not abdication - of key elements of the deciding function to the law clerk corps within the Supreme Court."[3] David O'Brien and Richard Posner make explicit yet untested claims that the increasing presence of law clerks on the Court is related to the increasing frequency of separate opinion

---

[1]Edward Lazarus, *Closed Chambers: The First Eyewitness Account of the Epic Struggles Inside the Supreme Court* (New York: Times Books, 1998), p. 271.

[2]Bernard Schwartz, *Decision: How the Supreme Court Decides Cases* (New York: Oxford University Press, 1996), p. 257.

[3]Ibid., p. 257.

writing.[4]

Other Court observers suggest that the behavior of Supreme Court law clerks reflects a principal-agent type relationship in which the duties of the principal, in this case the justice, often become the tasks of the agent law clerks.[5] From this perspective, the clerks routinely implement the precise dictates of the justices. Moreover, even if the law clerks perform their duties as unbiased, judicial automatons, the law clerk's agency is an important and necessary element in the process of deciding cases and issuing opinions. In this chapter, I develop a theory of law clerk behavior that characterizes the clerks as much more than neutral instruments of the justices' demands.

Although compelling observations for scholars who wish to account for the historical increase in nonunanimous opinion writing, the authors offer no empirical evidence that the presence of law clerks is linked to the Court's production of dissenting, concurring, and separate opinions. Modeling this relationship is the principle task of this book. Conceptually prior to this task, however, is an explanation as to why the law clerks have come to perform functions so inextricably linked to the Court's principle activities. It is my objective in this chapter to articulate a theory regarding the development of the law clerk tradition on the Supreme Court and how that development explains changing patterns of opinion writing. Without identifying causal mechanisms to account for a law clerk-nonconsensual opinion relationship, conclusions about a causal linkage between these variables would be little more than a conjectural inference based entirely on statistical correlation.

---

[4]David O'Brien, *Storm Center: The Supreme Court in American Politics* (New York: W.W. Norton Company, 1990), p. 170; Richard A. Posner *The Federal Courts: Challenge and Reform* (Cambridge: Harvard University Press, 1996), p. 357.

[5]see Jim Chen, "The Mystery and Mastery of the Judicial Power," *Missouri Law Review* 59 (1994), p. 286; Jan Palmer and Saul Brenner, "The Law Clerks' Recommendations and the Conference Vote On-The-Merits," *The Justice System Journal* 18 (1995): 187

Formal and Informal Structures in the Organizational Milieu

Social scientists, generally, and political scientists, in particular, casually identify Congress, the executive branch, and the Supreme Court as organizations. It is, however, not insignificant that the Supreme Court is properly defined as an organization. Indeed, that there is general agreement that the Court is an organization is essential to my belief that a theory of informal processes explains much of the behavior of law clerks. Talcott Parsons states that "[a]s a formal analytical point of reference, *primacy of orientation to the attainment of a specific goal* is used as the defining characteristic of an organization that distinguishes it from other types of social systems."[6] It seems almost indisputable that the Supreme Court's principal goal is the deciding of cases. Closely allied to this task is the production of written justifications; i.e., written opinions containing reasons for case outcomes. Parsons explains that "[a]n organization is a system which, as the attainment of its goal, 'produces' an identifiable something which can be utilized in some way by another system; that is, the output of the organization is, for some other system, an input."[7] It seems beyond argument that the Supreme Court's decisions and written statements of the law function as inputs for other social systems, and ". . . make a difference to the functioning of some other subsystem of the society,"[8] including the larger system of government in the United States. Furthermore, James Eisenstein and Herbert Jacob present a detailed analysis of court workgroups that supports the proposition that judicial

---

[6]Talcott Parsons, *Structure and Process in Modern Societies* (New York: The Free Press, 1960), p. 17.

[7]Ibid., p. 17.

[8]Ibid., p. 17.

institutions are properly characterized as organizations.[9] Moreover, organizational theorists should be comfortable with this characterization of the Court as an organization.

Mathematicians and economists often identify as "elegant" those theories which offer the virtues of both simplicity in their formulation and comprehensiveness in their depictions of practical relationships. Although lacking the formalistic qualities of logical or mathematical axioms, the theoretical constructs of formal and informal organization offer to scholars of public organizations much in terms of explanatory elegance.[10] The concept of informal organization is implicit to much research on judicial behavior, although it is not often made explicit in research on Supreme Court practice.[11] Herbert Jacob argues that the concept of informal organization is implicit to studies of Court behavior that focus on the behavior of nominal inferiors. Jacob offers as an example studies of associate justices exercising authorities formally assigned to superiors such as chief justices.[12] Jacob offers as examples of this type of research investigations of bargaining, coalition building, and leadership on the Court. Arguably, the performance by an associate justice of duties formally assigned to the chief justice may seem like delegation of responsibility as well as constituting the creation of an informal structure. However, assignment of key decision making and opinion writing tasks to

---

[9] James Eisenstein and Herbert Jacob, *Felony Justice: An Organizational Analysis of Criminal Courts* (Boston: Little, Brown and Compamy, 1977), pp. 61-3.

[10] Two important works on the subject are Peter M. Blau and W. Richard Scott, *Formal Organizations* (San Francisco: Chandler Publishing, Co., 1962) and Henry Mintzberg, *The Structuring of Organizations* (Englewood Cliffs, N.J.: Prentice-Hall Publishers, 1979).

[11] The author is aware of only one explicit application of the formal-informal organization distinction in Supreme Court practice. See Herbert Jacob, "Courts as Organizations," in Keith O. Boyum and Lynn Mather, eds., *Empirical Theories About Courts* (New York: Longman Press, 1983).

[12] Ibid, pp. 194-5.

the law clerks is something more than delegation; it is patently outside the boundaries of the Court's formal structure. Furthermore, Professor Jacob agrees that the significance of the law clerk role is entirely consistent with the concept of informal structures. In his discussion of the importance of court work groups as informal structures, Jacob suggests that "on the U.S. Supreme Court, a work group consisting of law clerks clusters around each justice; it is as significant (although not as powerful) as the work group consisting solely of the nine justices assembled in their conference room."[13]

But what defines informal and formal organization? Herbert Simon distinguished the formal, procedural coordination of an organization's activities. He differentiates formal organization from the informal organization of public agencies. Simon explains that informal organization "refers to the interpersonal relations in the organization that affect decisions within it but either are omitted from the formal scheme or are not consistent with that scheme."[14] Informal structures are those relationships and interactions among organizational actors that are beyond the formal procedures and offices designated as responsible for the realization of the organization's goals and purposes. Yet, as Simon indicates, informal structures perform an instrumental function in complex organizations. Simon suggests that ". . . it probably would be fair to say that no formal organization would operate effectively without an accompanying informal organization."[15] Chester Barnard argues that "[a]ttitudes, institutions, customs, of informal society effect and are partly expressed through formal organization. They are interdependent aspects of the same phenomena - a society is structured by formal organizations, formal organizations are vitalized and conditioned by informal

---

[13]Ibid., pp. 195-6.

[14]Herbert A. Simon, *Administrative Behavior: A Study of Decision Making Process in Administrative Organization* (New York: The Free Press, 1957), p. 148.

[15]Ibid., pp. 148-9.

organizations."[16]

Similarly, Gortner, Mahler, and Nicholson explain that informal organizations are ". . . composed of groups that form outside of or in spite of the formal structure" and   ". . . play a significant role in determining the perceptions and attitudes of group members, as well as establishing the values and norms of behavior" in the organization.[17] Barnard states that ". . . formal organizations arise out of and are necessary to informal organization; but when formal organizations come into operation, they create and require informal organizations."[18] Thus, in public organizations formal and informal structures interact in complex ways and often facilitate the operation of formally created structures and goals.

Herbert Simon cogently related the complexity of linkages between formal and informal structures. Simon explains that "the formal structure performs no function unless it actually sets limits to the informal relations that are permitted to develop within it. . . . Perhaps a more positive function of the formal, in relation to the informal, structure is to encourage the development of the former along constructive lines."[19] Moreover, Simon posits a conclusion similar to the aforementioned scholars - that formal structures and informal structures are devised such that the former checks the latter and the latter, in turn, augments the effectiveness of the former.

Perhaps most important to this study, informal structures have a very specific importance for organizational theorists' understanding of the behavior of the individual in the institutional milieu. Anthony Downs argues that informal structures arise, in part, as a consequence of self-

---

[16]Chester Barnard, *The Functions of the Executive* (Cambridge: Harvard University Press, 1968), p. 120.

[17]Harold F. Gortner, Julianne Mahler, and Jeane Bell Nicholson, *Organization Theory: A Public Perspective* (Chicago: The Dorsey Press, 1987), p. 72.

[18]Barnard, p. 120.

[19]Simon, p. 149.

interested behavior on the part of individuals. Downs suggests that formal institutional structures do not permit the full expression of human motives and behaviors. As a result, Downs argues, the boundaries of formal organizational structures are inevitably violated by individuals' personal, extra-organizational ambitions. Downs invokes Selznick's statement:

> From the standpoint of organization as a formal system, persons are viewed functionally, in respect to their roles, as participants in assigned segments of the cooperative system. But in fact individuals have a propensity to resist depersonalization, to spill over the boundaries of their segmentary roles, to participate as wholes. The formal systems cannot take account of the deviations thus introduced.[20]

Downs goes on to explain that informal structures arise because individual members of an organization mutate official institutional procedures and policies "so as to establish some personal significance and power of their own that will stay with them. . . ."[21] Further, Downs hypothesizes that "the creation of informal structures always involves a certain amount of discretion. . . . Whenever officials have any discretion, they will use at least some of it to advance their own interests rather than the formal interests of the organization."[22] Thus, Downs asserts the importance of actors' personal-psychological qualities in the establishment of informal structures. What, however, does Downs suggest are the institutional factors that trigger the establishment of informal structures?

Downs agrees with Simon and Barnard that informal structures are

---

[20]Phillip Selznick, "Foundations of the Theory of Organization," *American Sociological Review* 13 (1948): 26. Quoted in Anthony Downs, *Inside Bureaucracy* (Prospect Heights, IL: Waveland Press, 1967), p. 61.

[21]Downs, p. 62.

[22]Ibid., p. 64.

necessitated by the fact that formal policies and procedures are not exhaustive guides to the fulfillment of organizational purposes. Downs explains that "some informal devices spring up as a means of implementing the organization's goals by filling 'gaps' in the formal rules or adapting those rules to fit peculiar situations. No set of rules can specify in advance every situation an organization encounters. Hence, members of every bureau are called upon to implement the formal purposes of the organization in ways above and beyond those set forth in the formal rules."[23] Thus, if Downs is correct, the proliferation of informal structures and procedures is both individually and collectively rational. Moreover, the establishment of informal mechanisms stabilizes an organization's internal social environment, allowing the organization to achieve its goals and purposes. As Chester Barnard explains, informal organization has two key effects. First, it establishes certain attitudes, understandings, customs, habits, institutions. Barnard states that "the most general effects of informal organization are customs, mores, folklore, institutions, social norms and ideals. . ."[24] which guide the organization in its daily operations. Second, informal organization "creates the conditions under which formal organizations may arise,"[25] thus creating the conditions for organizational success.

I conclude that the organizational theory literature indicates that the establishment of informal structures is both inevitable and in most instances essential to the realization of the organization's goals and purposes. Downs argues that informal structures originate as creatures of the self-interested behaviors of individual actors but become important factors in the organization's efforts to meet its goals and purposes. Thus, as Downs explains, informal structures often function symbiotically with the formal structures of public organizations. Ira Sharkansky's characterization seems apt. He states: "Informal organization refers to

---

[23]Ibid., p. 63.

[24]Barnard, p. 116.

[25]Ibid., p. 116.

how things really work, despite what the formal rules indicate."[26]

The Development of Informal Procedures on the Supreme Court

Herbert Jacob is correct that interactions within work groups consisting of law clerks and justices constitute informal structures important to the behavior of the Supreme Court. Jacob does not, however, offer a detailed examination of law clerk behavior within these work groups. Doing so is essential to fully appreciating the linkage between law clerk behavior and the performance of the Court's principal functions. Moreover, it is important that the law clerks' formal, or perhaps statutory duties are distinguished from those activities that may be described as informal. Several judicial scholars argue that the scope of the law clerk's legitimate, formal authority does not extend to the acts of selecting cases for oral argument and authoring judicial opinions. In an effort to dispel suspicions that Supreme Court law clerks are charged with opinion drafting responsibility, former law clerk Alexander Bickel explained that the duties of a law clerk are to "generally assist their respective justices in researching the law books and other sources for materials relevant to the decision of cases before the Court."[27] Thus, by Bickel's account, it would seem law clerks should not and have not historically assumed opinion writing tasks on the Supreme Court. If Bickel's account is assumed as the full range of the law clerk's official duties, opinion writing by law clerks would constitute behavior beyond the boundaries of the formal structures of the institution.

Bickel's interpretation squares with what is commonly known about the selection of law clerks. Selected solely by the justices themselves, law clerks are not political appointees and are not subject to Senate

---

[26]Ira Sharkansky, *Public Administration: Agendas, Policies, and Politics* (San Francisco: W.H Freeman and Co., 1982), p. 30.

[27]Alexander Bickel as quoted in Bernard Schwartz and Stephan Lesher, *Inside the Warren Court* (Garden City, N.Y.: Doubleday and Company, 1993), p. 37.

confirmation proceedings. It was this fact that formed the basis of Justice Douglas's objections to granting to the law clerks increased authority over the case selection processes. In a memo to Chief Justice Burger, Justice Douglas laments the expanding scope of the law clerks' activities:

> The law clerks are fine. Most of them are sharp and able. But, after all, they have never been confirmed by the Senate and the job here is so highly personal, depending upon the judgement, discretion, experience and point of view of each of the nine of us that in my view the fewer obstacles put in our way, the better."[28]

The development of a law clerk institution that performs extensive case selection and opinion writing duties constitutes the establishment of informal procedures. Furthermore, both the development of informal organization and the expansion of the law clerk institution are consequences of two facts of organizational life. First, workload management problems encourage the development of adaptive mechanisms. Second, individual actors seek autonomy and personal significance in the organizational milieu. In the Supreme Court, both institutional responses to a burgeoning workload and the self-interested pursuit of autonomy by the law clerks account for the development of important informal procedures. These informal procedures facilitate the realization of the Court's principle tasks of deciding cases and writing judicial opinions, including those opinions expressing dissensus among the justices.

My suspicions about the decentralizing effects of these informal norms are contrary to the perspective of at least one Court observer. In his discussions of conflict on the Supreme Court, Phillip Cooper suggests that despite exponential growth in the Court's size and complexity, "the Court remains an organization where informal norms and unwritten rules of

---

[28]Melvin I. Urofsky, ed., *The Douglas Letters: Selections from the Private Papers of Justice William O. Douglas* (Bethesda, MD: Adler and Adler, Publishers, Inc., 1987), p. 141.

conduct are extremely important [in mitigating conflict]."[29]   Although Cooper argues that a set of "basic facts" of Supreme Court life along with the realities of group dynamics, the character of the justices, and "longstanding efforts to separate personal and professional disagreement" serve to mitigate conflict, he presents no sound empirical or theoretical explanation as to how these features of the institution are linked to the magnitude of conflict on the Court.   Cooper does not consider that inasmuch as specific unwritten norms ameliorate decentralizing tendencies, certain aspects of the Court's informal organization may be linked to the *decline* of consensus in the Court's decision making practices. Suggesting that informal norms and unwritten rules mitigate conflict does little to inform public law specialists' search for theoretical principles that will guide scholarly understanding of long-term trends in decision making and opinion writing behavior.   Moreover, careful examination of the informal aspects of the Court organization reveals patterns of activity that inform efforts to model conflict on the Court.

In contradistinction to Cooper, I suspect that an application of the concept of *informal structures* may reveal the causal mechanism associated with the frequency of conflict on the Court. I argue that the evolution of informal Court structures turned on the increasing presence of the law clerks.   Further, I submit that the establishment of these informal structures is instrumental in the justices' willingness and ability to produce both increasing numbers of written opinions and, most important, increasing numbers of opinions which express a concurring or dissenting view. Thus, the evolution of the law clerk tradition and the informal structures engendered in that tradition explain, in part, notable changes in the justices' opinion writing behaviors. Unlike Cooper, I suspect that the establishment of these informal structures *facilitates* the written expression of conflict among the justices. Specifically, then, what explains the current status and role of the law clerk on the United States Supreme Court? The current role of law clerks on the Court is a product of both adaptation to changing demands on the institution and the clerks'

---

[29]Phillip J. Cooper, *Battles on the Bench: Conflict Inside the Supreme Court* (Lawrence, KS: University Press of Kansas, 1995), p. 153.

self-interested desire for autonomy.

The Workload Explanation

Supreme Court law clerks perform duties beyond the scope of their formal authorities. Arguably, appellate law clerks are formally assigned some minimal range of authority in processing petitions for appeal and preparing for judges and justices working drafts of written opinions. However, when such authority expands to include substantial influence over the justices in case selection procedures and the content of final written opinions, that behavior constitutes the archetypical informal structure. Moreover, on the Supreme Court such behaviors are routinized, fully institutionalized means of conducting Court business. Law clerks are instrumental actors in the tasks of case selection and opinion writing. Both tasks require the sort of discretionary authority charged to the justices.

Why are law clerks entrusted with a central role in these core tasks? The most widely accepted explanation for the use of law clerks in the case selection and opinion drafting processes could be labeled the "workload crisis" problem. This perspective suggests that the increased numbers of law clerks on the Court and the use of law clerks in case selection and opinion writing tasks is an institutional response to exponential increases in case filings and, relatedly, an overburdened corps of justices. From this perspective, it seems that the development of the law clerk institution has followed an evolutionary course, steered by the historical increases in the numbers of case filings in each Court term.

The current role of law clerks is fundamentally different from that of clerks in the late nineteenth century. In Chapter 1, I commented that the role played by law clerks on today's Supreme Court is fundamentally different than that of law clerks in 1882, the year Justice Horace Gray hired the institution's first clerk. According to the memoirs of Samuel Williston, Justice Gray's first law clerk, "Gray employed clerks exclusively as sources of inspiration and criticism. . . contributing ideas but not documents to Gray's work as a judge."[30] Chester Newland explains that from the earliest days of the law clerk tradition, clerks were to be anything from research aids to "baggage carriers," but were by occupational description to exercise no substantive influence on the work of the justices. Newland's characterization of the first Supreme Court law clerks is echoed by Paul Baier. Baier states that William Rogers, law clerk to Justice Reed, defined the official duties of the clerks in the modern era as ". . . performing the drudgery of judging - looking up citations, examining old cases for apt quotations, and doing general research. This liberates the justices for their own important work."[31]

In the most recent published account of the work of law clerks, a much different portrait of the clerk's role emerges. Edward Lazarus states that while serving as Justice Blackmun's law clerk during the 1988 term:

> the vast majority of opinions the Court issued were drafted exclusively by clerks. Indeed, only Justices Scalia and Stevens made it a regular practice to participate in first drafts. The other Justices consigned themselves to a more or less demanding editor's role.[32]

Lazarus's observation is corroborated by the accounts of other Supreme Court law clerks. Sean Donahue, former law clerk to Justice Stevens, states:

> as has been widely reported, the clerks do a great deal of the

---

[30]John B. Oakley and Robert S. Thompson, *Law Clerks and the Judicial . Process: Perceptions of the Qualities and Functions of Law Clerks in American Courts* (Berkeley: University of California Press, 1980), p. 14.

[31]Paul Baier, "The Clerks: Profile of an Institution." *Vanderbilt Law Review* 26 (1973): 1125-39.

[32]Edward Lazarus, *Closed Chambers: The First Eyewitness Account of the Epic Struggles Inside the Supreme Court* (New York: Times Books, 1998), p. 271.

Court's opinion drafting. I estimate that well over half of the text the Court now produces was generated by law clerks. The most common practice is to have a clerk write the first draft of an opinion, followed by editing, rewriting and perhaps reorganization by the Justice. This process varies enormously from case to case; it may result in a near total rewrite or in only minor changes."[33]

David O'Brien argues that the devolution of opinion writing responsibility to the law clerks is a response to increasing workload. O'Brien states that "the managing of chambers and supervising of paperwork consumes more time than in the past"[34] and thus has encouraged the use of law clerks in the opinion drafting process. Thus, it seems almost indisputable that law clerks are key participants in the Court's opinion writing tasks. The connection between increasing workloads and the use of law clerks in the Court's principal duties becomes more patent when considering the role of clerks in the case screening process.

Much like the role of law clerks in the opinion drafting process, work done by clerks in reviewing certiorari petitions[35] appears to be a direct response to a workload problem. That law clerks originated and continue to work as assistants to justices in case processing and research activities is part of the Court's historical and contemporary record.[36] However, much like the role of law clerks in the opinion writing process, it is probable that the clerks' span of authority in this process has

---

[33]Sean Donahue, "Behind the Pillars: Remarks on Law Clerks," *The Long Term View, Massachusetts School of Law* 3 (1995): 77-84.

[34]David O'Brien, p. 124.

[35]The term "certiorari petitions" refers to those requests prepared by litigants in state or lower federal court proceedings who now seek the justices' approval in having their cases heard by the Supreme Court. It is entirely within the Court's discretion to issue the writ of certiorari.

[36]See Oakley and Thompson, p. 14.

changed since the genesis of the law clerk tradition. Oakley and Thompson explain that early in the history of the law clerk tradition, clerks were charged with responsibility for initial review of case filings. The authors explain that Samuel Williston, the first law clerk employed by the Supreme Court, "was expected to review all of the newly filed cases as would a judge, and formulate a recommended disposition which would be discussed with the justices in advance of the Court's Saturday morning conferences."[37]

More recently, former Chief Justice Vinson indicated that the clerks' primary role on the Court included reading petitions for certiorari and writing to their justice memoranda listing the facts, legal issues raised in the petition, and a recommendation indicating an appropriate action in the matter. This assignment appears to be more than a matter of mere convenience to the justices. Henry Abraham states that Justice Stevens responded to the severity of the Court's workload crisis by assigning substantial authority to his clerks. Abraham states that in his 1982 address to the American Judicature Society, Justice Stevens explained that he "found it necessary to delegate a great deal of the responsibility in the review of petitions [for certiorari] to his clerks." Abraham explains that Justice Stevens went on to note that "they examine them all and select a minority that they believe I should read myself. As a result, I do not even look at the papers in over 80 percent of the cases that are filed."[38] Such statements are not found in earlier accounts of the clerks' activities.

Justice Stevens' account of the work of law clerks is corroborated by former Stevens law clerk, Sean Donahue. He suggests that processing petitions for certiorari comprised approximately thirty percent of his working hours. Donahue states:

> In the 1993 term, the Court disposed of a record 6675 requests for review (in 6513 of the cases, by declining the invitation). The

---

[37]Oakley and Thompson, pp. 14-15.

[38]Henry Abraham, *The Judicial Process* (New York: Oxford University Press, 1993), p. 243.

menu is also expanding: Ten years earlier, the annual tally was only 4162 petitions. Although may of these petitions are not difficult or time consuming, the need to review well over one-hundred petitions a week is a major, unrelenting chore for the Court. Not surprisingly, law clerks are central to the Court's selection process. They are likely to remain so, as the influx of cert petitions shows no sign of decreasing.[39]

In a similar vein, Gregory Katsas, law clerk to Justice Thurgood Marshall during the Court's 1991 term, observed that "the justices don't have the resources to focus on 6,000 petitions like they do on 90 opinions."[40] Schwartz and Lesher observe that all justices use law clerks in reviewing and preparing memoranda for the large number of certiorari petitions that arrive at the Court each week. The authors state that "the clerks possess enough discretion in handling cert[iorari] memos to constitute a Court-within-a-Court when it comes to what will be heard. Because fewer than 10 percent of the cases presented are heard by the Court, clerk power is mighty indeed."[41] Justice Jackson commented that as regards the processing of certiorari petitions, "the clerks constitute a kind of junior court. . . ."[42] Thus, the need to process an ever-increasing number of certiorari petitions has served to increase the authority and autonomy of the law clerks in one of the Court's key decision making activities. David O'Brien comments that "the expanded role of the law clerks in screening cases is significant and problematic. Although bright, the law clerks are much less experienced than the justices."[43] Furthermore, O'Brien reports that the role of law clerks in the case

---

[39]Sean Donahue, p. 79.

[40]Johnathan S. Greene, "Supreme Insights: A Look Inside the Most Prestigious Judicial Clerkship of All" *Student Lawyer* 24 (1996): 28.

[41]Schwartz and Lesher, p. 40.

[42]Justice Robert H. Jackson, as quoted in Schwartz and Lesher, p. 37.

[43]O'Brien, p. 223.

screening process is most significant in the two or three month period before the justices' first conference when the clerks independently prepare memos for about one-fifth of the Court's total docket for the term. O'Brien explains that of these cases, "over four fifths of those cases are screened out by law clerks and are never collectively discussed and considered by the justices."[44]

In the middle and later months of each term, the law clerks exercise no less authority over the case screening process. Arguably, the authority of the law clerks in the case selection process is magnified by the 1972 "cert pool" innovation. Adopted pursuant Chief Justice Burger's concerns about efficiency in the processing of case filings, the decision to create the "cert pool" is evidence of a perceived workload management problem. The "cert pool" consists of the law clerks from eight of the nine chambers cooperatively dividing and preparing for the justices memoranda on each case filing.[45] The result is that each case filing receives comprehensive attention from the clerks from only one chamber. In considering the merits of the term's case filings, eight of the Court's nine chambers will have comprehensively considered only one-eighth of the case filings. It follows that in considering the merits of certiorari petitions, each justice's impressions are substantially informed by the memoranda prepared by law clerks under the employ of other chambers. Thus, vis-a-vis any individual justice's role in the case selection process, the law clerk institution exercises profound influence.

Other accounts of the case selection process speak to the profound significance of the law clerk institution. Professor O'Brien indicates that the Court typically grants oral argument to fewer than three percent of the total number of cases filed.[46] Excluding those cases disposed of by per

---

[44]Ibid., p. 224.

[45]Justices Steven's clerks do not participate in the "cert pool." During his lengthy tenure on the Court, at no time did Justice Marshall participate in the "cert pool."

[46]David M. O'Brien, *Storm Center: The Supreme Court in American Life* (New York: W.W. Norton, 1996), p. 256.

curiam opinion, approximately ninety-nine percent of the roughly 7,000 case filings that come to the Court each term do not move beyond the point of the law clerks' memoranda. Only a small number of case filings move beyond the justices' review of the clerks memoranda and are placed on a "discuss list" for more careful consideration at the justices' weekly conferences. Recall Justice Stevens's suggestion that in a given term he reads few of the certiorari petitions. Bernard Schwartz offers a similar observation. He relates the impressions of Judge Kenneth Starr: "The justices themselves rarely read the certiorari documents that parties go to great trouble and expense to prepare; the law clerks do that for them. Like congressmen, justices have learned to rely on staff."[47] Evidence supports the conclusion that in each term the law clerks today enjoy an almost unfettered autonomy in the handling of well over 7,000 case filings.

Empirical studies suggest that the central role of the law clerks in the case selection process significantly influences the relatively few case selection decisions made by the justices at weekly conferences. Several studies reveal that law clerk handling of case filings is linked to the justices' decisions about which cases will eventually be placed on the Court's docket of cases granted full oral argument. Studies by Provine,[48] Brenner, [49] and Brenner and Palmer[50] provide indications that the law clerks recommendations to the justices on matters of case selection, most commonly through memos expressing the merits of litigants' certiorari

---

[47]Bernard Schwartz, *Inside the Warren Court*, p. 257.

[48]Doris Provine, *Case Selection in the U.S. Supreme Court* (Chicago, University of Chicago Press, 1980)

[49]Saul Brenner, "Error Correction on the U.S. Supreme Court: A View from the Clerks' Memos," *The Journal of Social Science* 34 (1997): 1-9.

[50]Saul Brenner and Jan Palmer, "The Law Clerks' Recommendations and Chief Justice Vinson's Vote on Certiorari,"*American Politics Quarterly* 18 (1990): 70.

petitions, are useful guides to the justices' conference votes.[51]

Thus, it is recognized by sitting justices and judicial scholars that law clerks manage one of the Court's principle decision making activities. Arguably necessitated by an ever-increasing number of case filings, the law clerk authority in the case selection process has proven to be a convenient platform for what Bernard Schwartz refers to as "clerk power." Moreover, the "workload crisis" explanation of the law clerk foray into the Court's decision making processes is supported by Schwartz's observations of the certiorari process. The author observes that the exclusive law clerk handling of the certiorari petitions was forced upon the Court by an ever-expanding number of requests for review. Schwartz argues that "sheer volume, if nothing else, made this the normal practice."[52]

Data presented in Figure 3.1 confirm Schwartz's observation that the Court's workload has increased in dramatic fashion. During the period 1935 to 1995, total docketed cases increased from fewer than 2000 per term to roughly 8000 per term. Although case filings steadily increased during this entire period, two portions of this period deserve particular mention. During the period 1950 to 1970 the number of docketed cases

---

[51]Despite these findings, controversy surrounds the of issue of law clerk influence over votes to grant certiorari and votes on the merits. Applying principle-agent theory to justice-law clerk interactions, Palmer and Brenner examined the bench memoranda written by Justice Burton's law clerks. The authors find a significant degree of convergence between the clerks' recommendations in the memoranda and Justice Burton's conference votes on the merits. The authors conclude that "the Court is an efficient organization and that the clerks are trying to help rather than influence their employer; i.e. the clerks do not use their positions to pursue ideological goals." see Jan Palmer and Saul Brenner, "The Law Clerks' Recommendations and the Conference Votes On-The-Merits in the U.S. Supreme Court," *Justice System Journal* 18 (1995): 185.

[52]Schwartz, *Decision*, p. 258.

Figure 3.1 Total Cases on the Supreme Court Docket, 1935-1995

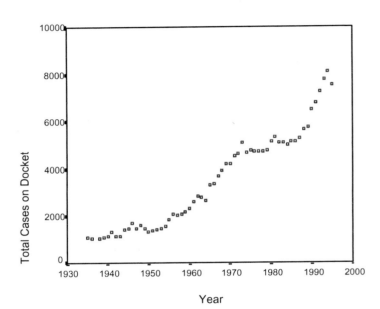

doubled. Also, since the mid 1980s, the numbers of cases on the docket has increased at a rate greater than in any previous two decades. Thus, not only have case filings increased during the period 1935-1995, but the rate of increase is not uniform throughout the period.

From these observations, I find that a workload management problem has triggered increasing devolution of principal decision making activities, namely opinion writing and case selection duties, from the hands of the justices into the purview of the law clerks. How then is the "workload crisis" condition on the Court and the consequent growth of the law clerk institution related to the proliferation of nonconsensual opinions? I suggest that the increasing presence of law clerks on the Court, although intended as a response to a workload management problem, ultimately creates the time and available resources for the justices to write nonconsensual opinions. A recent study by Sandra Wood supports the notion that increases in the numbers of law clerks on the Court enhances the justices' ability to produce written work. Wood presents empirical evidence that the number of law clerks on the Burger Court is directly related to the justices' willingness to write inter-chamber memos.[53]

Figure 3.2. Dissents and Concurrences Issued Without Opinion, 1935-1972[54]

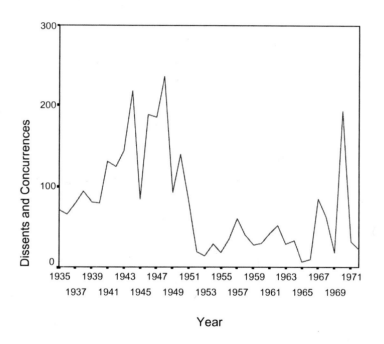

[53]Sandra L. Wood, "Bargaining on the Burger Court: Of Memos, Changes, and Endorsements" (Paper presented at the Midwest Political Science Association Conference. Chicago, Ill, April, 1998).

[54]Data Source: Albert P. Blaustein and Roy M. Mersky, *The First One-Hundred Justices: Statistical Studies of the Supreme Court of the United States* (Hamden, CT: Archon Books, 1978), pp. 140-1.

A brief consideration of the Court's voting and opinion writing activities supports the proposition that over the last several decades the justices have become increasingly able to produce written opinions. As Figure 3.2 indicates, during the period 1935 to 1972, Supreme Court Justices issued a decreasing number of concurring and dissenting votes unaccompanied by a written opinion. However, Figure 3.2 reveals that the number of dissents and concurrences without opinion changed substantially during the late 1940s. During the 1935-1949 period, the justices issued an average of 124.94 dissents and concurrences without opinion per term. Between 1950 and 1970, that number fell to an average of 46.96 dissents and concurrences per term. During the period 1950 to 1972, however, the frequency of dissents and concurrences without opinion diminished only slightly. Generally, these data indicate that during the 1935-1972 period dissents and concurrences, when issued, were at an increasing rate attached to a written justification. This change parallels the historical growth in the number of law clerks. In fact, the number of dissents and concurrences without opinion is related in a linear, statistically significant way to the number of law clerks on the Court. A Pearson correlation of -0.369 (statistically significant at the .05 level) indicates that as the number of law clerks on the Court has increased, the number of dissents and concurrences issued without opinion has decreased.

Figure 3.3 reveals that during the 1935-1995 period the Supreme Court produced an increasing number of nonconsensual opinions per case disposed of by signed opinion. In 1935, the justices produced an average of 0.13 nonconsensual opinions per case disposed of by signed opinion. In 1995, the Court produced an average of 1.38 nonconsensual opinions per case disposed of by signed opinion. The increase in nonconsensual opinion writing and the decrease in numbers of dissents or concurrences without opinion suggests that members of the Court have become increasingly willing and able to produce opinions expressing a view distinct from the opinion issued by a majority or plurality. Most important, the data in Figure 3.3 indicate that the justices are increasingly willing and able to access those resources needed to produce increasing numbers of nonconsensual opinons.

Figure 3.3 Average Nonconsensual Opinions per Case Disposed of
by signed Opinion, 1935-1995[55]

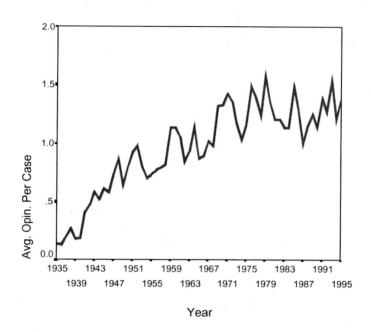

This interpretation is consistent with what public law scholars know
about strategic behavior on the Court. In *The Elements of Judicial
Strategy*, Walter Murphy argues that Supreme Court justices enjoy a finite

[55]Data Source: Data on the total number of nonconsensual opinions were
collected by David O'Brien from the *Annual Statement of the Number of Printed
Opinions*, Office of the Clerk, United States Supreme Court. Data on the number
of cases treated by signed opinion are provided by the Administrative Office of the
United States Court, *Cases on the Docket, Disposed Of, and Remaining on the
Dockets in the Supreme Court of the United States*, October Terms, 1935-1995.

stock of resources which may be used in pursuing policy goals.[56]   It follows that a decision to engage in one activity necessarily engenders an opportunity cost; resources spent on one duty may not be directed at the completion of another task.   Murphy explains that the strategic justice engages in the activities most likely to yield favorable policy outcomes.[57]

It also follows that expansion in the workload demands on a Supreme Court justice requires that additional resources be employed in order that the justice can complete central tasks and pursue policy goals. Furthermore, the introduction of additional case processing and opinion writing resources in the form of increasing numbers of law clerks eases the organization's workload burdens and supports the strategic-minded, policy-oriented justice's desire to produce written manifestations of desired case outcomes.

Finally, the Court's response to a workload management problem accounts for one important aspect of the Court's informal organization - the use of law clerks in the opinion writing and case selection processes. This response engenders behaviors among law clerks beyond the formal authorities originally assigned to law clerks. Although presumably aimed at meeting the demands of increasing numbers of case filings, I suspect that this institutional response to a burgeoning workload has had the unintended consequence of affording the justices increased personal and institutional resources for the drafting of dissenting and concurring opinions. In short, the rise of the Supreme Court law clerk has afforded the justices increased opportunities to act individually. Moreover, former Supreme Court law clerk Alexander Bickel predicted this result. In his response to proposals that additional law clerks be added to the Court to relieve the justices' workload management problems, he stated:

> The drawback to adding law clerks would be to accelerate a tendency in each expanding office to "turn the center of gravity inward. . . depersonalize the work, and jeopardize the collegial

---

[56]Walter Murphy, *The Elements of Judicial Strategy* (Chicago: The University of Chicago Press, 1964), p. 202.

[57]Ibid., p. 43

character of the Court's labors," with the end result of changing the Court into a "federation of nine corporate aggregates or charters."[58]

Judge Richard Posner presents a similar observation on the connection between Supreme Court law clerks and the ability of individual justices to draft opinions. He states: "Given the increase in caseload per justice or judge since 1960, the average length of opinions and the number of footnotes, citations, and concurring and dissenting opinions would probably have had to decline if the number of law clerks had not increased."[59] Posner also notes: "Granted there is no direct correlation between number of clerks and my measures of judicial output."[60] Considering that Judge Posner presents no empirical data to support his assertion, I will test his conclusion. Whether the numbers of law clerks on the Court are linked in a statistical sense to the frequency of nonconsensual opinion writing is the subject of the fourth and subsequent chapters.

Law Clerks and the Search for Autonomy

A second, less generally agreed to explanation for the expansion of the duties of law clerks might be labeled the "clerk autonomy" factor. This explanation relies on the postulation that informal structures arise, in part, from the self-interested behavior of individual actors within an organization. The organizational theory literature instructs that informal structures and self interested behavior are concurrent inevitabilities.

---

[58]Alexander Bickel, *The Caseload of the Supreme Court And What, If Anything, to Do About It* (Washington, D.C.: American Enterprise Institute, 1973), p. 9. Bickel's statement is a response to the *Report of the Study Group on the Caseload of the Supreme Court* (Washington, D.C.: Federal Judicial center, 1972).

[59]Richard A. Posner, *Federal Courts: Challenge and Reform*, p. 155.

[60]Ibid., p. 155.

Chester Barnard explains "that informal organizations are necessary to the operation of formal organizations as a means of communication, of cohesion, and of protecting the integrity of the individual."[61] Furthermore, Anthony Downs states that "individual officials are motivated by self-interest as well as by the organizational interests assigned to them in their formal roles."[62] Downs argues that this assertion is founded on Selznick's belief that in seeking personal significance, individual actors violate the boundaries of their formal authorities. Selznick explains:

> From the standpoint of organization as a formal system, persons are viewed functionally, in respect to their roles, as participants in assigned segments of the cooperative system. But in fact individuals have a propensity to resist depersonalization, to spill over the boundaries of their segmentary roles, to participate as wholes. The formal system. . .cannot take account of the deviations thus introduced.[63]

Thus, the concept of formal organization does not characterize the full range of individual behavior in public organizations. A comprehensive portrait of organizational behavior includes images of self-interested actors seeking personal significance in the organizational milieu. This search for personal significance and autonomy is, at least in part, associated with the establishment of informal structures which exist beyond the boundaries of formally specified roles and duties. Moreover, a complete description of organizational life must include consideration of the self-interested behavior of individual actors and the impact of that behavior on the work product of the institution.

The principle that self-interested behavior produces informal

---

[61]Barnard, p. 123.

[62]Downs, p. 61-2.

[63]Philip Selznick, "The Foundations of the Theory of Organization," *American Political Science Review* 13 (1948): 26. Quoted in Downs, p. 61.

structures is immediately applicable to the behavior of law clerks in the Supreme Court organization. I argue that pursuant the self-interested goal of increased influence over the decision making process, law clerks eagerly assist the justices in the opinion writing process. For the self-interested law clerk seeking significance in the Court organization, the justice's willingness to author a separate opinion affords the clerk an opportunity to implant into this opinion their own policy predilections. Lazarus agrees with this characterization of law clerk behavior. He writes: "Some clerks encourage these independent writings. After all, every opinion represents another opportunity (through his or her justice) to make an impression on the law and to achieve a sliver of immortality as the ghostwriter for portions of the U.S. Reports."[64]

Apparently, the law clerks accurately identify their role as "ghostwriters" to the justices as the most efficient vehicle to influence the substantive content of Supreme Court decisions. Lazarus states:

> . . . the prevalence of editorial justices means that most of the text of most Court opinions - the key words and phrases that make up the crux of a ruling - has been chosen and crafted by clerks. . . . And it is here, in wielding the enormous power of the first draft and, specifically, in the selection of words, structure, and materials, that clerks may exercise the greatest influence.[65]

Most important, Lazarus goes on to explain that in seeking this influence, many law clerks express no reticence about violating the formal boundaries of their office. He writes: "Given the deep schism at the Court, the ideological fervor on both sides, the atmosphere of mutual resentment and distrust, and the docket of polarizing cases, those so inclined readily have found (and continue to find) a compelling motive

---

[64]Lazarus, pp. 271-2.

[65]Ibid., p. 273.

to greatly overstep the appropriate role of a clerk."[66] It is here that the self-interested behavior of the law clerks, i.e., the "clerk autonomy" factor, is firmly wed to the violation of the Court's formal structural arrangements; self-interest on the part of the clerks explains, in part, the establishment of an informal structure - a clerk-driven opinion drafting scheme.

The law clerks' self interested motives, a brand of motive identified by Downs as antecedent to some informal structures, actually serve to fulfill the formal purposes of a Supreme Court confronted with decision making obligations that outmatch the personal resources of the justices. Much like Downs' argument that informal structures augment formal procedures in order to achieve organizational purposes, the informal procedures of which the law clerks are so integral a part have a substantially instrumental value. More specifically, the law clerks' pursuit of personal autonomy is inextricably linked to the justices' need to process thousands of certiorari petitions and produce written opinions in cases granted full review. I maintain that the law clerks' search for autonomy and the informal authorities which result yields a corps of justices who enjoy the time and personal resources to produce increasing numbers of separate opinions expressing individual policy perspectives.

Thus, it would be erroneous to conclude that the Court institution is entirely harmed by law clerk influence in the decision making environment. Indeed, the law clerks' search for autonomy and significance facilitates the Court's primary tasks. Furthermore, self-assertion on the part of law clerks may accrue to the decision making process certain tangible benefits, particulary to the extent that self-interested clerks challenge the thought of justices. Henry Abraham suggests that law clerks perform a valuable function as both foil and critic to their justice.[67] Alexander Bickel argues his experiences as a law clerk affirmed in his mind that "the law clerks' contribution - even if

---

[66]Ibid., p. 273-4. Lazarus generally looks disfavorably on the degree of law clerk influence on the substance of Supreme Court opinions.

[67]Abraham, p. 243.

labeled 'influence' - is toward enhancement of the intellectual integrity of the judicial process."[68]

Toward Increased Professionalization of the Law Clerk Role: A Link to the Law Clerk Autonomy Factor

Both individually and collectively, the Supreme Court law clerks manifest several traits recognized by political scientists as typical of professional groups or groups in the process of attaining professional status. The corps of Supreme Court law clerks exhibit the trait of expertise in performing the duties of their office. They also observe a unique set of formally stated ethical standards. Additionally, Supreme Court law clerks follow a distinct path of professional preparation prior to arriving at the Court, rationally choosing those experiences which prepare them for a positions at the top of the nation's legal and judicial hierarchies Moreover, these characteristics contribute to the law clerks' autonomy and significance in the Court organization.

Joseph Raelin identifies several characteristics of the behavior of professional groups. Raelin suggests that professional groups are characterized by autonomy, expertise, commitment, identification, ethics, and a means of standards enforcement.[69] Using Raelin's criteria and considering Amitai Etzioni's discussion of what he labels the "semi-professions,"[70] Barbara Romzek and Jennifer Utter characterize congressional legislative staff as an emerging profession or quasi-

[68]Alexander Bickel, "The Court: An Independent Analysis," *New York.Times*, April 27, 1958, section 6 (Magazine). Quoted in Baier, p. 1126.

[69]Joseph Raelin, *The Clash of Cultures: Managers Managing Professionals* (Cambridge, MA: Harvard Business School Press, 1991).

[70]Amitai Etzioni, *The Semi-Professions and Their Organization: Teachers, Nurses, and Social Workers* (Ann Arbor, MI: Books on Demand, 1969).

profession[71] - a group demonstrating some but not all of the characteristics identified by Raelin. Similarly, in his discussion of public organizations, Frederick Mosher includes in a model of professional occupations those "emergent professions" or public service occupations "which have not been so recognized and legitimized but which are valiantly and hopefully pulling themselves up by their vocational bootstraps to full professional status."[72] I submit that both individually and collectively, Supreme Court law clerks manifest several of the traits of a professionalized occupation. Supreme Court law clerks are described by the qualities of expertise, autonomy, and adherence to a recognized code of ethical conduct. Moreover, because they demonstrate many but not all qualities of an established profession, Supreme Court law clerks are best defined as an emerging professional group.

The law clerks' search for autonomy in the Court organization is typical of trends toward professionalization in public organizations. Mosher explains that one characteristic of what he labels the "public service professions" - those occupational identities employed predominantly by government agencies - is a continuing effort to "elevate the stature" of the profession.[73] Mosher suggests that one important means by which a prospective profession elevates its status is by "expanding the boundaries of work within which the members of the profession have exclusive prerogatives to operate."[74] In the previous section, I described in detail the law clerks' drive for increased autonomy in the Court's principal activities. Consistent with Mosher's discussion, I conclude that the law clerks' drive for increased autonomy in the Court's decision

---

[71]Barbara S. Romzek and Jennifer A. Utter, "Congressional Legislative Staff: Political Professionals or Clerks?" *American Journal of Political Science* 41 (1998): 1258.

[72]Frederick Mosher, "The Professional State," in Francis E. Rourke, ed., *Bureaucratic Power in National Policy Making* (Boston: Little, Brown, 1986), p. 78.

[73]Ibid., p. 78

[74]Ibid., p. 78.

making and opinion writing processes is evidence of a professionalizing occupation.

Federal law clerks, in general, and Supreme Court law clerks in particular, satisfy another of Raelin's criteria for a professional group; the law clerks are guided by an institutionally recognized system of ethical standards, created specifically for the unique environments of the nation's federal courts. Articulations of this code include the *Code of Conduct for Law Clerks* adopted in 1981 by the Judicial Conference of the United States.[75] This document follows the Judicial Conference's decision to extend to law clerks the 1973 American Bar Association Code of Judicial Conduct. Both are discussed in another broadly recognized statement of standards of conduct for law clerks, *The Law Clerk Handbook* prepared by Judge Alvin Rubin of the United State Court of Appeals for the Fifth Circuit.[76] This volume advises law clerks on subjects ranging from the confidentiality of pending cases to press relations and inter-chamber communications.[77]

Raelin posits that professional groups are characterized by expertise and specialized knowledge. The specialized knowledge and skills required of Supreme Court law clerks is further evidence that the clerks are manifesting professional traits. Indeed, the handling of thousands of certiorari petitions and the preparation of lengthy written opinions in a court of last resort is a combination of responsibilities found nowhere else in the legal community. With the exception of the justices in conference, Supreme Court law clerks are members of perhaps the most exclusive knowledge circle in the legal world. Furthermore, Lazarus's account of his experiences as a Supreme Court law clerk support this point. Referring to a set of guidelines provided to law clerks in Justice Blackmun's chambers, Lazarus explains ". . . we also received a forty-page

---

[75]See Alvin B. Rubin and Laura B. Bartell, *The Law Clerk Handbook: A Handbook for Law Clerks to Federal Judges* (Washington, D.C.: Federal Judicial Center, 1989), pp. 12, 165-9.

[76]Ibid., pp. 11-2.

[77]Ibid., pp. 165-9.

memorandum 'Helpful Hints for Blackmun Law Clerks,' that explained in detail what our Justice expected of us as incoming cases made their way through the Court's cycle of business."[78] Arguably, the law clerks are the only members of the legal world skilled in the task of implementing in the case selection and opinion writing dimensions of the Court's work the attitudinal proclivities of Supreme Court justices.

Closely linked to the knowledge and expertise exclusive to the Supreme Court law clerks is the narrowly defined professional experiences that qualify one for a clerkship at the nation's High Court. The unique preparatory training and employment experiences of Supreme Court law clerks distinguishes them as a fully differentiated group in the legal world. Prospective Supreme Court law clerks adhere to what is perhaps the most narrow course of professional preparation in the whole of public service. Moreover, sound theoretical principles suggest that the importance of this narrow path as a prerequisite to a Supreme Court clerkship influences the behavior of prospective law clerks.

Prospective clerks recognize the importance of clerkships on certain lower federal courts and rationally choose to follow these paths toward entrance into the professional group of Supreme Court law clerks. Patricia Wald, Associate Judge on the United States Court of Appeals for the D.C. Circuit explains that judges rely on the prospective clerks' recognition of a distinct path to a position in the Supreme Court organization. Judge Wald explains:

> A judge's reputation among his own colleagues may in part reflect his ability to garner the most highly-credentialed clerks under his banner so that he can maintain a reputation as a "feeder" of clerks to the Supreme Court. Correlatively, the stronger an appellate (or district) judge's reputation for channeling clerks to the High Court, the more attractive he will be to many understandably ambitious, qualified clerk applicants.

---

[78]Lazarus, p. 28.

Some judges have long friendships with justices [of the Supreme Court] so that their clerks have an edge simply by virtue of that friendship.[79]

Anthony Downs' discussion of how bureaucratic officials link personal goals to patterns of behavior in the organizational milieu is instructive to this point. Anthony Downs argues that when staffing an agency, managers encounter a dilemma. First, the bureau requires personnel that will be successful and productive in their organizational duties.[80] Yet, as Downs explains, candidates for positions "cannot be directly appraised in terms of their contribution to the ultimate value of [the organization's] output."[81] Thus, in seeking promotion within an agency, an official may demonstrate that "he can score well on whatever objective standards are used for appraising his promotional qualifications. This means attending the right schools, getting good grades, *acquiring experience in the right jobs*, and so on [italics mine]."[82] These, Downs explains, are the "paths to promotion" for the "climber" - the individual seeking to "maximize his own power, income, and prestige. . . ."[83]

I presume that the discussion in the previous section allows law clerk behavior to be discussed in the Downsian language of "climbers" and "power maximizers." How, then, might these motives find expression in the clerk's professional behavior prior to coming to the Court? One possibility is that, consistent with Downs' general theory of bureaucratic behavior, the law clerks seek those professional experiences most likely to yield a Supreme Court clerking opportunity. I suspect this motive is related to a professionalization of the law clerk vocation.

---

[79]Patricia M. Wald, "Selecting Law Clerks," *Michigan Law Review* 89 (1990): 154.

[80]Downs, p. 92

[81]Ibid, pp. 92-3.

[82]Ibid, p. 93

[83]Ibid., p. 92

Although not found in the criteria posited by Raelin, the criteria of professional background is one which follows from studies of state legislatures. Scholars studying the historical development of American political institutions presented testable criteria for determining the extent to which legislative organizations are professionalized.[84] Peverill Squire suggested that a member's salary, number of staff, and total length of each session are important indicators of the degree of professionalization of a state legislature.[85] Missing from these criteria, however, are measures of individual members' vocational histories. Whether examining legislative or judicial organizations, the prior training and vocational experience of decision making members, beyond mere academic training in the law, seems an obvious element of an institution's professional flavor.

I believe that the pattern of recruitment of Supreme Court law clerks is suggestive of a professionalization of the law clerk role and may reveal the clerks' identities as "climbers" in the federal judicial system. The route toward attaining what Johnathon Green describes as " . . . the most prestigious judicial clerkship of all"[86] is patently identifiable. That all Supreme Court law clerks are law school graduates, and nearly all from the nation's top academic institutions, is not instructive to this point. Indeed, evidence of professionalization of the law clerk role is found in more subtle relationships.

Of law clerks serving on the Court during recent terms, all but a few share common professional experiences. A few points of the shared

---

[84]Useful discussions of this research include: John G. Grumm, "The Effects of Legislative Structure on Legislative Performance," in *State and Urban Politics,* Richard I. Hofferbert and Ira Sharkansky, ed. (Boston: Little, Brown, 1971); Nelson W. Polsby, "Legislatures," in *The Handbook of Political Science, Volume 5: Government Institutions and Processes,* Fred I. Greenstein and Nelson W. Polsby, ed. (Reading, MA: Addison-Wellesley, 1975).

[85]Peverill Squire, "Legislative Professionalization and Membership Diversity in State Legislatures," *Legislative Studies Quarterly* 17 (1992): 71.

[86]Johnathon S. Green, "Supreme Insights: A Look Into the Most Prestigious Judicial Clerkship of All," *Student Lawyer* (1996):27-31.

characteristics are, perhaps, intuitively obvious.[87]   First, Table 3.1 indicates that prior service in a judicial clerkship is all but essential. Of the 137 law clerks serving during the 1992-1995 terms, only two came to the Court without prior experience in a judicial clerkship. Second, based on the profile of law clerks serving during this four year period, clerkship appointments in the federal judiciary are, it seems, mandatory.

Table 3.1 Prior Clerkship Assignment of Supreme Court Law Clerks, 1992-1995[88]

Court assignment	Number of Clerks
U.S. Court of Appeals (1st Circuit)	10
U.S. Court of Appeals (2nd Circuit)	10
U.S. Court of Appeals (3rd Circuit)	3
U.S. Court of Appeals (4th Circuit)	16
U.S. Court of Appeals (5th Circuit)	3
U.S. Court of Appeals (6th Circuit)	0
U.S. Court of Appeals (7th Circuit)	6
U.S. Court of Appeals (8th Circuit)	1
U.S. Court of Appeals (9th Circuit)	28
U.S. Court of Appeals (10th Circuit)	1
U.S. Court of Appeals (11th Circuit)	0
U.S. Court of Appeals (D.C. Circuit)	47
One of the 94 Federal District Courts	6
S. C. Clerks w/no prior judicial experience	2

[87]Green's discussion of the background of law clerks serving in the 1996 term corroborates my findings regarding clerks serving during the 1992-1995 period. See Green, p. 30.

[88]Data Source: Public Information Office of the United States Supreme Court.

These data indicate that during the 1992-1995 terms, all clerks with prior judicial experience served in one of the lower federal courts. Third, prior service on the U.S. Courts of Appeals is practically required; 124 of the 137 clerks had previously served in one of the 13 circuits. Of the remaining thirteen clerks, all had served in one of the ninety-four U.S. District Courts.

Less obvious, however, is that the circuits are not equally represented among Supreme Court law clerks. As Table 3.1 indicates, law clerks coming out of the Ninth and D.C. Circuits are noticeably over-represented. Forty-seven, or 34.3 percent, of the 137 clerks serving in this four year period previously served on the U.S. Court of Appeals for the D.C. Circuit. Twenty-eight, or 20.4 percent, of the 137 law clerks served on the Ninth Circuit Court of Appeals. Thus, four times as many clerks had served on the D.C. Circuit as on either the First or Second Circuits. Moreover, fifty-five percent of law clerks serving during the period 1992-1995 came to the Court armed with either Ninth or D.C. Circuit experience. Clerks arriving at the Court from several of the other circuits are few in number. The Sixth, Eighth, Tenth, and Eleventh Circuits have received little or no representation.

Although based on a limited number of data, it seems logical to conclude that experiences on the Ninth and D.C. Circuits favor a prospective Supreme Court law clerk's candidacy. What accounts for this trend? A complete answer to that question is beyond this scope of this chapter. However conjectural at this point, two explanations seem plausible. First, the Supreme Court justices may favor the type of experiences brought to the Court by clerks who served on these Circuits. Henry Abraham refers to the D.C. Circuit as "the second most important federal tribunal. . . ."[89] The Court of Appeals for the D.C. Circuit is charged with handling appeals from both the U.S. District Court in Washington D.C. and many of the decisions of the federal administrative agencies. By virtue of its geographic location, the D.C. Circuit hears a disproportionate load of appellate cases involving constitutional issues and matters of federal statutory interpretation. If Henry Abraham is correct, the work of the Court of Appeals for the D.C. Circuit

---

[89]Abraham, p. 163.

may be preferred training for cases handled by the Supreme Court.

Second, personal and ideological affinity with associates on these circuits may account for law clerk recruitment patterns. Four of the ten justices serving during the 1992-1995 period previously sat on either the Ninth or D.C. Circuit Court of Appeals. Justices Ginsburg, Thomas, and Scalia came to the Court from the D.C. Circuit Court of Appeals. Justice Kennedy served on the Ninth Circuit prior to his Supreme Court appointment. It may also be that recruitment patterns reflect ideological kinship with judges in these circuits. During the 1992-1995 terms, ten law clerks serving the most ideologically conservative justices - namely, Justices Scalia, O'Connor, Kennedy, and Thomas - previously clerked for the stridently conservative Judge Lawrence Silberman of the D.C. Circuit Court of Appeals.[90]

In either instance, the law clerks' collective pre-Court experiences are homogenized by these recruitments patterns. Whatever unique skills and experiences are brought to the Court by law clerks from the Ninth or D.C. Circuits, this preparatory path is approaching an institutional norm. Most important, this trend is evidence of the narrow professional channels along which travel the cadre of Supreme Court law clerks.

The unique prerogatives enjoyed by former Supreme Court law clerks is additional evidence that they assume a unique professional identity. Service as a Supreme Court law clerk is a shared experience of many attorneys who practice beyond the Supreme Court bar. In fact, service as a Supreme Court law clerk is an invaluable preparatory element in building a practice at the Supreme Court bar. Karen O'Connor and John R. Hermann examined post-clerkship professional activities of attorneys who once clerked for a Supreme Court justice. The authors report that of law clerks serving during the period 1958-1985, more than half would later participate, on at least one occasion, as counsel or amicus before the

---

[90]Brisbin reports that while serving on the Circuit Court of Appeals for the D.C. Circuit, Scalia and Judge Silberman's votes agreed in 92.3 percent of cases decided. see Richard A. Brisbin, *Justice Antonin Scalia and the Conservative Revival* (Baltimore, Johns Hopkins Press, 1997), p. 37.

Court.[91] Perhaps most important, O'Connor and Hermann explain that during the period 1969-1979, former Supreme Court law clerks were almost twice as likely as their similarly educated and employed law school classmates to appear as counsel or amicus before the Court.[92] Thus, a law school graduate who aspires to argue before the nation's highest court is well advised to follow an efficient path to a Supreme Court clerkship. O'Connor and Hermann elaborate: "Clerks become part of an elite Supreme Court community. The clerks understand the internal decision-making processes of the justices as well as the Court. With this in mind, both government and private law firms actively recruit clerks to act later as players before the Court."[93] Moreover, law school graduates who seek a regular association with the Supreme Court bar and the government and private organizations who regularly appear before the Court rationally seek entrance to the law clerk pipeline. Further, the "climber" rationally seeks a clerkship in particular federal courts and the tutelage of what are often called "feeder judges."

Conclusion

In this chapter, I present a theoretical explanation of how it is that the law clerks have come to exercise authority in the Court's principle tasks of case selection and opinion writing. The important decision-making functions performed by law clerks requires something more than the amount of authority originally intended at the genesis of the law clerk tradition. That such decision-making functions are contrary to the non-decision making description of the law clerk position represents a departure form the formal structure and procedure of the Supreme Court's work. The evolving role of law clerks as opinion writers and case petition

---

[91]Karen O'Connor and John R. Hermann, "The Clerk Connection: Appearances Before the Supreme Court by Former Law Clerks," *Judicature* 78 (1995): 249.

[92]Ibid., p. 249.

[93]Ibid., p. 249.

processors represents the adoption of informal procedures. I argue that the establishment of these informal procedures is explained by institutional responses to an ever increasing workload and the law clerks' efforts to attain autonomy and significance in the Court organization. That Supreme Court law clerks aspire to autonomy in the Court organization is, along with the adoption of an ethics code specific to the clerks and the expertise gained by the clerks in a unique set of professional experiences, evidence that processes of professionalization are closely linked to the establishment of these informal procedures. Most important, I suggest that the evolution of the law clerks' role has increased the justices' stock of opinion writing resources, facilitating the production of increasing numbers of dissenting and concurring opinions.

In the next chapter, I examine statistical relationships between increasing numbers of law clerks on the Court and the historical increases in the frequency of nonconsensual opinion writing.

CHAPTER 4

Law Clerks, Support Personnel, and Nonconsensual Opinion Writing: Examining Basic Relationships

Introduction

In this chapter, I test one key explanation for historical increases in the various indicators of nonconsensual opinion writing: I suspect that the expansion in the size of the Court work group is related to the production of written opinions. I test specific hypotheses associated with H1, the general proposition that increases in the numbers of law clerks and support personnel are related to historical increases in the number of nonconsensual opinions produced by the Supreme Court during the 1935-1995 period. The purpose of this chapter is limited to the presentation of descriptive statistics and bivariate correlation coefficients which address the empirical plausibility of each hypothesized relationship. I also present explanations of the statistical and substantive importance of each finding. Prior to testing each hypothesized relationship, I present a brief discussion of historical changes in each variable.

In later chapters, I test H2 and its associated hypotheses, presenting several multivariate regression models of nonconsensual opinion writing. These multivariate models are designed to test the importance of law clerks and support personnel when controlling for the effects of the various competing explanations of nonconsensual opinion writing. In the final chapter, I present multivariate regression models which include as independent variables each of the competing measures of dissensus as well as measures of the law clerk and support personnel variables.

The Proliferation of Supreme Court Opinions

Figure 4.1 indicates that the total number of Supreme Court opinions written in each term generally increased between 1935 and the middle 1980s. Between 1935 and 1952, the justices' opinion production is marked by substantial variation, with the total number of opinions at 170 in 1935, increasing to 260 in 1944, and declining to 182 in 1951. With a few exceptions, however, the total number of opinions increased steadily prior to 1985, ranging from a low of 132 in 1953 to a high of

Figure 4.1. Total Supreme Court Opinions and Caseload[1], 1935-1995

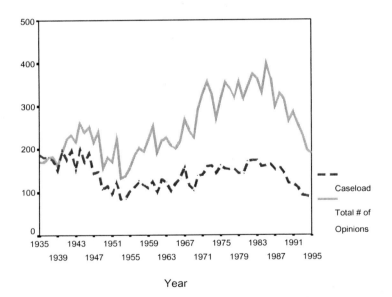

Year

[1]Caseload is defined as the number of cases disposed of by signed opinion in each term. Data for the number of cases disposed of by signed opinion in each term is provided by The Administrative Office of the United States Courts, *Cases On the Docket, Disposed of, and Remaining on the Dockets of the Supreme Court*, 1935-1995. Figures for each term are found in Appendix A.

398 in 1985. Since 1985, the number of written opinions has steadily declined, returning in 1995 to a level similar to that of the late 1930s. The notable decline in total opinion production between 1986 and 1995 is possibly linked to the decrease in the number of cases disposed of by signed opinion since 1986. As Figure 4.1 indicates, the justices disposed of 164 cases by signed opinion in 1986 but in 1995 treated only 87 cases by signed opinion. Thus, it is possible that between 1986 and 1995, the justices encountered a decreasing number of "opportunities" to draft opinions. Table 4.1 presents these data in a slightly different way. Table 4.1 indicates the average number of opinions written during selected periods since 1935. With the exception of declines in the 1950s and the 1990s, the average number of opinions written per term has increased gradually during the last seven decades rising from 172.6 in the later 1930s to 237 in the first half of the 1990s. In fact, the average number of opinions written per term during the 1980s is twice the average number of opinions written per term during the period 1935-1939. Furthermore, although the average number of opinions written during the period 1990-1995 represents a 31 percent decrease from the 1980s, the mean of 237 opinions during the 1990s is still higher than that of any decade prior to the 1970s.

What do sustained increases in the number of written opinions signal about the behavior of Supreme Court justices? Generally, increases in the numbers of written opinions produced by the Court signals an erosion in the norm of consensual opinion writing. Recall from Chapter 2 that an opinion for the court is defined as a written explanation for a decision, the substance of which is approved by at least a majority of the justices. Typically, the Court produces a maximum of one opinion for the Court[2] for each case treated with full written opinions.[3] Further, as Figure 4.1

---

[2]Recall from Chapter 2 that an opinion for the Court is one which reflects the disposition of at least a bare majority of justices.

[3]David O'Brien explains that in 1990, the Court handed down the first decisions in which "there were two opinions announcing different (and somewhat contradictory) parts of the Court's ruling for two different majorities." O'Brien cites *Arizona v. Fulimante* (1991) and *Gentile v. State Bar of Nevada* (1991) as

indicates, the number of cases disposed of by signed opinion in each term has remained essentially stable throughout much of the 1935-1995 period.[4] Moreover, Figure 4.1 reveals that opinion production is at most only modestly linked to the Court caseload. Thus, logic dictates that increases in the number of written opinions is caused, at least in part, by

Table 4.1. Average Total Opinions in Selected Periods

Period	Average Total Opinions	% Change From Previous Period
1935-1939	172.6	----
1940-1949	222.6	+29%
1950-1959	180.7	-18%
1960-1969	225.5	+25%
1970-1979	326.8	+45%
1980-1989	344.1	+5%
1990-1995	237.0	-31%

increasing numbers of separate, dissenting, and concurring opinions. As I discussed in Chapter 2, separate opinions are those written opinions that have different, shifting majorities assenting to different parts of the same opinion.

In Figure 4.2, I present another indication of the increase in opinion production. Figure 4.2 reveals the average number of written opinions per case disposed of by signed opinions during the period 1935-1995. These data suggest that during the 1935-1995 period, for each case disposed of

---

examples. See David M. O'Brien, *Storm Center: The Supreme Court in American Politics* (New York: W.W. Norton and Company, 1990), pp. 321-322.

[4]The Court disposes of cases in one of several ways. In addition to denials of appeal or denials of petitions for certiorari, cases reviewed by the Court are treated with either an unsigned *per curiam* opinion, by memorandum order, by signed opinion (plenary treatment),or in rare instances without opinion.

by signed opinions, the average number of written opinions increased steadily. Furthermore, the data in Figure 4.2 reveal a large amount of variation in the average number of opinions written per case. In 1935, the justices produced an average of 0.9 opinions per case.[5] By

Figure 4.2 Average Total Opinions per Case Disposed of By Signed Opinion, 1935-1995

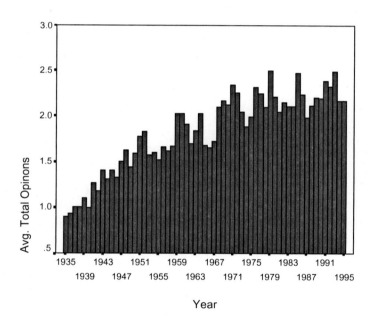

1952, that figure had more than doubled, with the Court producing an average of 1.83 opinions per case. By the late 1960s, the justices were writing an average of more than two opinions per case disposed of by

[5]In some instances, one signed opinion disposes of more than one case. See Walker, et. al., *The Supreme Court Compendium,* p. 85.

signed opinion. In 1979, the justices wrote the largest number of opinions per case, producing an average of 2.5 opinions for each case disposed of by signed opinion. Thus, historical increases in the numbers of written opinions are not strongly related to changes in the number of cases disposed of by signed opinion, or, as I suggest, the number of opportunities for the justices to respond to cases in the form of written opinions. I conclude that increases in the number of written opinions during the period 1935-1995 must be linked to factors other than the size of the Court's docket of cases which receive full oral argument and signed written opinions.

Considering the data presented in Figure 4.2, increases in the average number of written opinions produced by the Court per case disposed of by signed opinion leads immediately to the conclusion that the justices are authoring increasing numbers of opinions reflecting dissensus. David O'Brien presents data consistent with this conclusion. He finds that while the total number of opinions written by the justices has increased dramatically since the 1930s, the number of opinions for the Court has increased only slightly.[6] Further, employing O'Brien's opinion writing data, I indicate in Figure 4.3 that opinions for the Court represent a declining portion of the Court's total opinion production. Consistent with O'Brien's argument, I find that opinions for the Court have become a less typical means of announcing Supreme Court decisions. Most important, because the Court is producing increasing numbers of opinions per case disposed of by signed opinion, and the numbers of opinions for the Court and majority opinions have historically declined, other types of written opinions must account for the general increase in the total numbers of opinions produced by the Court each term. In short, the proportion of total opinion production in each term accounted for by dissents, concurrences, and separate opinions is equal to 1 minus the proportions reported in Figure 4.3. Thus, dissents, concurrences, and separate opinions have historically accounted for an increasing proportion of the Court's yearly opinion production.

---

[6]O'Brien, p. 319.

Figure 4.3 Opinions for the Court as a Percentage of Total Opinions, 1935-1995

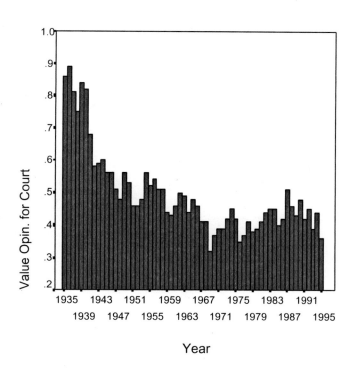

It is agreed among scholars attempting to model the decline in consensus norms that the numbers of separate, dissenting, and concurring opinions have increased since the late 1930s.[7] In his discussion of changes

---

[7]See Thomas G. Walker, Lee Epstein, and William Dixon, "On the Mysterious Demise of Consensual Norms on the United States Supreme Court," *Journal of Politics* 50 (1988):362; Stacia Haynie, "Leadership and Consensus on the U.S. Supreme Court," *Journal of Politics* 54 (1992):1159; Gregory A. Caldeira and Christopher J.W. Zorn, "Of Time and Consensual Norms in the United States Supreme Court," *American Journal of Political Science* 42 (1998): 874.

in opinion writing activities, O'Brien presents a graphical indication of the increase in the actual numbers of separate, dissenting, and concurring opinions. I submit that O'Brien's method of illustrating the demise of the institutional opinion offers only a partial description of the historical change in opinion writing behaviors.

In an original application of O'Brien's data, I present a more complete description of long-term trends in opinion writing activity. In his discussion of historical increases in the numbers of dissents, concurrences, and separate opinions, Professor O'Brien considers the actual numbers of each type of opinion written in each term. I examine both actual numbers and the number of each type of opinion as a percentage of the Court's total opinion production in each term. For the moment, I restrict my analysis to the data presented in Table 4.2.

Table 4.2 shows that both in actual numbers and as a percentage of the Court's total opinion production, separate, dissenting and concurring opinions became increasingly prominent during the 1935-1995 period. Separate, dissenting, and concurring opinions have not only increased in absolute terms but have also increased as a percentage of the Court's total opinion production. Dissents range from a low of twenty in 1935 to a high of 136 in 1985. Concurrences increased from a low of four in 1935 to thirty-four in 1945, peaking at sixty-three in 1970. Separate opinions have increased from single digits in the 1935 to 1955 period to seventy in 1980. Overall, separate, dissenting, and concurring opinions have increased from a combined 14% of total opinion production in 1935 to 65% of total opinion production in 1995.

This application of O'Brien's data supports his argument that Supreme Court justices have increasingly replaced institutional opinions with those expressing a view not commanded by a majority of the Court. Moreover, I submit that my application of opinion writing data offers a slightly different, yet uniquely important view of the decline in the consensus norm. I present evidence that nonconsensual opinions have not only increased in frequency but have become increasingly prominent elements in the Court's yearly opinion production.

Table 4.2 Dissents, Concurrences, and Separate Opinion Writing in Selected Terms*

Term	Dissents	(% of Tot.)	Concur	(% of Tot.)	Sep.	(% of Tot.)
1935	20	12	4	2	1	0.1
1940	25	13	4	2	6	3
1945	64	27	34	14	6	3
1950	54	31	32	18	4	2
1955	52	33	19	12	4	3
1960	94	37	33	13	16	6
1965	57	28	32	16	15	7
1970	91	31	63	22	28	10
1975	98	31	51	16	36	11
1980	92	29	35	11	68	21
1985	136	34	33	8	70	18
1990	78	29	45	17	15	6
1995	63	34	50	27	7	4

* The second figures indicate the number of dissenting, concurring, or separate opinions as a percentage of the total opinion production in that term.

Law Clerks, Support Staff, and Nonconsensual Opinion Writing

Posner, O'Brien, and Wald assert, but do not present empirical data to support a relationship, between nonconsensual opinion writing and the number of law clerks available to the author justices.[8] Their argument is intuitively appealing: written opinions are possible only where opinion writing resources are available to the justices. Specifically, then, how does the availability of opinion writing resources inform our understanding of opinion writing norms? Logic dictates that: (1) the justices always had the resources to write increasing numbers of opinions and the decision to do so reflects a change in behavioral expectations among the justices independent of changes in the amount of opinion writing resources; or (2) the opinion writing resources available to the justices increased, facilitating previously unrealized desires to write increasing numbers of opinions; or (3) the opinion writing resources available to the justices increased and this change is associated with the justices desires to write increasing numbers of opinions, altering opinion writing norms. Each of these possibilities speak, at least in part, to the justices underlying aspirations and desires vis-a-vis opinion writing. The second and third possibilities suggest that increasing numbers of law clerks and support staff, both elements of an important change in organizational resources, are key institutional features that mold the purposive behavior of individual Supreme Court justices. Either possibility is consistent with claims made by Judge Posner - that the availability of institutional resources influences the justices' decisions to produce written opinions. Furthermore, Hypothesis H1 and its associated hypotheses test, in part, the theoretical proposition articulated by Rogers Smith that "institutions are expected to shape the interests, resources, and ultimately the conduct of political actors, such as judges. . . ."[9]

---

[8]David M. O'Brien, p. 170; Richard A. Posner, *The Federal Courts: Challenge and Reform* (Cambridge: Harvard University Press, 1996), p. 357; Patricia M. Wald, "Selecting Law Clerks," *Michigan Law Review* 89 (1990): 153.

[9]Rogers M. Smith, "Political Jurisprudence, The 'New Institutionalism' and the Future of Public Law," *American Political Science Review* 82 (1988): 91.

Law Clerks and Support Staff: Increasing the Size of the Supreme Court Work Group

Figure 4.4 indicates that the numbers of Supreme Court law clerks has increased from three in 1935 to thirty-eight in 1995; in 1995 the Court employed twelve-and-a-half times the number of clerks working for the justices in 1935.[10] During the years 1935-1995, several periods deserve particular mention. First, a notable change took place during the 1940-1941 period. In 1941, the number of law clerks increased from six to eleven.[11] A second change took place between the 1946 and 1947 terms. In 1947, the numbers of law clerks increased from nine to thirteen - a change which coincided with the ascension of Fred Vinson as chief justice.[12] Thus, between 1935 and 1947, numbers of law clerks increased from three to thirteen, a change that provided at least one clerk for every

The 1969 and 1970 terms represent a third period of notable change. During the 1969 term the Court employed twenty-three law clerks. In 1970, the number of law clerks increased to thirty, gradually increasing until 1990, when the Court employed thirty-six clerks. This notable change in the number of law clerks is attributable to Justice Byron White's request that Congress provide the Court with the necessary staff assistance to dispose of a growing workload. Justice White explains that ". . .the burden must be met by providing additional help and this can be best accomplished by allotting each justice an additional law

---

[10]This Figure reflects only those law clerks assigned to active justices. Recall that I include in the study those law clerks assigned to retired justices. During the 1995 term, four law clerks were so assigned.

[11]John P. Frank indicates that Chief Justice Stone was provided with additional law clerks. See John P. Frank, *The Marble Palace: The Supreme Court in American Life* (New York: Alfred A. Knopf, 1958), pp.. 115-8.

[12]Ibid, pp. 115-8.

clerk."[13] Justice White informed U.S. Senators that law clerks are ". . . an indispensable aid in managing the ever increasing flow of petitions, briefs, and evidentiary records."[14] This sudden increase in the numbers of law clerks in the early 1970s also coincides with notable changes in the frequency of dissenting opinion writing. Another obvious feature of

Figure 4.4 Law Clerks Employed by the Supreme Court, 1935-1995

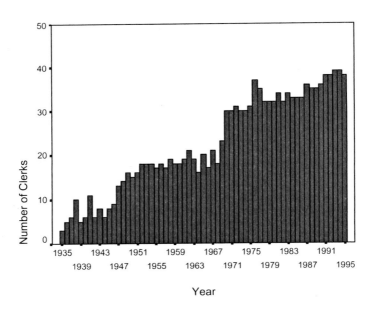

[13]U.S. Senate Committee on Appropriations, *Senate Hearings Before the Committee on Appropriations, State, Justice, Commerce, the Judiciary, and Related Agencies*, 90th Congress, 2[d] Session, FY 1969, p. 159. Y4.Ap6/2:St2/976 pt. 1.

[14]Ibid., p. 159.

these changes is that both developments coincide with the appointment of Chief Justice Warren Burger. The significance of this fact is discussed later. Figure 4.5 indicates that the number of support personnel employed by the Court has increased dramatically since the 1930s. In 1995, 345 persons were employed by the Supreme Court. This figure is more than six times the number of support personnel at the Court in 1935. The size of the Court as an institution has increased despite no sustained increase in

Figure 4.5 Number of Support Personnel Employed by the Court, 1935-1995

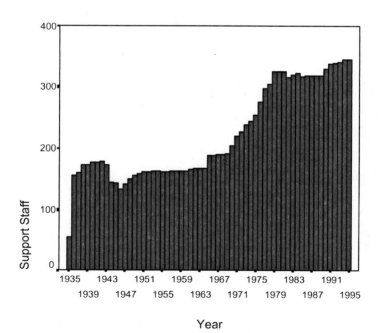

Year

the magnitude of the Court's plenary docket. Further, the sustained growth in the size of the Court work group has taken place absent a significant change in the Court's statutorily-defined appellate responsibilities. The only significant change in the business of the Supreme Court during the previous six decades is the exponential increase in the number of case filings. Herein lies the Court's reasons for requesting that Congress appropriate funds for additional support staff. In 1976, Justice White referred to the size of the Court's workload in explaining to a House of Representatives subcommittee on appropriations why additions were needed to the secretarial staff and the staff working in the office of the Reporter of Decisions. With regard to the Office of the Reporter of Decisions, he states: "This position is needed to provide secretarial assistance to cope with the case load of the Court and to assure that the Court's work will be done in a timely manner."[15] The importance of changes in workload and its relationship to both the growth in the size of the Court institution and changes in the consensus norm are topics for subsequent chapters.

Testing H1: Law Clerks, Support Staff and Measures of Nonconsensual Opinion Writing

Table 4.3 includes correlation coefficients for the variables: law clerks, support staff, and the various measures of nonconsensual opinion writing identified in Chapter 2. Coefficients are presented for both actual numbers of opinions produced per term and the various measures of opinion writing expressed as a percentage of the total number of opinions written per term.

Examining both measures of nonconsensual opinion writing is useful in examining linkages between law clerks, support staff, and changes in the opinion writing practices among the justices. Considering the actual

---

[15]U.S. House Appropriations Committee, *Hearing Before a Subcommittee of the Committee on Appropriations, House of Representatives*, 94th Cong., 1st sess., p. 433. Y4.Ap6/1:St2/976/pt.1.

Table 4.3. Bivariate Correlation Coefficients: Law Clerks, Support Personnel, and Measures of Nonconsensual Opinion Writing for 1935-1995 Terms

Measures of Nonconsensual Opinion Writing	Law Clerks	Support Personnel
Total Opinions	0.671**	0.678**
Opinions for the Court	0.022	0.242*
Opinions for the Court as a % of Total Opinions in Each Term	-0.762**	-0.564**
Separate Opinions	0.583**	0.608**
Separate Opinions as a % of Total Opinion in Each Term	0.602**	0.613**
Dissenting Opinions	0.647**	0.521**
Dissenting Opinions as a % of Total Opinions in Each Term	0.311**	0.061
Concurring Opinions	0.745**	0.623**
Concurring Opinions as a % of Total Opinions in Each Term	0.582**	0.429**

N=61; *p< .05 (one-tailed test).** p< .01 (one-tailed test).

numbers of opinions written by the justices in each term captures both the actual output of the Court and changes in the *type* of opinion writing work done by the Court. Thus, I believe that considering both measures of nonconsensual opinion writing provides insights into the impact of law clerks and support personnel on the nature of the Court's opinion writing output in each term. Expressing each measure of opinion writing as a percentage of the Court's total opinion production facilitates discussion about how the independent variables are related to changes in the composition of the Court's yearly collection of written opinions. Moreover, this second perspective on opinion writing reveals that important changes have taken place not just in the volume of opinion writing activity but effectively reveals key changes in Court behavior.

Support is found for each of the specific hypotheses associated with H1; increases in the size of the Court work group are associated with measures of nonconsensual opinion writing. Table 4.3 indicates support for H1a, the proposition stating that the numbers of law clerks and support staff are related in a statistically significant way to the total number of opinions written by the justices in each term. A correlation coefficient of 0.671 characterizes the association between law clerks and total opinions. The degree of association between support personnel and total opinions is evidenced by a correlation coefficient of 0.678. Both coefficients reflect a direct relationship between independent and dependent variables. Both coefficients are moderate if not strong in magnitude.

H1b is supported by the statistics presented in Table 4.3. H1b indicates that as the numbers of law clerks and support personnel assigned to the Court increase, the number of opinions for the Court will decrease. A correlation coefficient of 0.022 indicates that the law clerks variable is not associated in a statistically significant way with the numbers of opinions for the Court written by the justices in each term. Contrary to H1b a coefficient of 0.242 indicates that the support personnel variable is related in a linear, statistically significant way to the number of opinions for the Court produced in each term. However, the alternative perspective on nonconsensual opinion writing indicates the correctness of H1b. Bivariate correlation coefficients indicate a statistically significant, inverse relationship between the numbers of law clerks on the Court and the number of opinions for the Court written by the justices. Further, a correlation coefficient of -0.546 reveals a moderately strong, statistically significant, inverse relationship between the numbers of support personnel and the number of opinions for the Court written in each term.

In every respect, the information presented in Table 4.3 supports H1c, the hypothesis linking the numbers of law clerks and support personnel, to the frequency of separate opinion writing. Law clerks are associated in a direct, positive, statistically significant way to both the numbers of separate opinions and the numbers of opinions as a percentage of total opinions, evidenced by correlation coefficients of 0.583 and 0.602, respectively. Similarly, a correlation coefficient of 0.608 indicates a moderate, direct relationship between the number of support personnel and the number of separate opinions written per term. Furthermore, a coefficient of 0.613 reveals a direct, positive, statistically significant relationship between the number of support personnel and separate opinions as a percentage of total opinions written in each term.

Hypothesis H1d proposes a positive relationship between the number of law clerks, support personnel, and the number of dissenting opinions written in each term. The statistics presented in Table 4.3 indicate support for H1d. Evidenced by correlation coefficients of 0.647 and 0.311, statistically significant, positive associations characterize the relationships between the number of law clerks and the number of dissenting opinions and dissenting opinions as a percentage of the total opinions written in each term. Interestingly, the coefficient of 0.061 reveals no statistically significant relationship between the number of support personnel and dissenting opinions as a percentage of the total opinion output in each year. However, a correlation coefficient of 0.521 indicates a moderately strong, statistically significant, positive relationship between the number of support personnel on the Court and the number of dissenting opinions written in each term. Due to these contradictory findings, I tentatively suggest that support personnel are in some way related to the Court's production of increasing numbers of dissenting opinions but are, apparently, not instrumental factors in altering the justices' decision to write a dissent versus another type of opinion. One possible explanation for this result is that the law clerks are, in a relative sense, more proximate than support staff to the justices' opinion writing decision. Although important as an institutional resource related to opinion writing tasks, support personnel may be unable to engage in the persuasive behaviors of the more ideologically committed law clerks.

Hypothesis H1e proposes a positive relationship between the number of law clerks, support personnel and the writing of concurring opinions: the data presented in Table 4.1 support this proposition. Correlation coefficients of 0.745 and 0.582 indicates that the numbers of law clerks and support personnel on the Court are related to the justices' tendencies to write increasing numbers of concurring opinions and to make concurring opinions an increasingly larger proportion to each term's opinion production. Similarly, correlation coefficients of 0.623 and 0.429 reveal positive, moderately strong, statistically significant relationships between the number of support personnel, the number of concurring opinions, and concurring opinions as a percentage of the total number of opinions written in each term.

Conclusion

While Posner, O'Brien, and Wald assert a relationship between law clerks and opinion writing,[16] I find empirical evidence to support the proposition that increasing numbers of law clerks are associated with increasing numbers of several non-institutional opinion types. Further, I present evidence that tentatively suggests that the size of the Supreme Court work group, which includes support personnel, is related in a linear, statistically significant way to the frequency of nonconsensual opinion writing. This finding is important evidence that processes of institutionalization are linked to the behavior of individual Supreme Court justices. Although the data presented thus far are not conclusive, this finding suggests that the structure of the Supreme Court institution is connected to the behavior of individual justices.

One might be tempted to explain these statistical relationships as instances of correlation without causation. On its face, this argument is no more persuasive than were I to suggest that these statistical correlations are indisputable proof of the correctness of my hypotheses. Indeed, I must test the correctness of these hypotheses while controlling for competing explanations for increases in nonconsensual opinions. Further, I must present the results of appropriate diagnostic tests to ensure that these statistical relationships are not merely products of serial correlation in the error terms associated with each model. Moreover, the practice of "good science" requires that I subject these findings to more thorough testing, for

---

[16]O'Brien, p. 170; Posner, p. 357; Patricia M. Wald, "Selecting Law Clerks," *Michigan Law review* 89 (1990): 153.

example, controlling for competing explanations of dissensus and attempting to find the true degree of statistical correlation between the independent and dependent variables. In the next chapter, I begin this process using regression analysis and calculating partial correlation coefficients in an effort to determine the independent effect of the law clerks and support personnel on patterns of dissent and dissensus.

CHAPTER 5

Analyzing Changes in the Membership of the Supreme Court: Toward a Multivariate Explanation of Nonconsensual Opinion Writing

Introduction

In Chapter 1, I noted that judicial scholars have long recognized the primacy of attitudinal and ideological factors as explanations of disagreement among justices. From C. Herman Pritchett's classic study in 1948 to Glendon Schubert's book, *The Judicial Mind*, ideological identities have proven useful as guides to points of disagreement on the Court.[1] Interestingly, studies of the decline in consensual norms on the Supreme Court offer a different view of the importance of attitudinal or ideological factors. Walker, Epstein, and Dixon argue that the sudden collapse in the consensus norm in 1941 is not accompanied by an episodic change in the degree of ideological conflict among justices.[2] The authors compare voting behavior between and within ideological blocs on the Hughes and Stone Courts. The authors suggest that dissensus is not driven exclusively by disagreement between ideological foes. Rather, they report that notable increases in dissension on the

---

[1]C. Herman Pritchett, *The Roosevelt Court: A Study in Judicial Politics and Values: 1937-1947* (New York: MacMillan Publishers, 1948); Glendon Schubert, *The Judicial Mind* (Evanston: Northwestern University Press, 1965).

[2]Thomas Walker, Lee Epstein, and William Dixon, "On the Mysterious Demise of Consensual Norms on the United States Supreme Court," *Journal of Politics* 50 (1988): 375.

Court during this period are also linked to disagreement *within* blocs of justices of the same ideological description.[3] Thus, Walker, Epstein, and Dixon report that disagreement between ideological factions on the Hughes and Stone Courts did not precipitate the sudden increases in nonconsensual opinion writing.

In her longitudinal study of the decline in consensual norms, Stacia Haynie found no evidence to support the proposition that partisan divisions are related to the frequency of nonconsensual opinion writing.[4] Haynie hypothesized that dissenting and concurring opinions increase as the Court becomes more factionalized along political party lines. Haynie proposed that dissensus would become less frequent with increases in the size of the majority party coalition on the Court. However, Professor Haynie found no support for this hypothesis. If Haynie is correct, ideological tensions, as measured by the partisan composition of the Court, are not important factors in the historical decline in the consensus norm.

Another examination of the connection between ideology and dissensus yielded an interesting observation. In their cross-judicial study of dissent behavior in the federal courts, Scott Gerber and Keeok Park consider how changes in the ideological setting in which justices work influences their tendencies toward written expressions of dissensus. The authors find that regardless of their particular ideology or the ideological bent of the lower court on which they served, upon arriving at the Supreme Court the Rehnquist Court justices demonstrate a greater propensity to

---

[3]Ibid., p. 375.

[4]Stacia Haynie, "Leadership and Consensus on the U.S. Supreme Court," *Journal of Politics* 54 (1992): 1166. Haynie's use of partisanship is a good strategy for capturing the effects of judicial ideologies and attitudes on dissensus. Segal and Spaeth observe that partisanship is a viable surrogate for judicial attitudes. The authors note that partisanship is ". . . useful for predicting attitudes. . . ." See Segal and Spaeth, p. 232.

produce nonconsensual opinions.[5] This is an important finding. Inasmuch as Professors Gerber and Park argue that variation in the ideological composition of the judicial body in which justices serve is not significantly related to dissent behavior, it does leave unanswered the question of how the context specific to the Supreme Court makes all justices more dissent prone, regardless of how agreeable or disagreeable they find the Court's ideological climate. The authors note:

> [t]he implication of this finding may be that virtually all justices become more dissent prone after they come to the Supreme Court and that the individual justices' ideology   affects their nonconsensual behavior more on the Supreme Court than it does on the lower appellate courts.[6]

My point is not that the ideological composition of a judicial organization is unrelated to dissent behavior. Rather, if Gerber and Park are correct, Supreme Court justices may encounter an institutional context which facilitates the written expression of ideological conflict. Paul Brace and Melinda Gann Hall present a similar argument in their study of dissent behavior on state supreme courts. The authors write:

> The results indicate that justices' decisions to dissent reflect significantly more than attitudinal disagreement, reactions to various types of case facts or responses to contextual forces. Rather, dissents are the product of all of these types of variables, interacting with institutional rules and procedures.[7]

---

[5]Scott D. Gerber and Keeok Park, "The Quixotic Search for Consensus on the U.S. Supreme Court: A Cross-Judicial Empirical Analysis of the Rehnquist Court Justices," *American Political Science Review* 91 (1997): 396.

[6]Ibid, p. 396.

[7]Paul Brace and Melinda Gann Hall, "Integrated Models of Judicial Dissent," *Journal of Politics* 55 (1993): 914.

The research by Gerber and Park and Brace and Hall encourage the view that the strength of a connection between ideological composition and nonconsensual opinion writing may be context-specific; the causal importance of an ideological variable may be closely associated with the presence of other variables, including institutional features. Thus, I include in the same regression model measures of institutional change, such as increases in the numbers of law clerks and support personnel employed by the Court, and a variable which measures changes in the ideological composition of the Court.

Inclusion of an ideological composition variable in the model of nonconsensual opinion writing is important for additional reasons. The studies by Walker, Epstein, and Dixon and Haynie are not conclusive with regard to the importance of ideological or partisan divisions as a source of nonconsensual opinion writing. That Walker, Dixon, and Epstein consider only a brief period of Supreme Court history does little to explore the connections between changes in the ideological composition of the Court and long term trends in nonconsensual opinion writing. Indeed, it is unlikely that ideological factors are of uniform influence on opinion writing practices in all eras of the Court's history.

Haynie's use of the size of the majority party coalition on the Court as a measure of ideological divisiveness may be a less than optimal approach to operationalizing this important concept. Haynie identifies each justice as either a Democrat or Republican. This approach fails to capture the true extent of ideological divisiveness among justices. An example makes this problem more obvious. It is conceivable that two justices, say Justices White and Stewart, each weakly identified with two different political parties, may be more ideologically proximate than, say, Justice Brennan, who was among the most liberal of Democratic identifiers on the Court, and Justice White, a Democrat with more centrist tendencies. In Haynie's model, the two weak identifiers are treated as being ideologically distinct while Justices Brennan and the notably more conservative Frankfurter would be treated as ideological twins. Under Haynie's scheme, the ideological "distance" between two justices of the same partisan identity but with very different attitudinal proclivities is entirely lost. In short, Haynie's scheme is not sensitive to the actual range or variation in ideological leanings among the Court's members.

Should Haynie's approach to measuring ideological tension on the Court be discarded? To do so would ignore an important proxy measure of attitudinal or ideological tension among the justices.[8] Thus, I include a partisan-composition variable in the models of nonconsensual opinion writing when an alternative method of accounting for ideological conflict on the Court violates the assumptions of the data analysis methods employed to test the hypotheses.

Other than the use of a partisan composition variable, there is another way of accounting for the importance of ideological composition as a factor in the decline of consensual norms on the Court. The ideological heterogeneity score identified in Chapter 2 serves the interests of both measuring ideological conflict over a lengthy period of time and accounts for the actual range of ideological dispositions among the justices. Pursuant to my criticism of Haynie's partisan competition variable, this ideological heterogeneity measure is designed to capture the actual magnitude of value differences between justices whether they are of the same or different party identifications. The ideological heterogeneity score also allows examination of the effects of changes in ideological composition during the period 1946-1995, a period much longer than that considered by Walker, Epstein, and Dixon. A more complete explanation of the ideological heterogeneity variable is included in a later section of this chapter.

Of course, one might argue that my proposition linking ideological heterogeneity and dissensus is little more than a truism. Intuition suggests that a Court beset by ideological division will always produce written expressions of dissent more frequently than one characterized by ideological homogeneity. However, such an argument fails on at least the following point: written expressions of dissent are possible only where the resources exist to produce such documents. Again, my suspicion about the intercorrelation between nonconsensual opinion writing and institutional factors is supported. Implicit in H2a, is my suspicion that the law clerks

---

[8]See the discussion by Jeffrey A. Segal and Harold J. Spaeth, *The Supreme Court and the Attitudinal Model* (Cambridge: Cambridge University Press, 1993), p. 232.

and support personnel constitute an institutional environment enabling the justices to produce written opinions in numbers proportional to the extent of ideological tension.

Correlates of Conflict: Changes in the Chief Justice's Seat

Several studies directly test the proposition that the historical decline in the consensus norm is attributable to the behavioral expectations of the chief justice. Stacia Haynie's study of historical increases in the frequency of nonconsensual opinion writing reveals the importance of Chief Justice Harlan Fiske Stone's arrival on the Court for alterations in the consensus norm.[9] Walker, Epstein, and Dixon present a similar finding, stating that ". . . much of the responsibility for changing the operational norms of the Court from institutional unity to permitting free expression of individual views can be attributed to the leadership of Harlan Fiske Stone."[10]

Professors Caldeira and Zorn present the most vigorous argument in support of the proposition that variations in the occupant of the chief justice's seat are primarily responsible for historical changes in rates of dissent and dissensus.[11] The authors argue that nonconsensual opinion writing is part of a dynamic process in which different chief justices influence the extent to which consensual norms constrain dissent behavior.[12] Similar to previous studies, Caldeira and Zorn attribute the origin and persistence of high rates of dissent to the chief justiceship of Harlan Fiske Stone. Caldeira and Zorn conclude that "[n]o other external event or institutional change. . . accounts for the explosion of conflict

---

[9]Haynie, pp. 1158-69.

[10]Walker, Epstein, and Dixon, pp. 384.

[11]Gregory Calderia and Christopher J.W. Zorn, "Of Time and Consensual Norms in the Supreme Court," *American Journal of Political Science* 42 (1998): 874-902.

[12]Ibid., p. 900.

under Stone and its persistence from 1941 to the present."[13]

In light of these studies, it seems almost axiomatic that the historical decline in the consensus norm is attributable to changes in the occupant of the chief justice's seat. Furthermore, it seems that the leadership of Chief Justice Stone is an especially important factor in the alteration of consensual norms. I noted in Chapter 1 that historical and anecdotal treatments of Supreme Court history indicate that the service of Chief Justice Burger is also likely to be associated with discord and dissent.

Although previous studies present convincing arguments in support of the proposition that changes in leadership are most closely associated with changing patterns of dissent and dissensus, this monocausal explanation is problematic if not implausible. For example, Caldeira and Zorn recognize that a permanent change in the consensus norm occurred during Stone's tenure and that different chief justices in varying degrees have caused the consensus norm to constrain the behavior of the Court. However, Caldeira and Zorn fail to mention an obvious quality of the decline in consensual norms: the rate of nonconsensual opinion writing increased steadily for five decades, irrespective of the occupant of the chief justice's seat. Although Stone's presence on the Court is undoubtedly linked, as the authors suggest, to the permanent change in the consensus norm, it seems improbable that the influence of any one or all chief justices wholly accounts for the increasing rates of nonconsensual opinion writing which occurred during each of the services of Chief Justices Stone, Vinson, Warren, and Burger. Thus, I suspect that the "chief justice" effect is overstated. The data presented in Table 5.1 and the discussion which follows support this conclusion.

Also, it seems that Professors Caldeira and Zorn ignore the important findings of Scott D. Gerber and Keeok Park. Gerber and Park's conclusion implies that the frequency of nonconsensual behavior on the Supreme Court is conditioned by the justices' *ability* to produce independent expressions. The authors observe that upon arrival at the Supreme Court, the newly appointed Rehnquist Court justices produced more dissents and concurrences than they did while serving in other judicial posts. Gerber and Park state:

---

[13]Ibid., p. 875.

Consistent with the neoinstitutional perspective, we surmise that this behavior change is due to the modern Supreme Court being unique, a court on which the members feel it is desirable, necessary, and *possible* to express policy disagreements with the majority via separate opinions and votes [italics mine]."[14]

It is also important to note that Caldeira and Zorn reserve final judgement about other causes of dissent behavior. The authors explain: "Thus, in our reading of the results, consensual norms, far from being a fixed canon of judicial conduct, are a *dynamic* process: norms both influence, and are in turn influenced by, changes in the politics, *procedures,* and personnel on the Court [emphasis mine]."[15] Caldeira and Zorn's argument is entirely consistent with my general proposition that whatever the cause of the decline in the consensus norm and the historical trend toward nonconsensual opinion writing, procedural changes in the Court's organization, which are arguably linked to changes in the availability of institutional resources, fuel manifestations of this changing norm. In other words, assuming that Professors Caldeira and Zorn are correct, and that chief justices are responsible for on-going alterations in the consensus norm, a procedural shift caused by the rise of a law clerk institution is a likely factor in the full realization of the changing consensus norm.

The Variables: Operationalization and Measurement

In this section, I identify the operational definitions, specific measurement issues, and preliminary evidence related to inclusion of the ideological conflict and chief justice variables in regression models. In a later section, I present a similar treatment of the turnover and inexperience variables.

The meaning of the ideological heterogeneity score deserves careful explanation. Recall from Chapter 2 that the ideological heterogeneity

---

[14]Gerber and Park, p. 390.

[15]Calderia and Zorn, p. 900.

score for each term is calculated using the ideological values of the justices on the Court during that term.[16] A justice's ideological value may be any number between -1.0 and +1.0. Justices determined to be the most conservative were assigned a score of -1.0. Conversely, the most liberal justices were assigned a score of +1.0. All but a few justices were assigned scores somewhere between these extreme values. For example, Justice Rehnquist was assigned a value of -0.91 while Justice Black was assigned as score of +0.75. A complete listing of the ideological scores is found in Appendix A.

The ideological heterogeneity score for any particular term is defined as the standard deviation of the ideological scores assigned to each serving justice during that term. Thus, the ideological heterogeneity score for a specific term represents the average amount of deviation from the mean ideological score for that term. Considering that the largest value which may be assigned to any justice has an absolute value of 1, ideological heterogeneity scores may take on any value within the range 0 to 1. The most ideologically heterogeneous Courts are those with scores approaching 1, while a Court with a score approaching 0 is one characterized as relatively homogenous. For example, the standard deviation of ideological scores for the justices serving in the 1967 term is 0.33. In contrast, the standard deviation of ideological scores for the justices serving during the 1972 term is 0.78. Thus, relative to the 1967 term, the justices serving during the 1972 terms were more ideologically divided. An ideological heterogeneity score of 1 would result only where scores for an even number of justices were utilized and the justices were heterogeneous. Only on a Court where all justices were assigned the same ideological value would an ideological heterogeneity score of 0 result. In

---

[16]As I noted in Chapter 2, the ideological heterogeneity score is calculated using the ideological values provided by Segal and Cover. See Jeffrey A. Segal and Albert Cover, "Ideological Values and the Votes of Supreme Court Justices," *American Political Science Review* 83 (1989): 557-65. Additional values are also taken from Walker, et. al., The Supreme Court Compendium. Because Segal and Cover have not determined scores for justices serving prior to 1946, use of the ideological heterogeneity score limits the universe of study to the terms 1946-1995.

no instance was any Court determined to have an ideological heterogeneity score of either 0 or 1. Appendix B includes a complete explanation of the methods used in calculating ideological heterogeneity scores for each term, 1946-1995. The ideological heterogeneity score is useful because it reflects both the range of ideological scores as well as the ideological proximity of the Court's members. Utilizing only a measure of range would produce scores that emphasized those justices assigned extreme ideological values. The method of calculation I use considers one justice's score and ideological position to be as important as that of any other justice when determining the degree of ideological heterogeneity on the Court.

How, then, has the degree of ideological heterogeneity on the Court changed during the period 1946-1995? Figure 5.1 reveals that ideological heterogeneity varied noticeably between 1946 and 1995, ranging from a low of 0.33 in the early 1960s to a high of 0.78 in the early 1970s. Perhaps most interesting is that the degree of ideological heterogeneity on the Court increased markedly in the 1969 term. In fact, during the period 1946-1968, ideological heterogeneity scores never exceeded 0.46; the average score during the period 1946-1968 is 0.38. During the period 1971 to 1986, ideological heterogeneity scores never fell below 0.77. The average score during the period 1969 and 1989 is 0.74, almost twice that of the 1946-1968 period. In 1990, the ideological heterogeneity score dropped to 0.38 and increased slightly to 0.48 in 1995.

What do these changes in ideological heterogeneity scores suggest about historical changes in the ideological composition of the Court? The average ideological heterogeneity score of 0.38 during the 1946-1968 period indicates that the justices were more closely grouped around a mean ideological heterogeneity score than in the 1969-1989 period. The average ideological heterogeneity score of 0.74 during the 1969-1989 period indicates that during this later period, the justices were, in an ideological sense, more broadly scattered around an ideological mean. Thus, relative to the earlier period of 1946-1968, the Court during the years 1969-1989 is characterized by a higher degree of variability among justices in terms of their ideological values. In this sense, it can be seen that the Court during the latter period (1969-1986) was typically more

Figure 5.1. Ideological Heterogeneity Scores, 1946-1995

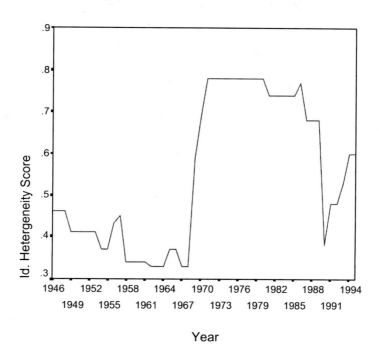

Year

ideologically heterogenous than during the previous period (1946-1968), a fact, I suspect, that is linked to the frequency of nonconsensual opinion writing.

Prior to testing a model of nonconsensual opinion writing and controlling for the effects of changes in the ideological composition on the Court, it is important to conduct a preliminary assessment of any linkage between the degree of ideological heterogeneity on the Court and the frequency of nonconsensual opinion writing. Based on the data presented in Figure 5.1, I separated the period 1946-1995 into two shorter periods, 1946-1968 and 1969-1989. I have identified 1946-1968 as a period of low ideological heterogeneity while 1969-1989 is identified

Table 5.1 Nonconsensual Opinion Writing in Periods of High and Low
Ideological Heterogeneity

| | Average Number of Opinions Per Term* | | |
	Concur.	Dissents	Separate Opin.**
1946-1968			
(Low Id. Hetero.)	28.7	67.87	8.96
	(0.24) (0.57)	(.08)	
1969-1989			
(High Id. Hetero.)	45.86	105.33	42.48
	(0.30) (0.70)	(.28)	
Difference of	t=-1.72	t=-7.57	t=-6.56
Means Tests	(p<.05	(p<.01	(p<.01
	1-tailed test)	2-tailed test)	2-tailed test)

* The numbers in parentheses indicate the average number of opinions
written per case disposed of by signed opinion. The figures for the
number of cases disposed of by signed opinion are taken from the
Administrative Office of the United States Courts, Statistics Division. See
*Supreme Court of the United States, Cases on the Docket, Disposed of,
and Remaining on Dockets*, successive terms 1946-1989.

** Recall that O'Brien defines a separate opinion as one announcing the
decision of the Court, the whole of which is not joined by a same majority
coalition of justices. For example, in a separate opinion, the coalition of
justices that agrees to one part of a controlling opinion is different from
that coalition of justice that agrees to another part of the same controlling
opinion. O'Brien cites as an example Justices Powell's opinion in *Regents
of the University of California v. Bakke* (1978).

as a period of high ideological heterogeneity. For each period, I calculated the average numbers of dissenting, concurring, and separate opinions written by all the justices in each term. These data appear in Table 5.1.

Table 5.1 indicates that during the period of high ideological heterogeneity, 1969-1989, the average number of concurring opinions written by the justices is nearly twice that produced by the Court during the period of low ideological heterogeneity, 1946-1968. Similarly, during the period of high ideological heterogeneity, the justices wrote an average of 105.33 dissenting opinions compared to an average of 67.87 during the 1946-1968 period. Further, during the 1969-1989 period, the justices produced an average of 42.48 separate opinions in each term. This number is more than four-and-one-half times the number produced during the earlier period, the period of low ideological heterogeneity.

In addition, Table 5.1 indicates the t test statistics calculated to determine whether the differences in the average numbers of concurring, dissenting, and separate opinions between the two periods are statistically significant. Table 5.1 reveals that for each type of nonconsensual opinion writing, the difference in means between periods is statistically significant. This result supports the proposition that the justices produced significantly more nonconsensual opinions during the period of high ideological heterogeneity.

Table 5.1 also indicates the average numbers of dissenting, concurring, and separate opinions written by the justices per case disposed of by signed opinion. It indicates that the average number of concurring opinions written per case disposed of by signed opinion increased from 0.24 in the period of low ideological heterogeneity to 0.30 in the period of high ideological heterogeneity. In addition, the average number of dissents written per case disposed of by signed opinion increased from 0.59 in the period of low ideological heterogeneity to 0.70 in the period of high ideological heterogeneity. Also, the average number of separate opinions written per case disposed of by signed opinion increased from 0.08 in the period of low ideological heterogeneity to 0.28 in the period of high ideological heterogeneity.

What do the data in Table 5.1 suggest about the relationship between the degree of ideological heterogeneity on the Court and the frequency of nonconsensual opinion writing? These data do not indicate any causal relationship between the ideological composition of the Court and instances of concurring, dissenting, and separate opinion writing. From these data, however, I infer that the frequency of nonconsensual opinion writing varies markedly between periods characterized by different degrees of ideological heterogeneity among justices. Moreover, I believe that these data constitute sufficient evidence to include the ideological heterogeneity variable in models of nonconsensual opinion writing.

Including the ideological heterogeneity variable in the models of nonconsensual opinion writing is at times problematic. The ideological variable is strongly intercorrelated with the law clerk and support personnel variables. Also, recall that ideological heterogeneity variables are available only for the 1946-1995 terms. In order to ease the effects of multicollinearity and account for ideological tensions on the Court during the entire 1935-1995 period, I substitute the partisan-composition variable used by Haynie. The partisan-composition variable is operationally defined as the number of justices comprising the majority party on the Supreme Court in each term. For example, a term in which the Court is comprised of seven justices identified as Republicans and two justices identified as Democrats yields a value of "7" for that observation on the partisan composition variable. I anticipate a negative relationship between the partisan- composition variable and the number of dissenting, concurring, and separate opinions written by the Court in each term The party identification of each justice serving during the period 1935-1995 is determined using the listings prepared by Lisa Paddock in her 1996 book, *Facts About The Supreme Court of the United States.*[17]

The data presented in Table 5.1 are important in another way. Considering that the average number of dissenting, concurring, and separate opinions per case disposed of by signed opinion in each term increased between the periods of low and high ideological heterogeneity, I surmise that changes in the Court's production of nonconsensual

---

[17]Lisa Paddock, *Facts About The Supreme Court of the United States* (New York: H.W. Wilson Company, 1996), pp. 216, 235, 272, 273, 291, 312, 364, 365, 415.

opinions are not systematically influenced by the "opportunity" to draft additional opinions. The increases in dissenting, concurring, and separate opinions written per case disposed of by signed opinion suggests that the justices were not producing more nonconsensual opinions in the period of high ideological heterogeneity simply because more cases were being given plenary treatment by the Court.

Accounting for changes in the chief justice variable requires the use of several dummy variables. Dummy variables are used to capture the effects of the tenures of Chief Justices Hughes, Stone, Vinson, Burger, and Rehnquist. Each multiple regression model includes a dummy variable for each of Chief Justices Hughes, Stone, Vinson, Burger, and Rehnquist. For example, measures on the dummy variable for Chief Justice Rehnquist indicate a "1" for terms during the period 1986 to 1995 and a "0" for all other terms during the period 1935-1995.

The effect of Chief Justice Warren's tenure is measured by the constant term. To include a dichotomous dummy variable for all chief justices produces a perfectly correlated dummy variable, that is, a variable that is perfectly multicollinear with the constant term. The presence of perfect multicollinearity makes estimation of regression coefficients impossible.

In an earlier section, I discussed the close connection between the tenure of Chief Justices Stone and Burger and dissension on the Court. But which of the other chief justices are likely to be associated with high rates of dissensus? Table 5.2 provides an answer. I present in Table 5.2 the average number of concurring, dissenting, and separate opinion written during the tenures of Chief Justices Hughes, Stone, Vinson, Warren, Burger, and Rehnquist.

Chief Justice Stone's tenure is associated with notable increases in the frequency of nonconsensual opinion writing. During Stone's tenure, the Court produced an average of 22.8 concurrences per term, a number five times greater than the average number of concurrences produced per term during the tenure of Chief Justice Hughes. Also, during the tenure of Chief Justice Stone the Court drafted an average of 61 dissents per term. By contrast, during the tenure of Chief Justice Hughes the justices produced an average of 22.67 dissents per term.

Table 5.2. Average Nonconsensual Opinions Per Term During The Services of Chief Justices Hughes Through Rehnquist*

Chief Justice	Concur/ term	Dissents/ term	Sep. Opin./ term	Avg. Cases Disp. by Signed Op.**
Hughes (1935-1940)	4 (.02)	22.67 (.12)	4.5 (.03)	177.84
Stone (1941-1945)	22.8 (.13)	61 (.34)	8.2 (.05)	178.80
Vinson*** (1946-1951)	25.7 (.53)	69 (.19)	3.83 (.03)	133.0
Warren (1953-1968)	30.43 (.25)	66.06 (.56)	11.13 (.10)	115.0
Burger (1969-1985)	40.82 (.27)	107.41 (.70)	48.47 (.32)	152.41
Rehnquist (1986-1995)	62.4 (.50)	77.3 (.62)	14.3 (.12)	123.70

* Number in parentheses are the average number of opinions written per case disposed of by signed opinion. ** Source: Administrative Office of the United States Courts, Statistics Division, *Cases on the Docket, Disposed of, and Remaining on Dockets in the Supreme Court of the United States*, 1935-1995 terms. *** In the interests of convenience, the data in this table do not reflect opinion writing behavior in the 1952 term. Chief Justice Fred Vinson died on September 8, 1953. Per an interim appointment, Chief Justice Warren arrived at the Court on March 2, 1953, serving only during the final four months of the 1952 term. Warren's first full term as chief justice began in October 1953.

Table 5.2 also indicates the average number of concurring, dissenting, and separate opinions written by the justices per case disposed of by signed opinion. Table 5.2 reveals that while the Hughes Court produced an average 0.02 concurrences per case, the Stone Court produced an average of 0.13 concurrences per case. Further, the Stone Court produced an average of 0.34 dissents per case while the Hughes Court produced an average of only 0.12 dissents per case.

High rates of concurring opinions writing are associated with the tenure of Chief Justice Rehnquist while Chief Justice Burger's service is more closely linked to the production of written dissents and separate opinions. During the 1986-1995 terms, the Rehnquist Court produced an average of 62.4 concurrences per term or nearly two and one half times that of the Vinson Court. The Rehnquist Court of the 1986-1995 period wrote twice as many concurrences as the Warren Court and one and a half times as many as the Burger Court. Moreover, the Rehnquist Court justices issued an average of 0.50 concurrences per case disposed of by signed opinion despite operating in an ideological climate more favorable for consensus than that encountered by the Burger Court justices.

The Burger Court (1969-1985) produced an average of 107.41 written dissents per term. The Rehnquist Court of the 1986-1995 period produced an average of 77.3 dissents per term, while the Warren and Vinson Courts wrote an average of 66.06 and 69 dissents per term, respectively. Thus, the Burger Court produced nearly one and a half times more written dissents per term than either the Vinson, Warren, or Rehnquist Courts. Furthermore, the Rehnquist Court produced an average of 0.62 dissents per case, a figure exceeded only by the Burger Court justices who produced an average of 0.70 dissents per case.

The data in Table 5.2 reveal that the Court produces different levels of dissent under different chief justices. Could it be that different levels of dissent behavior are driven by the number of "opportunities" to dissent under different chief justices? Should it be expected, for example, that because the Stone Court treated more cases with signed opinions than the Rehnquist Court it should also produce more concurring, dissenting, and written opinions? Although the increased number of "opportunities" may have influenced nonconsensual opinion writing, I find that this factor is not strongly related to the production of dissenting, concurring, or separate opinions.

I explained above that the Stone Court produced many more dissenting, concurring, and separate opinions than the Hughes Court. However, the Stone Court disposed of an average of 178.8 cases by signed opinion per term compared to the average of 177.83 signed opinions produced by the Hughes Court per term. Moreover, the Hughes and Stone Court justices encountered essentially the same number of opportunities to produce nonconsensual opinions; the Hughes and Stone Courts are essentially equal in the average number of cases disposed of by signed opinion per term. This result indicates that the momentous increase in nonconsensual behavior which occurred during the tenure of Chief Justice Stone is not an artifact of an increased number of opportunities to disagree. It is, of course, possible that caseload is a more important factor for opinion writing in later terms.

In addition, the Vinson Court justices disposed of an average of 133 cases per term by signed opinion. Despite the fact that both the Hughes and Stone Courts issued signed opinions in an average of 45 more cases per term, neither Court produced as many dissents and concurrences as the Vinson Court justices. Similarly, the Warren Court justices disposed of an average of 115 cases per term by signed opinion. Thus, the Warren Court disposed of an average of 63 fewer cases by signed opinion per term than either the Hughes or Stone Courts. Yet, the Warren Court issued an average of 30.43 concurrences per term and 66.06 dissents per term, figures noticeably higher than the average number of concurrences and dissents issues by either the Hughes or Stone Courts.

The Burger Court justices issued an average of 40.82 concurrences per term, an average of 107.41 dissenting opinions per term, and 11.8 separate opinions per term. By contrast, the Stone Court issued an average of 22.8 concurrences per term, an average of 61 dissents per term, and an average of 8.2 separate opinions per term. Although the Burger Court justices produced more than twice the average number of nonconsensual opinions written by the Stone Court, the Burger Court disposed of an average of 152.41 cases per term, some 25 fewer cases per term than the average number of cases disposed of by signed opinion during the Stone Court years. Again, it does not appear that "opportunity" explains differences in the frequency of nonconsensual opinion writing.

The opinion writing behavior of the Rehnquist Court represents the most striking evidence that "opportunity," as defined by caseload, is not systematically related to the production of nonconsensual opinions. The data presented in Table 5.2 indicate that the Rehnquist Court treated an average of 123.7 cases disposed of by signed opinion per term. This figure is noticeably less than the average of 177.83 cases treated by the Hughes Court per term, the 178.8 cases treated by the Stone Court per term, the 133 cases treated by the Vinson Court per term, and the 152.41 cases treated by the Burger Court per term. The Rehnquist Court, however, produced a higher number of average concurrences per term than the Court produced under any other chief justice. Further, the Rehnquist Court produced an average of .50 concurrences per case, a figure higher than that of any Court in during the 1935-1995 period. Also, the Rehnquist Court justices produced an average of 77.3 dissents per term, a figure higher than that produced by either the Hughes, Stone, Vinson, or Warren Courts. Moreover, the Rehnquist Court justices, despite enjoying relatively few "opportunities" to issue nonconsensual opinions, are second only to the Burger Court in their propensity toward dissensus.

These findings confirm my point that historical increases in the frequency of nonconsensual opinion writing are not simply artifacts of an increasing number of opportunities to dissent. Rather, the justices of the Supreme Court demonstrated an increased propensity toward nonconsensual opinion writing for reasons unrelated, for the most part, to historical changes in the number of cases treated with signed opinions. Most important, this finding supports Caldeira and Zorn's decision to use the actual numbers of written opinions as measures on the dependent variable in their models of the historical decline in consensual norms. The authors explain that use of a measure of opinion production that is "normalized" according to the number of decisions of the Court in each term produces results substantially similar to those resulting from models which employ the raw numbers of nonconsensual opinions.[18] Thus, in

---

[18]Caldeira and Zorn, p. 881, n.3.

modeling the historical decline in consensual norms, I utilize the actual numbers of written dissents, concurrences, and separate opinions.[19]

This finding does not, however, fully resolve the question of whether "opportunity" is linked to the frequency of dissenting, concurring, and separate opinion writing. In Chapter 7, I included in the multiple regression models a measure of the Court's caseload that also captures changes in the number of opportunities to draft nonconsensual opinions.

Turnover and Inexperience

As I noted in Chapter 1, two additional measures of membership change are possibly linked to historical changes in the number of dissenting, concurring, and separate opinions produced by the Court. The extent of turnover and inexperience on the Court may be related to patterns of nonconsensual behavior. The degree of inexperience on the Court in each term is defined as the number of justices with three or fewer full terms of service on the Court.[20] This operational definition is similar to that used by Walker, Epstein, and Dixon.[21] As the authors hypothesize, "[a] disproportionately inexperienced Court may have difficulty maintaining

---

[19]The use of actual numbers of opinions is supported by the strong correlations between a measure of opinion writing that includes the number of "opportunities" to dissents and measures of opinion writing and the actual numbers of opinions written per term. I calculated an alternative measures of dissenting, concurring, and separate opinion writing in each term by dividing the actual number of each type of opinion by the number of cases disposed of by signed opinion in each term. A Pearson correlation coefficient of 0.922 is calculated for this measure of concurrences and the actual number of concurrences. A coefficient of 0.845 is calculated for this measure of dissents and the actual number of dissents. A coefficient of 0.983 is calculated for the number of separate opinions and the actual number of separate opinions.

[20]This differs from the Walker, Epstein, and Dixon study. The authors count each justice's first term, even if the justice joined after the opening of the term, as one full term.

[21]Walker, Epstein, and Dixon, p. 373.

allegiance to the ways [or consensual norms] of the past."[22] Walker, Epstein, and Dixon find that the highly conflictual Stone Court is characterized by having more inexperienced justices than any Court during the 1888-1946 period.[23] I extend the authors' analysis to include determination of the number of inexperienced justices during all terms in the 1935-1995 period.

The degree of turnover on the Court in each term is defined as the number of justices serving their first full term. Walker, Epstein, and Dixon defined an instance of turnover as the seating of a new justice on the Court.[24] Moreover, the authors find that the conflict-ridden Stone Court (1941-1945 terms) exhibited a higher rate of turnover than the relatively more consensual Fuller, White, Taft, and Hughes Courts of previous decades.[25] I propose to extend their analysis beyond the Stone Court years, testing the turnover hypothesis using opinion writing data from the Court's modern era. If the authors are correct, the turnover variable should be related in a direct, positive way to the frequency of nonconsensual opinion writing.

Table 5.3 includes data reflecting the extent of turnover and inexperience on the Court during the tenures of Chief Justices Hughes, Stone, Vinson, Warren, Burger, and Rehnquist. For the purposes of concise presentation, I use a turnover rate and inexperience index similar to Walker, Dixon, and Epstein. The use of the turnover rate and inexperience index is limited to this chapter. The actual numbers of newly appointed and inexperienced justices are used in the regression models estimated in Chapters 6 and 7. It is also important to note that my data differs from that presented by Walker, Dixon, and Epstein. When calculating the turnover rate and inexperience index, I count all new and inexperienced justices, including newly appointed chief justices. This

---

[22]Ibid., p. 373.

[23]Ibid, p. 373.

[24]Ibid., p. 372.

[25]Ibid., pp. 372-373.

method is preferable to that of Walker, Epstein, and Dixon because they include only newly appointed and inexperienced *associate* justices in their tabulations. Contrary to my approach, their method excludes from analysis the turnover and "inexperience" brought to the Court by Chief Justices Vinson (1946), Warren (1952), and Burger (1969). When compared to the opinion writing data in Table 5.2, the data presented in Table 5.3 do not suggest a systematic relationship between nonconsensual behavior and the extent of turnover and inexperience on

Table 5.3 Turnover and Inexperience on the Supreme Court from Hughes to Rehnquist

Chief Justice	Turnover Rate*	Inexperience Index**
Hughes (1930-1940)	0.64	20.4
Stone (1941-1945)	0.80	33.3
Vinson (1946-1952)	0.43	17.5
Burger (1954-1968)	0.35	13.1
Rehnquist (1986-1995)	0.50	18.8

* Turnover rate is the average number of new justices per term.

** The Inexperience Index is the percentage of Supreme Court seats occupied by justices who have served less than three full terms on the Court.

the Court. Despite being courts characterized by high rates of dissent and dissensus, there was relatively little turnover on the Burger and Rehnquist Courts. Turnover rates of 0.35 for the Burger Court and 0.50 for the Rehnquist Court are lower than the 0.64, 0.8, and 0.66 rates for the Hughes, Stone, and Warren Courts, respectively. However, a turnover rate of 0.80 on the Stone Court, the highest among the five courts examined, is consistent with the proposition that high turnover is linked to dissent behavior.

In addition, I find that instances of turnover, defined as the number of new justices on the Court in each term, are not strongly correlated with the numbers of dissenting, concurring, and separate opinion written by the justices in each term. A Pearson correlation coefficient of -.205 for the dissenting opinions variable, -0.82 for the concurrences variables, and -.334 (statistically significant at .01 level) for the separate opinion variable indicates that the extent of turnover on the Court is, in fact, weakly and negatively correlated with nonconsensual opinion writing. These data indicate that the frequency of turnover on the Court is not producing increasing numbers of nonconsensual opinions.

The extent of inexperience on the Court does not appear to be closely associated with historical increases in nonconsensual opinion writing. Recall from my earlier discussion of Table 5.2 that the Hughes Court demonstrated relatively low rates of nonconsensual opinion writing. Yet, the Inexperience Index of 20.4 calculated for the Hughes Court is higher than all post-Stone courts. Further, figures of 13.1 and 18.8 are calculated for the Burger and Rehnquist Courts, respectively. I noted in the discussion of Table 5.2 that both the Burger and Rehnquist Courts produced relatively high numbers of dissenting, concurring, and separate opinions. An Inexperience Index of 33.3 for the Stone Court is, however, consistent with the sudden increase in the numbers of dissenting and concurring opinions that occurred under the leadership of Harlan Fiske Stone.

Pearson correlations between the extent of inexperience on the Court, defined as the number of seats occupied by justices who have served less than three full terms on the Court, and the three measures of nonconsensual opinion writing suggest that inexperience is not strongly related to the Court's production of dissenting, concurring, or separate opinions. A correlation coefficient of -.298 (statistically significant at the .05 level) for the dissents variable, -.099 for the concurrences variable, and -.372 for the separate opinion variable (statistically significant at the .01 level) indicates that inexperience is weakly and negatively associated with instances of nonconsensual opinion writing. These data indicate that changes in the extent of inexperience on the Court are not producing increasing numbers of nonconsensual opinions.

These data do not, however, resolve the question of whether the turnover and inexperience variables are associated with historical changes in opinion writing practices. Thus, I include both variables in the multivariate models of nonconsensual opinion writing presented in Chapter 6.

Conclusions

In this chapter, I present preliminary evidence indicating that the extent of ideological conflict on the Court and changes in the occupant of the chief justice's seat may be important factors in the historical increase in the frequency of dissenting, concurring, and separate opinion writing. In addition, I present preliminary evidence which suggests that the "opportunity" to write individual opinions, as measured by the number of cases disposed of by signed opinion per term, is not obviously related to changing patterns of nonconsensual opinion writing. I also present preliminary evidence indicating that the extent of turnover and inexperience on the Court are not systematically related to historical increases in the numbers of dissenting, concurring, and separate opinions produced by the justices.

In the next chapter, I conduct a more rigorous test of the importance of each variable. Each variable is included in multiple regression models that estimate the effect of changes in the numbers of law clerks and support personnel on historical increases in nonconsensual opinion writing.

CHAPTER 6

Law Clerks, Support Personnel, and the Writing of Nonconsensual Opinions: Controlling for Changes in the Court's Membership

Introduction

In this chapter I use several multiple regression equations to test the independent effect of law clerks and support personnel on the frequency of nonconsensual opinion writing while controlling for several types of changes in the Court's membership. Specifically, I control for changes in the ideology of the justices on the Court, changes in the occupant of the chief justice's seat, changes in the number of inexperienced justices serving in each term, and changes in the extent of turnover in the number of newly appointed justices on the Court in each term. I employ multiple regression analysis to simultaneously test hypotheses H2a, H2b, H2c, and H2e.

    H2a is the hypothesis stating that the numbers of separate, dissenting, and concurring opinions written by the justices are related to a statistically significant degree to the increasing presence of law clerks and support personnel when controlling for changes in the ideological composition of the Court. H2b is the hypothesis stating that the numbers of separate, dissenting, and concurring opinions written by the justices are related to a statistically significant degree to the increasing presence of law clerks and support personnel when controlling for the relative turnover on the Court per term. H2c is the hypothesis stating that the numbers of separate, dissenting, and concurring opinions written by the justices are related to a statistically significant degree to the increasing presence of law clerks and support personnel when controlling for the relative inexperience of the justices on the Court in each term. H2e is the hypothesis stating that the numbers of separate, dissenting, and concurring opinions written by the justices are related to a statistically significant degree to the increasing presence of law clerks and support personnel when controlling for changes in the occupant of the chief justice's seat on the Court.

I also offer several of my conclusions regarding hypotheses H2a, H2b, H2c, and H2e. In the next chapter, I add to the multiple regression analysis two variables that measure historical changes in the substantive composition of the Court's docket and changes in the size of the institution's workload. It is from this model that I draw final conclusions regrading the relationship between law clerks, support personnel, and the historical decline in the consensus norm.

Procedures for Testing Hypotheses

In this section, I outline the procedures for testing the relationship between law clerks, support personnel, and the historical increase in the frequency of nonconsensual opinion writing. Prior to presenting the multiple regression equations, however, I examine the degree of linear association among the independent variables used in the multiple regression equations. This procedure involves constructing a correlation matrix containing each of the variables identified in H2a, H2b, H2c, and H2e.

Construction of the correlation matrix is necessary in order to anticipate the occurrence of multicollinearity in the regression models. Gujarati explains that multicollinearity is a condition that frustrates attempts to precisely determine the magnitude of regression coefficients, draw accurate conclusions about the statistical significance of t-ratios,[1] and assess the independent effect of explanatory variables. Yet, as William Berry explains, provided that no two independent variables are perfectly multicollinear, the assumptions of multiple regression are not

---

[1] Damodar N. Gujarati, *Basic Econometrics* (New York: McGraw-Hill, Inc, 1995), p. 327.

violated.[2]

Table 6.1 indicates the degree of intercorrelation among the independent variables identified in H2a, H2b, H2c, and H2e. A correlation coefficient of 0.904 indicates that the law clerk and support personnel variables are strongly intercorrelated. This correlation coefficient indicates that the law clerk and support personnel variables are strongly multicollinear, or approximate linear combinations of one another. Including both variables in the same model will frustrate the task of estimating the independent effect of either variable on the frequency of nonconsensual opinions. Moreover, I suspect that inclusion of this highly collinear pair of variables in the same regression models will frustrate hypothesis testing procedures.

Gujarati explains that multicollinearity among independent variables is often accompanied by OLS estimators with large variances, which are related to the expansion of confidence intervals used in hypothesis tests. This consequence biases hypothesis tests in favor of failing to reject the null hypothesis of a "0" or no relationship between variables. As a result, hypothesis tests conducted on multicollinear variables are unreliable.[3] Moreover, the presence of highly collinear or perfectly collinear variables compromises the precision of estimates produced by regression equations.

In order to conduct more reliable hypothesis tests, I examine the law clerk and support personnel variables in separate regression equations after confirming the presence of multicollinearity using the variance inflation factor statistics produced by SPSS when calculating regression equations. This approach is a necessary compromise position between (a) including the collinear variables and sacrificing the interpretability of the regression coefficients and (b) excluding from the analysis one of the collinear variables and suffering any resulting specification bias.

The law clerk and ideological heterogeneity variables are also noticeably collinear. A Pearson correlation coefficient of 0.721 indicates that the ideological heterogeneity and law clerk variables are, in a

---

[2]William D. Berry, *Understanding Regression Assumptions* (London: Sage Publications, 1993), p. 27.

[3]Gujarati, p. 327.

Table 6.1. Correlation Matrix: Variables Used in Testing H2a, H2b, H2c, and H2e

	Clerks	Pers.	Id.*	Inex.	Turn.	Vin	War	Bur	Rehn
Clerks	1.00	.904	.721	.237	-.136	-.268	-.228	.523	.576
Pers.	.904	1.00	.676	-.174	-.164	-.455	-.604	.389	.639
Id	*.721	.676	1.00	-.265	-.189	-.268	-.728	.821	.110
Inex.	-.237	-.174	-.265	1.00	.448	.044	.120	-.262	.132
Turn.	-.136	-.164	-.189	.448	1.00	-.061	.189	-.197	.066
Vinson	-.268	-.455	-.268	.044	-.061	1.00	-.277	-.290	-.202
Burger	.523	.389	.821	.262	-.197	.290	-.492	1.00	-.359
Rehnq.	.576	.639	.110	.132	.066	-.202	-.343	-.359	1.00
P.C.	-.240	-.162	----	.359	.123	.559	-.231	-.528	.254
Diss.	.674	.521	.751	-.298	-.205	-.043	-.194	.690	.029
Concur.	.745	.623	.340	.099	-.082	-.183	-.134	.198	.640
Sep.Op	.583	.617	.694	-.372	-.334	-.272	-.256	.813	-.124

* N=50. For all other correlations N=61.

statistical sense, closely related. However, the importance of examining the effect of the law clerk variable when controlling for the degree of ideological tension on the Court makes inclusion of either both variables or a proxy measure of ideology in a single model a necessary strategy for testing H2a.

Table 6.1 also indicates that the ideological heterogeneity variable and the Chief Justice Burger dummy variable are noticeably intercorrelated. A Pearson coefficient of 0.821 suggests that the degree of collinearity between the variables may be problematic for analysis of the partial regression coefficients. A Pearson correlation coefficient of -0.728 indicates that the ideological heterogeneity variable and the Warren dummy variable are noticeably collinear. For both sets of collinear variables, variance inflation factor statistics are calculated to assess the presence of problematic multicollinearity. If it is found that the ideological heterogeneity variable proves sufficiently collinear with the other independent variables, then the partisan composition variable discussed in Chapter 5 is entered in the model as a measure of ideological tension among the justices.

Partisan composition is defined as the number of justices comprising the majority party coalition on the Court in each term. Values on the partisan composition variable for the 1935-1995 terms are included in Appendix A. The partisan identifications of justices serving during the 1935-1995 terms are included in Appendix B.[4]

Testing Hypotheses: Multiple Regression Equations

When considered collectively, the tests for H2a, H2b, H2c and H2e indicate that the numbers of dissenting and concurring opinions written in each term are related in a statistically significant way to the number of law clerks employed by the Court when controlling for changes in the ideological heterogeneity among justices (H2a), changes in the degree of turnover on the Court (H2b), changes in the number of inexperienced justices on the Court (H2c), and changes in the occupant of the chief justice's seat (H2e). In short, these results suggest an independent, positive relationship among law clerks, support personnel, and two types of nonconsensual opinion writing. I do not find that the number of law clerks on the Court in each term is related to the frequency of separate opinions. Also, I find that the number of support personnel on the Court are not related in a statistically significant way to the numbers of dissenting and concurring opinions written by the justices. However, there is some evidence that the support personnel variable is statistically significant in a model estimating the number of separate opinions produced in each term.

---

[4]Note that Justice Felix Frankfurter (1939-1962) is sometimes identified as a an Independent. For the purposes of compiling the partisan composition variable, Frankfurter is treated as a Democrat. A complete explanation for this is found in Appendix B.

Most important, I find that the dependent variables differ in their relationship to the set of independent variables. Moreover, the independent variables are not uniform in their relationship to the frequency of written concurrences, written dissents, and separate opinions. As a consequence, three different sets of equations are presented to estimate the production of dissenting, concurring, and separate opinions and, relatedly, to test hypotheses H2a, H2b, H2c, and H2e. A complete discussion of the implications of the differences in the dissents, concurrences, and separate opinion models is presented in Chapter 7.

The first set of equations is presented in Table 6.2 and estimates the number of dissenting opinions written in each term. The second set of equations is presented in Table 6.3 and estimates the number of concurring opinions written in each term. The third set of equations is presented in Table 6.4 and estimates the number of separate opinions written in each term. Further, included in Tables 6.2, 6.3, and 6.4 are the partial regression coefficients, goodness-of-fit statistics, and Durbin-Watson d statistics for each multiple regression model. These tables include the statistics used to test each hypothesis.

Modeling the Frequency of Dissenting Opinions

Six multiple regression equations are presented in Table 6.2. The first equation includes as independent variables each of the variables identified in H2a, H2b, H2c, and H2e. This first equation takes the following form and is identified in Table 6.2 as equation 6A:

Dissents = Constant + b(Clerks) + b(Support Personnel) + b(Ideology) + b(Vinson) + b(Burger) + b(Rehnquist) + b(Turnover) + b(Inexperience) + error term

Because the ideological heterogeneity variable is calculated using scores from justices serving during the period 1946-1995, dummy variables for Chief Justices Hughes and Stone are eliminated from this first equation,

Table 6.2 Multiple Regression Equations Estimating the Frequency of Written Dissents

Ind. Var	Eq. 6A	Eq. 6B	Eq. 6C	Eq. 6D	Eq. 6E
Constant	31.384	144.33***	140.33***	117.744***	139.885***
law clerks	0.128	---------	0.248	1.295***	---------
supp. pers.	-4.13E-02	---------	---------	----------	2.86E-02
Id. Hetero.	96.386**	---------	---------	----------	----------
Party Comp.	------	-13.753***	-13.847***	-12.987***	-13.856***
Hughes	-------	-47.276***	-44.188***	-31.844***	-46.685***
Stone	-------	28.432**	31.305**	39.575***	28.863**
Vinson	-1.597	38.601***	39.807***	40.785***	39.431***
Burger	4.390	33.330***	29.966**	15.282**	30.318***
Rehnq.	-6.198	27.454***	23.022	--------	23.005*
Turnover	-1.286	0.129	0.148	0.120	0.355
Inexper.	-3.446	-0.615	-0.636	-0.869	-0.621
F	8.336***	24.876***	21.735***	23.771***	21.797***
Adj. R Sq.	0.545	0.761	0.757	0.752	0.757
				(.697)****	
Std. Err.	16.596	14.205	14.331	14.462	14.315
Durbin D	1.584	1.806	1.798	1.726	1.792
N	50	61	61	61	61

***$p<.01$; **$p<.05$; *$p<.10$

**** Adjusted R squared statistic produced when law clerk variable is removed from the equation.

and the sample size is limited to 50 cases.

In Table 6.2, Equation 6A indicates an F test statistic of 8.336 which is statistically significant. However, because of the presence of multicollinearity among variables, the ideological heterogeneity variable is the only independent variable that is statistically significant. Equation 6A suggests that the numbers of law clerks and support personnel are not related to the statistically significant increase in the frequency of written dissents. Recall, however, that Table 6.1 indicates strong correlations between the law clerk and support personnel variables. Table 6.1 also reveals strong correlations between the ideological heterogeneity and Chief Justice Burger dummy variables as well as strong correlations between the law clerk and ideological heterogeneity variables. I suspect, consistent with Gujarati's admonitions, that these multicollinear relationships conceal the actual relationships between the frequency of written dissents and law clerks, support personnel, ideological heterogeneity, and the presence of Chief Justice Burger, a factor identified in Chapter 5 as closely related to the production of dissents. In addition, a strong collinear relationship is suggested by the variance inflation factor (VIF) of 15.315 for the Rehnquist dummy variable, 19.404 for the Burger dummy variable, 25.383 for the law clerk variable, 13.903 for the support personnel variable, and 8.474 for the ideological heterogeneity variable. The VIF reflects the magnitude of the coefficient of determination between two independent variables. As an indicator of the strength of the relationship between two independent variables, the coefficient of determination produced when regressing one independent variable on another reflects the magnitude of the variance of the regression coefficient on the particular independent variable. As the coefficient of determination (the adjusted R squared statistic) produced when regressing one independent variable on another approaches 1, the size of the VIF increases. A VIF of 1 indicates no collinearity between two independent variables. As Gujarati explains, "[a]s a rule of thumb," a VIF of 10 indicates that the variable is strongly collinear.[5] A VIF of 10 or more results only when the coefficient of determination produced when regressing one independent variable on another is equal to or greater than 0.90.

In recognition of the multicollinearity problem, I estimate equations which: (1) separately test the statistical significance of the law clerk and support personnel variables; and (2) substitute the partisan composition

---

[5]Gujarati, p. 339.

variable for the ideological heterogeneity variable. Doing so has the effect of increasing the universe of cases to include all terms of the Court during the 1935-1995 period. The increase in the universe of cases allows dummy variables for the tenures of Chief Justices Hughes and Stone to be added to the data analysis. Further, the partisan composition variable is significantly correlated with the ideological heterogeneity variable. A Pearson correlation coefficient of -0.463 (statistically significant at the .01 level) suggests the partisan composition variable is a viable surrogate for the ideological heterogeneity variable. The negative sign on the coefficient indicates that the more ideologically heterogeneous courts are those characterized by small majority party coalitions. This result is consistent with the design of both variables.[6]

Equation 6B estimates the number of dissenting opinions written by the Court in each term during the 1935-1995 period. Equation 6B includes the party composition variable in lieu of the ideological heterogeneity variable. Also, Equation 6B excludes the law clerk and support personnel variables; this equation is used as a benchmark from which to evaluate the explanatory importance of the law clerk and support personnel variables. In Equation 6B, partisan composition is related to the statistically significant increase in written dissents. The regression coefficient of -13.753 indicates a negative relationship between the size of the majority party coalition on the Court and the number of dissenting opinions produced by the Court in each term. This coefficient indicates that a one-justice decrease in the size of the majority party coalition is associated with an increase of 13.75 dissenting opinions.

The Hughes, Stone, Vinson, Burger, and Rehnquist dummy variables are statistically significant. Consistent with the data presented in Table

---

[6]Note that Table 6.1 includes Pearson correlations for the partisan composition variable and the other independent variables. Also note that a correlation coefficient of -.206 is calculated for the partisan composition and Hughes dummy variables. A coefficient of .464 is calculated for the partisan composition and Stone dummy variables. Further, Pearson correlations of 0.311, 0.019, and -0.502 are calculated between the partisan composition variable and the number of dissents, concurrences, and separate opinions, respectively.

5.2, the regression coefficient for the Hughes dummy variable indicates that relative to the Warren Court justices, the Hughes Court produced few written dissents. All other chief justice dummy variables possess a positively signed coefficient, which is consistent with the sustained historical increases in dissents beginning with Stone's appointment as Chief Justice in 1941. Turnover and inexperience are not related to the statistically significant increase in written dissents. A Durbin-Watson d test statistic of 1.806 indicates that autocorrelation is not present in the model.[7] The adjusted R squared statistic indicates that Equation 6B explains 76 percent of the variance in the frequency of written dissents.

In Equation 6C, the law clerk variable is added to the multiple regression model. Doing so, however, does not produce a reliable estimation of the magnitude or statistical significance of the law clerk variable. A VIF of 24.322 for the law clerk variable and 11.041 for the Rehnquist dummy variable suggests that these variables are strongly collinear. In addition, neither variable is statistically significant in Equation 6C. This result is suspicious considering the large number of dissents written by the Rehnquist Court justices. Thus, in order to conduct a more reliable test of the law clerk variable, an equation must be estimated which does not include the Rehnquist dummy variable.

Equation 6D removes the Rehnquist dummy variable from the multiple regression model. Equation 6D suggests that law clerks are related to the statistically significant increase in the frequency of written dissents, as are each of the remaining chief justice dummy variables. The regression coefficient on the law clerks variable is 1.295 which suggests that each additional law clerk assigned to the Court is associated with an increase of 1.295 dissenting opinions. This result is suggestive of only a weak linkage between law clerks and the frequency of written dissents. As expected, the partisan composition is statistically significant and the sign is in the negative direction. A coefficient of -12.987 indicates that a one-justice decrease in the size of the majority party coalition on the Court is associated with the production of 12.987 additional dissenting opinions. The Durbin-Watson test statistic is 1.726, indicating that the equation is

---

[7]Gujarati, p. 422.

not compromised by the presence of autocorrelation. The adjusted R squared statistic is 0.752. Removing the law clerks variable from Equation 6D produces an adjusted R squared statistic of 0.697. Thus, the presence of the law clerks variable adds 5.5 percent to the variance explained by the model.

Equation 6E is identical to Equation 6B, the benchmark equation, but for the addition of the support personnel variable. In equation 6E, partisan composition and all chief justice dummy variables are statistically significant and all signs are in the expected direction. The number of support personnel, however, are not linked to the statistically significant increases in written dissents.

What do the statistics presented in Table 6.2 suggest about the correctness of the H2a, H2b, H2c, and H2e? Each hypothesis is supported in that the number of law clerks is related in a positive, statistically significant way to the numbers of dissenting opinions written by the justices during the 1935-1995 period. However, the presence of multicollinearity in the model indicates that this finding must be accepted with caution. I do not find that the number of support personnel are related in a statistically significant way to the frequency of written dissents. Why might this be the case? In Chapter 4, I proposed that the law clerks are, in a relative sense, more proximate than support staff to the justice's opinion writing decisions. I also noted in Chapter 4 that support personnel may be unable to engage in the persuasive behaviors attributed to the more ideologically committed law clerks. Thus, law clerks may possess a greater ability to trigger the justices' decisions to write opinions squarely in opposition to the majority.

The connection between the size of the Court's majority party coalition and the production of written dissents is important. While not a revolutionary finding, this result is valuable in building a complete explanation of nonconsensual opinion writing. Furthermore, in the next section, data are presented suggesting that partisan composition is not related to production of written concurrences. This finding supports a view of dissents and concurrences as consequences of very different types of conflict.

Modeling the Frequency of Concurring Opinions

Table 6.3 includes five multiple regression equations which estimate the number of concurring opinions written by the justices in each term during the 1935-1995 period. The first equation, identified as Equation 6F, provides a benchmark from which to evaluate the explanatory significance of the law clerk and support personnel variables. In equation 6F the Hughes, Burger, and Rehnquist dummy variables are statistically significant and the signs are, as expected, in the positive direction, supporting the proposition that leadership influences the production of nonconsensual opinions. Unlike the equations which estimate the number of dissenting opinions produced by the Court per term, partisan composition is not related to the production of written concurrences. This finding suggests that written concurrences are not direct products of partisan or ideological conflict. By contrast, written dissents are artifacts of the attitudinal divisions captured by differences in partisan identity. Thus, concurrences are referents of disagreement not fundamentally ideological in description. Also, turnover and inexperience are not related to the production of written concurrences. Further, the Stone and Vinson dummy variables are not statistically significant. The adjusted R squared statistic of 0.656 indicates that the equation 6F accounts for 65 percent of the variance in concurring opinions written in each term during the 1935-1995 period. The Durbin-Watson d test statistic of 1.284 falls in the "zone of indecision,"[8] and does not conclusively indicate the presence or absence of positive autocorrelation. This result means that parameter estimates must be interpreted with caution.

Equation 6G adds the law clerk variable to equation 6F. In equation 6G, the law clerk variable is not statistically significant. However, because equation 6G includes the highly collinear Rehnquist dummy variable, no conclusion may be made about the statistical significance of the law clerk variable. Equation 6H, however, removes the Rehnquist variable from the model. Equation 6H indicates that the number of law

---

[8]See Gujarati, p. 422.

Table 6.3 Multiple Regression Equations: Estimating the Frequency of Written Concurrences

Indep. Var.	Eq. 6F	Eq. 6G	Eq. 6H	Eq 6H$_2$	Eq 6I
constant	27.870	39.640**	-3.804	26.379	47.073***
law clerks	--------	-0.792	1.288***	0.493***	--------
supp. pers.	--------	--------	---------	--------	-.123*
party comp.	-0.444	0.721	2.376	-0.559	0.890
Hughes	-26.432***	-35.504***	-11.735	-22.213***	-28.986***
Stone	-9.248	-17.688	-1.765	-3.244	-11.112
Vinson	-6.739	-10.283	-8.408	-4.160	-10.324
Burger	10.504*	20.383**	-7.886	--------	23.508***
Rehnq.	31.312***	44.329***	-------	21.757***	50.522***
turnover	-1.057	-1.112	-1.200	-1.339	-2.034
inexper.	0.491	0.552	0.103	0.455	0.515
F	15.303***	13.803***	11.668***	14.100***	15.889***
Adj. R sq.	0.656	0.658	0.587	0.636	0.691
				0.461****	0.623****
Std. Err.	11.307	11.208	12.386	11.632	10.721
Durbin d	1.284	1.420	1.097	1.189	1.489
N	61	61	61	61	61

$p<.01$; **$p<.05$; *$p<.10$ * Adjusted R Squared statistic produced after removal of the law clerks variable

clerks are the only predictor related in a statistically significant way to the number of concurrences written by the Court in each term. The regression coefficient on the law clerk variable is 1.288, indicating that the addition of one law clerk is expected to produce an additional 1.288 concurring opinions in each term. Again, this result suggests that law clerks exert little immediate influence on the justices' opinion writing practices. The Durbin-Watson d test statistic of 1.097 is slightly below the lower limit of the "zone of indecision," indicating that autocorrelation may be effecting the model. Including a lagged version of the dependent variable in the model remedies the autocorrelation. However, the presence of the lagged variable among the predictor variables produced a model with few statistically significant independent variables. Moreover, use of an autoregressive term severely compromised interpretation of regression coefficients and hypothesis tests. In light of the convincing theoretical basis upon which the law clerk - opinion writing hypothesis is founded, I chose to present and cautiously interpret equation 6H as supporting Hypothesis H2.

The adjusted R squared statistic of 0.587 indicates that Equation 6H explains 58.7 percent of the variance in concurring opinions. Removing the law clerk variable from Equation 6H produces a model with an adjusted R squared statistic of 0.461. Thus, the presence of the law clerk variable adds 12.5 percent to the explained variance in the number of concurring opinions written per term.

The significance of the law clerk variable must be interpreted with caution, however. In Equation 6H, the Burger dummy variable is not statistically significant and the sign is in the negative direction. In equation 6G the Burger dummy variable is statistically significant and the sign is in the positive direction. Further, I suspect that a multicollinear relationship between the law clerk and Burger dummy variables suppresses the importance of the Burger variable and deflates the importance of the law clerk variable. A Pearson correlation coefficient of 0.523 indicates a moderate to strong relationship between the law clerk and Burger dummy variables. However, variance inflation factors of 4.554 for the law clerk variable and 2.739 for the Burger dummy variable indicate that multicollinearity is not dramatically effecting the regression coefficients. Estimation of an additional equation indicates that this is correct.

In Equation $6H_2$, I remove the highly collinear Burger dummy variable from the model and substitute the Rehnquist dummy variable. Removal of the Burger dummy variable from the equation does not alter the fact that the law clerks variable is statistically significant. However, the regression coefficient of 0.493 (significant at 0.10 level) indicates that the number of law clerks is not as strongly related to the frequency of written concurrences as indicated in equation 6H. Removal of the law clerk variable from Equation $6H_2$ produces an adjusted R squared statistic of 0.623. This indicates that the presence of the law clerks variable adds 1.3 percent to the explained variance in the number of concurrences produced in each term. Thus, while the combined presence of the collinear law clerk, Rehnquist and Burger variables suppresses the statistical significance of the law clerks variable, the presence of the Burger dummy variable in the absence of the Rehnquist dummy variable also somewhat suppresses the strength of the relationship between the law clerk and concurrences variables.

I conclude that the importance of the law clerk variable is somewhat influenced by the presence of the Burger dummy variable. Indeed, the multicollinear relationship between the Burger and law clerk variables frustrates precise estimation of the impact of law clerks on the production of written concurrences. However, based on the data presented in equations 6H and $6H_2$, I cautiously conclude that the number of law clerk employed by the Court is a viable predictor of the number of concurring opinions produced by the Court in each term.

Equation 6I adds to Equation 6F, the benchmark equation, the support personnel variable. In equation 6I, the number of support personnel are related to the statistically significant increase in written concurrences, but a regression coefficient of -0.123, indicates a negative relationship between the number of support personnel employed by the Court and the frequency of concurring opinions produced by the Court in each term. Removal of the Rehnquist dummy variable[9] produces a regression coefficient of 8.924E-02 (statistically significant at 0.05 level) for the support personnel variable. In Equation 6I, the Hughes, Burger, and Rehnquist dummy variables are statistically significant and the signs on

---

[9] A Pearson correlation coefficient of .639 is calculated for the support personnel and Rehnquist dummy variables. This result indicates a collinear relationship that may account for the negative sign on the support personnel variable in Equation 6I.

the partial regression coefficients are in the expected directions. As in equation 6F, 6G, and 6H, the presence of Chief Justice Stone and Vinson are not related to the production of written concurrences. This result suggests that changes in the frequency of written concurrences is most closely associated with the tenures of Chief Justice Hughes, Burger, and Rehnquist when compared to the opinion writing behavior of the Warren Court justices.

What are the implications of the statistics presented in Table 6.3? First, consistent with H2a, H2b, H2c, and H2e, the number of law clerks employed by the Court in each term appears to be related in a statistically significant way to the number of concurring opinions written in each term during the 1935-1995 period. However, this finding must be taken with caution. The presence of serial correlation in Equation 6H and the presence of the collinear chief justice variables means that only tentative impressions can be drawn from these data. Consistent with hypotheses H2a, H2b, H2c, and H2e, I find a statistically significant relationship between support personnel and concurring opinions. However, this relationship is very weak; changes in the number of support personnel are not associated with a substantial increase the production of concurring opinions. Also, the equations in Table 6.3 indicate that not all chief justices are associated with changes in the frequency of written concurrences. This result differs from the equations presented in Table 6.2, where the regression models indicate that each chief justice is related in a statistically significant way to the number of dissents produced by the Court in each term. Moreover, it appears that unlike dissents, written concurrences are not artifacts of partisan conflict and the attendant attitudinal or ideological schisms.

Modeling the Frequency of Separate Opinions

Table 6.4 includes three multiple regression equations which estimate the number of separate opinions written by the Court in each term. Equation 6J serves as a benchmark equation, including the partisan composition variable along with the Hughes, Stone, Vinson, Burger, and Rehnquist dummy variables. Also included are the turnover and inexperience variables. In addition, Equation 6J includes a lagged version of the dependent variable. This variable is added to remedy the positive autocorrelation that otherwise plagues the separate opinion models.

In equation 6J, the Burger dummy and the lagged separate opinion variables are statistically significant. The importance of the presence of the Chief Justice Burger dummy variable is consistent with the statistics presented in Table 5.2. The adjusted R squared statistic of 0.813 indicates that the model accounts for 81.3 percent of the variance in the production of separate opinions. Much of the explained variance may be attributed to the presence of the lagged separate opinion variable. Thus, in the absence of this variable, the equation would explain far less of the variance in separate opinion writing.

Equation 6K tests the significance of the historical increases in the number of law clerks employed by the Court. In Equation 6K, the law clerks are not related to increases in the Court's production of separate opinions despite the removal of the highly collinear Rehnquist dummy variable. In Equation 6K, the Burger dummy variable remains statistically significant and, as expected, the regression coefficient of 15.687 indicates that the replacement of Chief Justice Warren with Chief Justice Burger produced an additional fifteen-plus separate opinions per term. The adjusted R squared statistic of 0.815 indicates that Equation 6K accounts for 81.5 percent of the variance in the number of separate opinions written by the justices in each term. In both equation 6J and 6K, the Durbin h statistics are calculated to test for the presence of autocorrelation. The Durbin h, as opposed to the Durbin d statistic, is used in models that contain a lagged version of the dependent variable. The Durbin h statistics calculated for both Equations 6J and 6K indicate no evidence of autocorrelation.

Equation 6L tests the significance of the support personnel variable. Equation 6L excludes the lagged separate opinion variable and, evidenced by the Durbin d test statistic of 1.143, does not conclusively indicate the presence or absence of autocorrelation. Equation 6L indicates that the number of support personnel, changes in partisan composition, and the presence of the Chief Justice Stone, Vinson, and Burger dummy variables are related to the statistically significant increase in the frequency of separate opinions. The regression coefficient of 0.124 on the support personnel variable indicates that an addition of

Table 6.4 Multiple Regression Equations: Estimating the Frequency of Separate Opinions

Indep. Var.	Eq. 6J	Eq. 6K	Eq. 6L
Constant	4.902	11.246	30.534**
law clerks	---------	0.239	----------
supp. pers.	---------	----------	0.124***
party comp.	0.496	-1.917	-6.955***
Hughes	-1.913	1771	-2.318
Stone	-2.367	7.506	20.457***
Vinson	-5.655	3.393	14.111*
Burger	-16.378***	15.679*** 21.768***	
Rehnq.	-3.587	---------	---------
turnover	-3.206	-3.164	-3.397
inexperience	-0.150	-0.160	-1.604
seplag1	0.571***	0.511***	---------
F	29.577***	29.802*** 27.021***	
Adj. R Sq.	0.813	0.815	0.776
			(0.688)****
Std. Err.	9.3876	9.3564	10.2616
Durbin h	-1.68	0.83	Durbin d=1.143
N	61	61	61

p<.01; **p<.05; *p<.10; * Adjusted R Squared statistic produced by the removal of the support personnel variable from the equation.

10 Court employees is associated with only an increase of 1.24 separate opinions per term. This finding is consistent with the view that support personnel are remote from the justices' decisions to produce written opinions. The Rehnquist dummy variable is excluded as it proved to be

strongly collinear with the support personnel variable. In equation 6L, the turnover and inexperience variables are not statistically significant. The R squared statistic of 0.776 indicates that the model explains 77.6 percent of the variance in separate opinions written in each term. Removing the support personnel variable from the model produces an adjusted R squared statistic of 0.688. This result indicates that the presence of the support personnel variable increases the explained variance by 8.8 percent. This finding, however, must be taken with caution because the removal of the support personnel variable also produces an equation with a Durbin-Watson d statistic of 0.851, a value which indicates the presence of positive autocorrelation. The importance of the support personnel variable will be considered further in Chapter 7.

What do the statistics presented in Table 6.4 suggest about hypotheses H2a, H2b, H2c, and H2e? These hypotheses are not confirmed because the number of law clerks employed by the Court is not related in a statistically significant way to the number of separate opinions drafted by the Court in each term during the 1935-1995 period. However, the number of support personnel employed by the Court is related in a statistically significant way to the number of separate opinions written by the Court in each term. As with the law clerk variable, the collinearity of the support personnel variable means that this result should be accepted cautiously. This result supports my earlier suggestion that the tasks of support personnel may influence the justices behavior in a way that differs from that of the law clerks. It seems possible that law clerks, who enjoy frequent, in-chambers contact with the justices, may fuel the ideological schisms among justices and provide research for the doctrinal clashes that result in written dissents. Increased numbers of support personnel may perform tasks which free the justices time for the writing of additional concurrences and separate opinions. Yet, time alone may not be the sufficient cause for large numbers of written dissents. It may be that large numbers of dissenting opinions require both additional time for writing and the type of advocacy which Edward Lazarus reports is typical of justice-law clerk interactions.[10]

---

[10]Lazarus, p. 6.

Rethinking the Chief Justice Hypothesis

In several equations in Tables 6.2, 6.3, and 6.4, the Rehnquist dummy variable is excluded from the analysis in order to remedy the presence of multicollinearity. Does removal of the Rehnquist dummy variable from any of the multiple regression models require the conclusion that H2a, H2b, H2c, and H2e are supported in only a qualified way? Evidence exists indicating that it does not. Furthermore, I find evidence that previous studies overstate the importance of changes in the occupant of the chief justice's seat for the historical decline of consensual norms.[11] Arguably, the results of these studies are products of a failure to recognize the importance of law clerk and support personnel contributions to the opinion writing process.

Where statistically significant, the Stone, Vinson, Burger, and Rehnquist dummy variables indicate that the presence of each chief justice is associated with an increase in the number of nonconsensual opinions. This finding seems inconsistent with the proposition that a change in the leadership on the Court results in a momentous change in the justices' observance of consensual norms. In short, each chief justice is associated with a notable change in the production of nonconsensual opinions. Considering the sustained increase in the frequency of nonconsensual opinion writing throughout most of the 1935-1995 period, removal of one or even all chief justice dummy variables from a model of nonconsensual opinion writing does not change the basic finding that law clerks have influenced nonconsensual opinion production. The data presented in Figure 6.1 provide support for my conclusion. These data reflect the number of nonconsensual opinions written during the

---

[11]See Thomas Walker, Lee Epstein, and William Dixon, "On the Mysterious Demise of Consensual Norms in the United States Supreme Court," *Journal of Politics* 50 (1988): 361-89; Stacia Haynie, "Leadership and Consensus on the U.S. Supreme Court," *Journal of Politics* 54 (1994): 1158-69; Gregory Caldeira and Christopher J.W. Zorn, "Of Time and Consensual Norms in the U.S. Supreme Court," *American Journal of Political Science* 42 (1998): 874-902.

Figure 6.1 Total Nonconsensual Opinions, 1935-1995

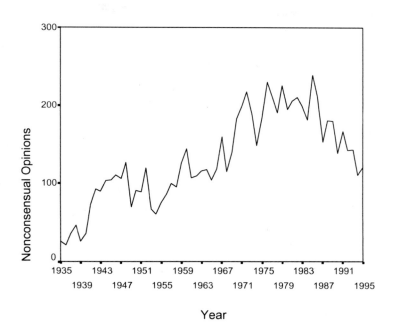

1935-1985 period.[12]

Figure 6.1 reveals the sustained upward trend in conconsensual opinion writing nonconsensual opinions increased *during* the tenures of Chief Justice Hughes, Stone, Warren, and Burger. For example, during the tenure of Chief Justice Stone, the Court in 1941 produced fewer than 50 nonconsensual opinions. By 1945, the Court had drafted 104 nonconsensual opinions. A similar trend is evident during the service of Chief Justice Warren. In 1953, the Court drafted 67 nonconsensual opinions. In 1968, the justices produced a total of 114 dissenting, concurring, and separate opinions. At the end of Chief Justice Burger's

---

[12]The number of nonconsensual opinions written in each term is the sum of the number of dissenting, concurring, and separate opinions written in each term.

tenure in 1985, the Court produced 239 nonconsensual opinions, the highest number of any term in Supreme Court history. These results do not support hypotheses that indicate change in the occupant of the chief justice's seat is the principal determinant of nonconsensual behavior.

What about the decline in the total number of nonconsensual opinions written after 1986, the beginning of Rehnquist's service as Chief Justice? Recall from my discussion of Table 5.2 that relative to the Burger Court, the Rehnquist Court reduced the number of cases disposed of by signed opinion in each term. Also, recall that Table 5.2 indicates the Rehnquist Court issued, on the average, fewer dissenting and separate opinions per term than the Burger Court justices. Yet, the Rehnquist Court issued on the average more concurring, dissenting, and separate opinions per term than either the Hughes, Stone, Vinson, or Warren Courts. In sum, the Rehnquist Court issued a declining number of total nonconsensual opinions. Yet, because it disposed of fewer cases by signed opinion, it is nonetheless among the most divisive of Courts during the 1935-1995 period. Thus, the Rehnquist Court is in some ways a special case. A cursory glance at the total number of nonconsensual opinions written per term suggests a reversal in the historical increase in nonconsensual behavior. A more careful examination, however, reveals opinion writing behavior consistent with the long-term erosion of the consensus norm.

The behavior of the Rehnquist Court is remarkable in another way. The justices of the conflict-ridden Rehnquist Court were, after 1990, predominantly Republican. In fact, the Rehnquist Court was comprised of seven Republicans during the 1990 term, eight Republicans during the 1991-1993 terms, and seven Republicans during the 1994 and 1995 terms. Yet, during the period 1990-1995, the Rehnquist Court justices produced an average of 0.58 concurring opinions per case disposed of by signed opinion. By contrast, the Burger Court, in which the majority party coalition never grew beyond five justices between 1970 and 1986, issued an average of 0.28 concurring opinions per case disposed of by signed opinion. Moreover, despite a partisan composition that favored consensus, the justices of the Rehnquist Court granted little deference to a consensus norm. This finding is consistent with the finding that partisan composition is more closely associated with the frequency of written dissents and not significantly related to the frequency of written concurrences.

What remains of the proposition that the historical decline in consensual norms is primarily influenced by changes in the Court's leadership? Assuming that different chief justices do, in fact, substantially alter the Court's observance of a consensus norm, it must be concluded that each chief justice, with the exception of Vinson, had the same basic impact on the frequency of written dissents, concurrences, and separate opinions; each chief justice caused among his colleagues an increased propensity toward nonconsensual behavior. Indeed, nonconsensual behavior increased throughout much of the 1935-1995 period, despite changes in the Court's leadership. Thus, the occupant of the chief justice's seat may be of less importance than reported in earlier studies.

How do the law clerk and support personnel variables perform in models that exclude the chief justice dummy variables? Table 6.5 indicates that law clerks and support personnel are related to the statistically significant increase in the numbers of dissenting, concurring, and separate opinions written by the justices per term. However, the coefficients on the law clerk variables are small indicating weak relationships between the number of law clerks on the Court and the frequency of nonconsensual opinion writing. A coefficient of 1.553 on the law clerk variable in equation 6M reveals that the number of law clerks are only weakly associated with increases in the number of dissents produced by the Court. Further, coefficients of 1.4 and 0.909 in equations 6O and 6Q, respectively, reveals that increases in the number of law clerks on the Court is weakly associated with increases in the numbers of written concurrences and separate opinions produced by the Court. The coefficients on the support personnel variables are also very small, indicating that increases in the number of support personnel employed by the Court are not associated with large increases in the frequency of nonconsensual opinion writing. Equations 6O, 6Q, and 6R suggests the significance of partisan composition for the drafting of concurrences and separate opinions. This result is inconsistent with the data presented in Tables 6.2, 6.3, and 6.4. The presence of autocorrelation in the models that exclude the chief justice variables

Table 6.5. Regression Models: Excluding the Chief Justice Dummy Variables From Equations Estimating the Importance of the Law Clerk and Support Personnel Variables

	Dissents		Concurrences		Separate Opinions	
Variables	(6M)	(6N)	(6O)	(6P)	(6Q)	(6R)
Const.	64.862**	69.725***	-16.689***	-13.357	42.906***	33.284***
Clerks	1.553***	------	1.400***	------	0.909***	-------
Sup. Pers.	-----	0.176***	-----	0.162***	-----	0.147***
Pty Comp..	-3.138	-4.332	3.181**	2.132	-6.162***	-6.538***
Turnover	-3.482	-2.291	-0.242	0.884	-7.330**	-6.022*
Inexper.	-2.051	-3.427	0.361	-0.859	-0.850	-1.409
F	11.906***	7.413***	20.650***	9.501***	15.812***	20.074***
Adj. R Sq.	0.421	0.299	0.567	0.36	0.497	0.560
Std. Err.	22.1082	24.3174	12.6839	15.4016	15.3883	14.3937
Durbin D	0.744	0.636	1.014	0.733	0.593	0.719
N	61	61	61	61	61	61

***<.01; **p<.05; *p<.10

means that estimates in the more inclusive, less "noisy"models are of greater reliability. Thus, the data presented in Table 6.5 do not displace the more plausible finding that partisan composition is not related to the production of written concurrences.

The Adjusted R squared statistics are noticeably smaller than those presented in Tables 6.2, 6.3, and 6.4. Thus, removing the chief justice dummy variables from the regression models leaves a linear combination of variables which account for much less explained variance in the frequency of nonconsensual opinion writing. However, because of the persistent increase in the numbers of nonconsensual opinions written per term during the 1935-1995 period, each chief justice dummy variable is necessarily associated with an increase in nonconsensual behavior. Thus, the chief justice dummy variables may not reflect the effects of changes in the occupant of the chief justice's seat, but may actually reflect the presence of an upward trend in the opinion writing data. Moreover, the supposed importance of a "chief justice effect" may be only an artifact of successive chief justices coming to the Court at different points during a period when there was a persistent increase in the numbers of dissenting, concurring, and separate opinions written by members of the Court for reasons unrelated to the leadership traits of each chief.

Additionally, the Durbin-Watson d test statistics of 0.744 in equation 6M, 0.636 in equation 6N, 1.014 in equation 6O, 0.733 in equation 6P, 0.593 in equation 6Q, and 0.719 in equation 6R, indicate the presence of positive autocorrelation in each of the regression models of nonconsensual opinion writing. This means that the equations presented in Table 6.5 allow neither reliable hypothesis tests nor definitive conclusions about the significance of the law clerk and support personnel variables.

What are the implications of the equations presented in Table 6.5? Although autocorrelation compromises tests for statistical significance, the equations presented in Table 6.5 suggest that changes in the numbers of law clerks and support personnel are of some importance for the Court's production of nonconsensual opinions. Additionally, the strength of the theoretical basis upon which the law clerk-opinion writing hypothesis is founded suggests that the data presented in this chapter provide some support for Hypothesis H2 and its associated hypotheses. Thus, while the chief justice dummy variables included in the equations found in Tables 6.2, 6.3, and 6.4 may be masking the effects of autocorrelation in the data, the presence of these control variables does not preclude the small importance of the law clerk and support personnel variables in the models of nonconsensual opinion writing.

If I am correct that changes in the occupant of the chief justice's seat are of less explanatory importance than previously suggested, the historical increase in the numbers of law clerks and support personnel represents a key change in both the size of the Court institution and composition of the Court work group. Most important, the sustained increases in the number of law clerks and support personnel reported in

Chapter 4 (Figures 4.4 and 4.5) coincide with the persistent, historical increase in nonconsensual opinion writing. As indicated in this chapter, some statistical support is found for the hypothesized connection between law clerks and two types of nonconsensual opinion writing. I conclude that whatever the importance of the law clerk and support personnel variables, these relationships hold despite changes in the Court's leadership. Thus, in Chapter 7, I include the chief justice dummy variables in regression models that also control for the effects of changes in docket composition and caseload.

Conclusion

Contrary to the assertions of Caldeira and Zorn, the frequency with which the justices of the Supreme Court produce dissenting and concurring opinions is in some measurable way related to an increase in the number of the law clerks. The statistics presented in Tables 6.2 and 6.3 indicate that the addition of one law clerk is associated with an increase of 1.295 dissenting opinions per term and an increase of 1.288 concurrences per term (or 0.493 concurrences per term as indicated in Equation 6H$_2$).[13] While each additional law clerk is not associated with a large increase in opinion production, the substantial growth in the number of law clerks during the 1935-1995 period does contribute to an explanation of why the Court has produced increasing numbers of nonconsensual opinions. For example, in 1951, the Court employed sixteen law clerks and produced sixty-eight dissenting opinions and seventeen concurring opinions. By contrast, in 1985, the Court employed thrity-three law clerks. In that year, the justices produced 136 dissents and thirty-three concurrences. In short, in a term in which the Court employed twice as many clerks, the justices produced exactly twice as many dissents and nearly twice as many concurrences. Moreover, the historical growth in the number of law clerks working for the justices parallels the marked changes in opinion writing behavior that characterize the last six decades of Supreme Court history.

---

[13]This, of course, presumes that the regression coefficients on the law clerks variables are not compromised by the presence of multicollinearity.

I find no statistical evidence that the number of law clerks employed by the Court is related to the number of separate opinions written by the justices in each term. In Chapter 7, I reexamine this finding in models that control for changes in docket composition and caseload. The number of support personnel employed by the Court is related in a statistically significant way to the number of separate opinions produced by the Court. The connection between the number of support personnel on the Court and the frequency of written concurrences, though statistically significant, is so weak as to be without substantive significance. In sum, statistical evidence exists supporting the conclusion that increases in the number of law clerks and support personnel are institutional changes linked to the historical decline in consensual norms on the Supreme Court.

Another finding is equally compelling. Dissenting, concurring, and separate opinions are each unique and in some ways discrete phenomena. Two key findings support this conclusion. Several scholars argue that the frequency with which Supreme Court justices produce written dissents and concurrences is driven by changes in leadership style on the Court as measured by changes in the occupant of the chief justice's seat. Although I present evidence which militates against the primacy of the "chief justice effect," I find that whatever the impact of leadership style changes, such changes do not uniformly effect all types of nonconsensual opinion writing. Whereas each chief justice is related in a statistically significant way to historical changes in the frequency of written dissents, Chief Justices Stone and Vinson appear to have exerted less influence than other chief justices on the frequency of written dissents. Also, Chief Justices Stone, Warren and Burger are most closely associated with changing patterns of separate opinion writing. The presence of Chief Justice Rehnquist is noticeably linked to the production of written concurrences, a fact that evinces the relative partisan accord of the Rehnquist Court.

I present quantitative evidence to suggest that ideological conflict as measured by the size of the majority party coalition on the Court is related to the production of dissenting opinions in a way not important for the drafting of written concurrences. In short, ideological or partisan conflict among the justices drives dissent behavior but does not appear to increase the frequency of written concurrences. This finding suggests that concurrences reflect a type of conflict among justices that is not principally driven by differences in ideology. Changes in partisan composition are also associated with the production of separate opinions, an indication that the same type of ideological conflicts that are related to the production of written dissents also yield unstable majority voting coalitions. These findings should give pause to scholars such as Haynie and Walker, Epstein, and Dixon who reject the argument that underlying attitudinal, ideological, or partisan tensions on the Court are not significantly related to historical changes in the frequency of nonconsensual opinion writing.

Finally, these findings are to be accepted only after considering one or two additional points. The multiple regression models presented in this chapter account for neither changes in the composition of the Supreme Court's docket of formally decided cases nor historical increases in the size of the Supreme Court's caseload. The task of accounting for these changes is the focus of the next chapter.

CHAPTER 7

Modeling the Effects of Law Clerks and Support Personnel on the Writing of Nonconsenseual Opinions: Controlling for Changes in Caseload and Docket Composition

Introduction

In this chapter, I extend the multivariate modeling begun in Chapter 6 to include measures of caseload and changes in the number of civil liberties cases reviewed by the Court in each term. I begin by briefly revisiting several studies which test the importance of caseload and docket composition variables in models of nonconsensual opinion writing. Second, I present preliminary quantitative evidence indicating that workload and docket composition variables should be included in a study which seeks to account for historical changes in the frequency of nonconsensual opinion writing. Third, I add measures of caseload and docket composition to the multiple regression models presented in Chapter 6. Last, I discuss several conclusions regarding the importance of competing explanations for the decline in consensus norms. Most important, I present conclusions regarding the role of law clerks and support personnel as determinants of nonconsensual opinion writing.

The civil liberties and caseload variables are added to the regression equations in order to test hypotheses H2d and H2f. Hypothesis H2d indicates that increases in the numbers of separate, dissenting, and concurring opinions written by the justices in each term are related in a statistically significant way to the increasing presence of law clerks and support personnel when controlling for changes in the composition of the docket of cases granted plenary review. Hypothesis H2f indicates that increases in the numbers of separate, dissenting, and concurring opinions written by the justices in each term are related to a statistically significant degree to the increasing presence of law clerks and support personnel when controlling for changes in the Court's workload.

Docket Composition and Dissensus

In Chapter 1, I discussed Richard Pacelle's observation that from the early 1930s to the early 1970s the proportion of the Supreme Court's docket devoted to civil liberties cases had increased from less than ten percent to nearly sixty percent.[1] Is this change in docket composition related to the historical decline in the consensus norm? Is the growth in the numbers of civil liberties cases linked to the increasing numbers of dissenting, concurring, and separate opinions written by the justices during the period 1935-1995?

In their study of the decline in consensual norms, Thomas Walker, Lee Epstein, and William Dixon ". . . reject the notion that case mix changes ushered in the dissent-prone period after 1941."[2] Further, they explain that while the number of civil liberties cases doubled between the 1939-1940 and 1941-1942 periods, the Hughes and Stone Courts heard civil liberties cases that were nearly identical in factual descriptions. Thus, the authors find no linkage between an increase in the number of civil liberties cases during the 1939-1942 period and differences in nonconsensual opinion writing practices in the Hughes and Stone Courts.

Did the historical increase in civil liberties cases contribute to the

---

[1]Richard L. Pacelle, *The Transformation of the Supreme Court's Agenda* (Boulder, CO: Westview Press, Inc., 1991), pp. 137-8.

[2]Thomas G. Walker, Lee Epstein, and William J. Dixon, "On the Mysterious Demise of Consensual Norms in the United States Supreme Court," *Journal of Politics* 50 (1988):370. The authors use the term "case mix" to indicate the issue content of the Court's yearly docket of plenary treated cases.

gradual, persistent increase in the numbers of dissenting, concurring, and separate opinions during the 1935-1995 period? In her longitudinal study of the decline in consensual norms, Stacia Haynie finds that "[n]o relationship was present between the decline of economic issues and the rise of civil rights and liberties issues and the increase in concurring and dissenting opinions."[3] Based on the findings of Walker, Epstein and Dixon and Haynie, Caldeira and Zorn chose to omit a docket composition variable from their model of opinion writing.[4]

Do these findings preclude the use of a docket composition variable in the model of nonconsensual behavior? I believe they do not. Why? First, Segal and Spaeth find that "judgements of the Court," - decisions in which only a plurality of the justices agree to both the outcome and rationale for the outcome - are strongly associated with cases involving civil rights and civil liberties decisions.[5] Moreover, the authors link an "unusual amount of conflict" to judgments of the Court and the civil liberties issues which precipitate these types of decisions.[6]

Second, in a later section of this chapter, I present data suggesting that Walker, Epstein, and Dixon do not account for all types of civil liberties cases in their tabulations of changes in case mix. Their approach masked the extraordinary, and important, increase in the number of civil liberties cases encountered by the Stone Court. In short, I find that the sudden increase in the number of civil liberties cases during the Stone Court years cannot be dismissed as an event without a consequence for nonconsensual opinion writing. I hypothesize that the sheer volume of civil liberties cases heard by the Stone Court may be

---

[3]Stacia L. Haynie, "Leadership and Consensus on the U.S. Supreme Court," *Journal of Politics* 54 (1992): 1166.

[4]Gregory Caldeira and Christopher J. W. Zorn, "Of Time and Consensual Norms in the United States Supreme Court," *American Journal of Political Science* 42 (1998): 878.

[5]Jeffrey A. Segal and Harold J. Spaeth, *The Supreme Court and the Attitudinal Model* (Cambridge: Cambridge University Press, 1993), pp. 290-1.

[6]Ibid., p. 291.

more important for the level of conflict on the Court than previously discovered.

Third, even if changes in case mix are not linked to the changes in opinion writing behavior that occurred after Stone became chief justice, increases in the numbers of civil liberties cases may be linked to nonconsensual opinion writing in other eras. As Pacelle explains, "[a]fter 1957, the pace of the growth of Civil Liberties on the Court's agenda hastened dramatically. The Court took almost two decades to increase the agenda space granted Civil Liberties by 20 percent, but an equal rate of change took only a half- dozen more terms [after 1957]."[7] Thus, changes in docket composition did not occur at a rate uniform to all eras in the Court's modern history. Moreover, the between-terms rate of change in docket composition may be an important factor linked to patterns of dissensus. In order to test for this possibility, I include in the regression analysis a measure of the between-terms change in the proportion of the Court's docket allocated to civil liberties cases.

The Workload of the Supreme Court: Implications for Nonconsensual Behavior?

In Chapter 3, the historical increases in the number of case filings was discussed. Did this exponential growth in the number of case filings impact the justices' ability or willingness to reach consensus on cases granted plenary treatment? Might a justice routinely forgo the time-consuming search for consensus in order to review an immense number of yearly case filings? Robert Bennett observes that this may be an accurate depiction of the impact of workload on nonconsensual opinion writing practices. With regard to the increasing frequency of dissent behavior, he writes: "Some blame the increasing caseload, and it is plausible that the process of reaching agreement among nine judges may be more time consuming than the production of additional opinions."[8]   Walker,

---

[7]Pacelle, p. 139.

[8]Robert W. Bennett, "A Dissent on Dissent," *Judicature* 74 (1991): 260.

Epstein, and Dixon test this proposition. They speculate:

> As demands on the Court increase, the justices lose the luxury of
> ample time to build consensus and construct the compromises
> that hold the Court together. Constant pressure exists to arrive
> at a decision and move on to address the next case. It is no
> longer advantageous to expend substantial resources to convince
> a dissenting or concurring justice to join the majority."[9]

Yet, Walker, Dixon, and Epstein do not find empirical support for this
proposition. They explain: ". . . dissent rates are not systematically
affected by caseloads since the surge in the former actually *precedes* the
period of strongest growth in case filings [italics mine]."[10] Their analysis
reveals that the most rapid increases in case filings began in the 1950s, two
decades after the sudden increase in dissenting opinions that occurred in
the early 1940s.[11] Moreover, Walker, Epstein, and Dixon write: ". . .
caseload levels and individual expression are not causally related with one
another."[12] Haynie indicates that her analysis of caseload and dissenting
opinion data confirms the results reported by Walker, Epstein, and
Dixon.[13]

Do these results preclude the use of a workload variable in a model
of the decline in consensual norms? They do not. Both studies limit
examination of caseload to the number of case filings in each term. This
method crudely neglects another dimension of the Court's caseload; the
Walker, Epstein, and Dixon study, and the Haynie study, fail to test the
connection between the number of cases granted plenary treatment in each
term and the production of nonconsensual opinions. It may be that as the

---

[9]Walker, Epstein, and Dixon, pp. 366-7.

[10]Ibid., p. 367.

[11]Ibid., p. 367.

[12]Ibid., p. 368.

[13]Haynie, p. 1165.

number of cases disposed of by signed opinion increases, the justices encounter additional "opportunities" to disagree and produce the written manifestations of that disagreement. Is this proposition supported by the data analyses presented in Chapters 4 and 5?

In Chapter 4, I noted that the during the 1935-1995 period the justices drafted increasing numbers of opinions per case disposed of by signed opinion. In Chapter 5, I presented descriptive statistics indicating that during the 1935-1995 period the justices generally became increasingly dissent prone regardless of the number of cases disposed of by signed opinion in each term. These findings, however, do not resolve the question of whether this important dimension of the Court's caseload is related to the historical increase in nonconsensual opinion writing. Moreover, it may be that this important measure of the Court's caseload is linked to the frequency of written dissenting, concurring, and separate opinions in a way not detectable by examination of the descriptive statistics presented in Chapters 4 and 5.

To conduct a more rigorous test for the presence of a relationship between the "opportunity"for individual expression and instances of nonconsensual opinion writing, I include in the multiple regression models a measure of "opportunity," or the number of cases disposed of by signed opinion in each term. Moreover, hypothesis H2f proposes a direct, positive relationship between this measure of caseload and the frequency of written dissents, concurrences, and separate opinions.

The Docket Composition Variable: Measurement and Preliminary Evidence

The docket composition variable is operationally defined as the percentage change in the Court's docket allocated to civil liberties cases during the 1935-1995 period. Each observation reflects the particular term's percentage increase or decrease in the proportion of docket space allocated to civil liberties cases. This operational definition is preferred because use of the actual percentage of cases raising civil liberties issues in each term produces a variable highly correlated with the law clerk and support personnel variables. The proportion of civil liberties cases in each term is equivalent to the number of cases raising civil liberties issues divided by the total number of orally argued cases disposed of by a signed or per curiam opinion of one page or more in length as printed in the *United States Reports*.[14]

Figure 7.1 indicates a gradual upward trend in the proportion of docket space allocated to civil liberties cases during the 1935-1971 terms. In 1935, 5.8 percent of the Court's docket was comprised of civil liberties cases. In 1971, 66.1 percent of the Court's docket was comprised of civil liberties cases, a figure eleven times greater than in 1935. Since the early 1970s, the proportion of docket space allocated to civil liberties cases has remained relatively stable. Since the mid 1980s, the amount of docket space allocated to civil liberties cases has decline somewhat. In 1995, 52.2 percent of the Court's docket was comprised of civil liberties cases. What lessons can be drawn from these data in Figure 7.1? First, the historical rise in nonconsensual behavior indicated in Figure 6.1 and the long-term increases in civil liberties cases define both the Supreme Court's opinion writing behavior and substantive focus during much of the 1935-1995 period. Second, the Court has increasingly devoted itself to the consideration of issues found by Segal and Spaeth to be disproportionately associated with conflict among the justices. Third, when informed by Segal and Spaeth's finding, these data seem inconsistent with Walker, Epstein, and Dixon's finding that case mix is entirely unrelated to nonconsensual opinion writing practices.

Recall that Walker, Epstein, and Dixon indicate that an increase in the number of dissenting opinions issued in civil liberties cases between the last two terms of the Hughes Court (1939-1940) and the first two

---

[14]These data are provided by Richard Pacelle. Pacelle defines civil liberties cases as involving due process, substantive rights, or equality issues. Due process cases include issues of criminal procedure and due process issues in administrative proceedings. Substantive rights cases involve First Amendment issues and individual rights to abortion, privacy, the rights of conscientious objectors, and the rights of alleged Communists. Equality cases include issues of discrimination based on race, gender, age, or disability. See Pacelle, pp. 208-9.

Figure 7.1. Percentage of Court's Docket Allocated to Civil Liberties
Cases 1935-1995

terms of the Stone Court is not linked to changes in case mix. Despite

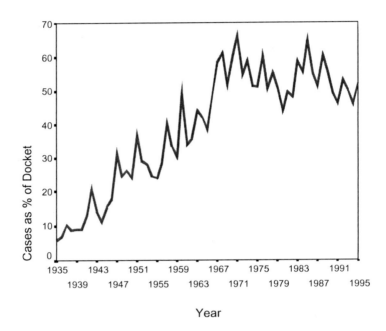

Year

the doubling in number of civil liberties cases in the latter period, the
authors maintain that the "case-mix" hypothesis is not supported given that
the justices heard essentially the same type of civil liberties cases and
encountered almost identical litigant types in the civil liberties cases of the
two periods. In short, the authors argue that there is no variation in the
types of civil liberties cases heard by the Hughes and Stone Courts. They
conclude that disparities in dissenting opinion writing in these cases were
due to changes in the Court's leadership.   The authors assign no
importance to the general impact of an increase in the sheer numbers of
civil liberties cases.

The data in Table 7.1 indicate that Walker, Epstein, and Dixon may
have erred in dismissing the "case mix" hypothesis in favor of an

Table 7.1 Nonconsensual Opinions and Civil Liberties Cases, 1935-1995*				
Chief Justice	Avg. % Docket Allocated. To Civil. Lib	Avg. Concur/ term	Avg. Diss./ term	Avg. Sep.Op./ term
Hughes (1935-1940)	8.28	4.0 (.02)	22.67 (.12)	4.5 (.03)
Stone (1941-1945)	15.0	22.8 (.13)	61.0 (.34)	8.2 (.05)
Vinson (1946-1951)	27.06	25.7 (.53)	69.0 (.19)	3.83 (.03)
Warren (1953-1968)	39.52	30.34 (.25)	66.06 (.56)	11.3 (.10)
Burger (1969-1985)	54.87	40.82 (.27)	107.41 (.70)	48.47 (.32)
Rehnquist (1986-1995)	51.96	62.4 (.50)	77.3 (.62)	14.3 (.12)

* Number in parentheses are the average number of opinions written per case disposed of by signed opinion. For data source see table 5.2.

Table 7.2. Percentage of Docket Space Allocated to Civil Liberties Cases and Total Nonconsensual Opinions on the Hughes and Stone Courts, 1935-1945

Chief Justice	Term	% Docket Space Allocated to Civil Liberties Cases	Total Noncons. Opinions*
Hughes	1935	5.8	25
	1936	6.8	21
	1937	10.3	35
	1938	8.7	46
	1939	9.0	25
	1940	9.1	35
	------	-----	----
Stone	1941	13.2	72
	1942	20.7	92
	1943	14.3	89
	1944	11.2	103
	1945	15.5	104

* Total nonconsensual opinions = total number of dissenting, concurring, and separate opinions per term.

explanation which relies exclusively on the importance of the chief justice. Table 7.1 reveals that the average proportion of the docket allocated to civil liberties cases increased from 8.28 during Hughes's service as chief justice to 15.0 cases during Stone's service as chief justice. Further, as Table 7.2 indicates, in the Stone Court's 1942 term, 20.7 percent of the Court's docket was allocated to civil liberties cases, a figure twice that of any term during Hughes's service as chief justice. Table 7.2 indicates that of the cases given plenary treatment in the 1943, 1944, an 1945 terms, the

Stone Court encountered civil liberties issues in 14.3, 11.2, and 15.5 percent, respectively. The largest proportion of the docket allocated to civil liberties cases during the Hughes Court years was 10.3 percent (1937). Thus, the Hughes Court consistently encountered a docket consisting of noticeably fewer civil liberties issues than the Stone Court. Even if, as Walker, Epstein, and Dixon suggest, the justices heard nearly identical civil liberties cases during both the Hughes and Stone Courts, the effect of an increase in the actual numbers of civil liberties cases cannot be summarily dismissed.

Most important, Walker, Epstein, and Dixon exclude from their tally of civil liberties cases the many criminal rights cases which came before the Court during the Hughes and Stone Court years. The authors do not explain this method of tabulating civil liberties cases. Had the authors included criminal rights cases in their tally of the number of civil liberties cases considered by the Hughes and Stone Courts, they may have arrived at a very different conclusion. Moreover, the criminal rights cases of the Stone Court era produced many dissenting opinions.

Using Walker, Epstein, and Dixon's data, I calculated for the 1939-1940 terms of the Hughes Court a total of 21 civil liberties cases (this includes criminal rights cases) wherein the justices produced 25 dissenting opinions. For the 1941-1942 terms of the Stone Court, the justices heard 43 civil liberties cases (this also includes criminal rights cases) and issued 90 dissenting opinions in those cases. Moreover, in the 1939-1940 terms, the Hughes Court justices issued 1.19 dissenting opinions per civil liberties case while the Stone Court justices issued 2.09 dissenting opinions per case. Thus, Walker, Epstein, and Dixon's decision to exclude criminal rights cases from the category of civil liberties cases yields an analysis much more favorable to the proposition that docket composition is not linked to patterns of dissensus. Defining civil liberties cases in a more conventional way, as I have done, produces a somewhat different result.[15]

---

[15] Judicial scholars often consider criminal rights issues as an important component of civil liberties law. Two examples are Craig Ducat, *Constitutional Interpretation* (St. Paul, MN: West Publishing, 1995); Otis H. Stephens and John M. Sheb, *American Constitutional Law* (Belmont, CA: West / Wadsworth, 1999).

Other implications of these data are equally compelling. When the total number of civil liberties cases doubled, the dissent rate within this subject area of cases doubled. This suggests that something in addition to docket composition is related to instances of nonconsensual opinion writing during this period. Walker, Epstein, and Dixon attribute such changes in opinion writing to the difference in leadership styles of Chief Justice Hughes and Stone. I suspect, however, that an increase in the actual number of civil liberties cases from 21 to 43 represents a profound qualitative change in the Court's task environment that may have challenged the norm of consensual behavior. Moreover, the effects of changes in the number of civil liberties cases decided by the Court deserves more rigorous testing. I include in the regression analysis a civil liberties cases variable that measures the between-terms changes in the percentage of docket space allocated to civil liberties cases. Also, the operational definition of this variable includes a broader range of cases than that used by Walker, Epstein, and Dixon. The civil liberties variable I use is operationally defined to include cases raising criminal rights issues in addition to those cases raising issues of First Amendment freedoms, due process issues in administrative proceedings, privacy issues including abortion rights, the rights of alleged communists, and the rights of conscientious objectors.

The data in Table 7.1 are important in yet another way. Table 7.1 reveals that while the percentage of docket space allocated to civil liberties cases increased, the average number of concurrences and the average number of dissents produced by the Court in each term increased steadily. Furthermore, the average number of dissents and concurrences written per case disposed of by signed opinion generally increased throughout the 1935-1985 period. These data also reveal that each succeeding chief justice serving during the 1935-1985 period encountered dockets increasingly devoted to civil liberties cases. This suggests that the chief justice dummy variables and the percentage of the Court's docket allocated to civil liberties cases variables would be strongly collinear in a multiple regression model, a fact that may have suppresses the importance of civil liberties cases in the model estimated by Haynie.[16] Thus, unless a different measure of docket composition is employed, multiple regression analysis may not reliably estimate the independent impact of either factor on the frequency of nonconsensual opinion writing.

The Caseload Variable: Measurement and Preliminary Evidence

The caseload variable is operationally defined as the number of cases disposed of by signed opinion per term. This measure of caseload is preferable to simply counting the number of cases granted oral argument per term. The latter measure would include in the analysis the many orally argued cases which are disposed of by per curiam opinion. Orally argued per curiam decisions are unique decisions reflecting the unanimous disposition of the Court and are disposed of using short, typically anonymous opinions that lack substantial legal reasoning.[17] Moreover, such a measure would include in the analysis cases that do not present the individual justices with the "consensus" versus "individual expression" debate that obtains in plenary treated cases. In short, a caseload variable that includes all cases disposed of by signed opinion eliminates from the study those cases that by definition do not present the opportunity for dissenting, concurring, or separate opinion writing.

In a manner similar to Walker, Dixon, and Epstein, I superimpose a graph of caseload data on the frequency of nonconsensual opinion writing. Figure 7.2 indicates the number of cases disposed of by signed opinion and the total number of nonconsensual opinions written by the justices during the 1935-1995 period. In 1935, the Court disposed of 187 cases by signed opinion. The number of cases treated with full opinions decreased dramatically until the early 1950s. In 1954, the Court treated only 86 cases with signed opinions. From 1955 until the early 1980s,

---

[16]Haynie, p. 1166.

[17]Unanimous decisions announced by signed opinion, as opposed to a per curiam opinion, are included in the analysis.

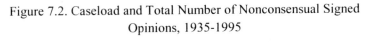

Figure 7.2. Caseload and Total Number of Nonconsensual Signed Opinions, 1935-1995

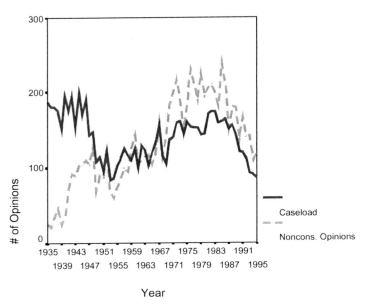

the Court issued full signed opinions in an increasing number of cases, reaching a figure of 174 cases in 1983. Since the 1983 term, the number of cases disposed of by signed opinion has diminished. In 1995, the justices disposed of only 87 cases by signed opinion, the lowest figure in over four decades.

Figure 7.2 also indicates that the increases in nonconsensual opinion writing which characterize the early 1940s occurred during a period in which there was no systematic increase in the number of cases disposed of by signed opinion. In fact, the number of cases disposed of by signed opinion appears to be inversely related to the number of nonconsensual opinions written during the 1935-1945 period. Contrary to Walker,

Dixon, and Epstein, however, I do not immediately conclude that the frequency of nonconsensual opinion writing is unrelated to changes in caseload.

From the early 1950s until the early 1980s, both the total number of nonconsensual opinions and the number of cases disposed of by signed opinion increase in a gradual and sustained way. Also, from the middle 1980s until 1995, both caseload and nonconsensual opinions decreased steadily. Further, a Pearson correlation coefficient of 0.73 is calculated for the caseload and total nonconsensual opinion measures during the period 1946-1995. Thus, caseload and the frequency of nonconsensual opinion writing may be related in some way. This finding warrants the inclusion of this caseload measure in regression models estimating relationships between law clerks, support personnel, and the patterns of nonconsensual opinion writing.

What type of relationship do I anticipate between the number of cases disposed of by signed opinion per term and historical changes in the numbers of dissenting, concurring, and separate opinions written in each term? Based on the data presented in Figure 7.2, I suspect that increases in the number of cases disposed of by signed opinion in each term is directly, yet modestly related to the historical increase in nonconsensual opinion writing. Moreover, I suspect that caseload may be inversely related to nonconsensual opinion writing during the 1930s and 1940s, while directly linked to nonconsensual opinion writing during the more lengthy 1946-1995 period.

Multivariate Regression Models: Estimating the Impact of Law Clerks on Nonconsensual Opinion Writing

In this section and the section which follows I present tables that include several multivariate regression equations. Each table includes three multiple regression equations in which I have added the civil liberties cases and caseload variables to those factors examined in Chapter 6. The equations in this chapter are designed to present the varying impact of the law clerk and support personnel variables on each type of nonconsensual opinion after adding the civil liberties and caseload variables to the models. Table 7.3 includes the law clerk variable in three multivariate regression equations estimating the numbers of dissenting, concurring, and separate opinions written by the justices in each term during the 1935-1995 period. Table 7.4 includes the support personnel variable in three multivariate regression equations estimating the numbers of dissenting, concurring, and separate opinions written by the justices in each term.

Table 7.3 indicates that law clerks are related to a statistically significant increase in the number of dissenting, concurring, and separate opinions written by the justices in each term. Equation 7A estimates the number of dissenting opinions written in each term and indicates a regression coefficient of 0.851 for the law clerk variable. Thus, Equation 7A indicates that for each additional law clerk employed by the Court, the justices draft an additional 0.851 opinions per term.   Moreover, a regression coefficient of 0.851 indicates that the employment of an additional 20 law clerks is associated with the production of 17 additional written dissents.   This finding takes on a greater significance when comparing opinion writing behavior in two actual Supreme Court terms. For example, in the 1957 term the Court employed 17 clerks and the justices produced 74 written dissents.   In 1976, when 37 clerks were employed by the Court (an increase of 20 clerks since 1957), the justices produced 117 written dissents or 43 more dissents than were written in 1957.   Thus, Equation 7A estimates that the increase in law clerks accounts for 17 of the additional dissents drafted by the justices in the 1976 term.

In Equation 7A, the partisan composition, Hughes, Vinson, Burger, and caseload variables are also statistically significant and the signs are in the expected directions. Consistent with the findings presented in Chapter 6, the highly collinear Rehnquist dummy variable is removed from regression equations that include the law clerk variable. Further, a coefficient of -7.151 on the partisan composition variable indicates that a one-justice decrease in the size of the majority party coalition on the Court is associated with the production of 7.151 additional dissenting opinions per term. Also, a regression coefficient of 0.354 on the caseload variable indicates that each additional case disposed of by signed opinion is associated with the production of an additional 0.354 dissenting opinions per term.   Changes in the percentage of the Court's docket allocated to civil liberties cases are not related to changes in frequency of

Table 7.3. Multiple Regression Equations: Estimating the Impact of Law Clerks on the Frequency of Nonconsensual Opinion Writing When Controlling for Caseload and Docket Composition.

Indep. Var.	Equation 7A (Dissents)	Equation 7B (Concurrences)	Equation 7C (Separate Opinions)
constant	51.811***	-44.079**	7.367
law clerks	0.851**	1.018***	0.606*
Part. Comp.	-7.151**	5.840*	-3.107
Hughes	-55.708***	-27.961***	-3.196
Stone	-0.750	-26.662*	8.370
Vinson	19.931*	-20.806*	1.424
Burger	11.956*	-9.952*	22.423***
Turnover	0.120	-1.234	-4.664
Inexper.	-1.009	0.393	-2.103
C. Lib	9.434E-02	-4.59E-02	-1.28E-02
Caseload	0.354***	0.217**	0.127
F	22.640***	9.986***	16.501***
Adj. R Sq.	0.793	0.604	0.724
	(0.733)****	(0.553)****	(0.708)****
Std. Err.	12.9044	11.9730	11.4090
Durbin d	1.813	1.078	0.966
N	61	61	61

*** $p<.01$; ** $p< .05$; *$p<.10$

**** Adjusted R Squared statistic produced when the law clerk variable is removed from the regression equation.

written dissents.

An adjusted R squared statistic of 0.793 indicates that the linear combination of variables accounts for 79.3 percent of the variance in dissenting opinions produced by the Court in each term. Removing the law clerk variable from Equation 7A produces an adjusted R squared statistic of 0.733. This indicates that the presence of the law clerk variable adds 6.0 percent to the explained variance in the number of dissenting opinions written in each term. The Durbin-Watson d statistic of 1.813 indicates that the model is not compromised by the presence of autocorrelation.

Equation 7B indicates that law clerks are related to a statistically significant increase in the number of concurring opinions written by the justices in each term. The regression coefficient of 1.018 for the law clerk variable indicates that the number of law clerks are more strongly related to the production of concurring opinions than dissenting opinions. Moreover, Equation 7B indicates that each additional law clerk is associated with the production of one additional concurring opinion in each term. Equation 7B also indicates that the presence of Chief Justices Hughes, Stone, Vinson, and Burger is linked to a statistically significant increase in the frequency of written concurrences. In addition, caseload is linked to the historical increase in written concurrences. A regression coefficient of 0.217 indicates that each additional case treated by signed opinion is associated with the production of 0.217 additional concurring opinions.

Contrary to my expectations, a regression coefficient of 5.840 indicates that the partisan composition variable is related in a positive way to the frequency of written concurrences. This result, however, is an artifact of the highly collinear relationship between the partisan composition and Vinson dummy variables. Further, a correlation coefficient of -0.833 characterizes the relationship between the Vinson and partisan composition variables. When the Vinson dummy variable is removed from Equation 7B, the sign on the partisan composition variable is reversed, the regression coefficient is estimated at 0.615, and the variable is not related in a statistically significant way to the number of concurrences written by the justices in each term. This result is consistent with the findings presented in Chapter 6; partisan composition is not related in a statistically significant way to the drafting of concurring opinions. Also, this finding supports Walker, Epstein, and Dixon's assertion that ideological divisions on the Court are not related to written concurrences.[18]

The adjusted R squared statistic of 0.604 indicates that the linear combination of variables in equation 7B account for 60.4 percent of the variance in concurring opinions. Removing the law clerk variable from Equation 7B produced an adjusted R squared statistic of 0.553. This indicates that the presence of the law clerk variable adds 5.1 percent to the explained variance in the number of concurring opinions written per term. The Durbin-Watson d test statistic of 1.078 is in the "zone of indecision," indicating that this test is inconclusive with regard to the presence or absence of autocorrelation.

Contrary to the statistics presented in Table 6.4, Equation 7C reveals that an increase in the number of law clerks is weakly related to a statistically significant increase in the frequency of separate opinions. Because Equation 7C controls for changes in caseload, this finding supercedes that presented in Table 6.4. It may be that under conditions of an increasing caseload, the justices have less time to build stable majority opinion coalitions and, consequently, forgo a search for consensus and turn to law clerks as a resource in drafting separate opinions. In addition, the presence of Chief Justice Burger is related to the statistically significant increase in the number of separate opinions produced in each term. Recall that Table 5.2 indictaes that the Burger Court justices produced an average of 0.32 separate opinions per case disposed of by signed opinion, a figure higher than that of any Court in the 1935-1995 period.

Removal of the law clerks variable from the equation reduces the adjusted R squared statistic from 0.724 to 0.708. This indicates that the presence of the law clerks variable adds 1.6 percent to the explained variance in the frequency of separate opinion writing. Similar to Equations 7A and 7B, the civil liberties variable is not statistically significant. Moreover, the Durbin-Watson d test statistic of 0.966

---

[18]Walker, Epstein, and Dixon, p. 375.

indicates the presence of positive autocorrelation. Thus, no definitive conclusion can be made about the independent effect of law clerks on the production of separate opinions.

What are the implications of the data presented in Table 7.3? I cautiously conclude that these data support Hypotheses H2a, H2b, H2c, H2d, H2e, and H2f.[19] The data in Table 7.2 reveal a positive, statistically significant relationship between the number of law clerks on the Court and the frequency of dissenting and concurring opinions. Considering that these models control for a broader range of competing explanations, the findings suggested by Table 7.2 supercede those presented in Chapter 6. However, the presence of autocorrelation in equation 7C means that no definite conclusion can be made with regard to the impact of law clerks on the production of separate opinions. In addition, the presence of collinear relationships between the law clerk and chief justice dummy variables means that the independent effect of law clerks on written dissents and concurrences cannot be determined with absolute certainty. Yet, the relationships suggested by Table 7.3 cannot be dismissed in light of the fact that these data are consistent with the general theory of law clerk influence in the opinion writing process.

Although superceding the results presented in Chapter 6, the data presented in Table 7.3 support the findings presented in previous chapters; nonconsensual opinion writing is a multi-causal phenomena driven by the increasing numbers of law clerks employed by the Court, ideological tension among justices, changes in one measure of caseload, and changes in the occupant of the chief justice's seat. The data presented in Equations 7A, 7B, and 7C do not support the proposition

---

[19]In Table 6.5, I presented several regression models estimating the numbers of written dissents, concurrences, and separate opinions when removing the chief justice dummy variables from the equations. Table 6.5 reveals some support for the proposition that the numbers of law clerks and support personnel are significantly related to the Court's production of nonconsensual opinions. A similar result obtains when the chief justice dummy variables are removed from the models presented in Tables 7.3 and 7.4. The law clerk and support personnel variables are related in a weak, yet statistically significant way to the numbers of dissents, concurrences, and separate opinions written in each term.

that changes in the amount of docket space allocated to civil liberties cases are related in a statistically significant way to the production of nonconsensual opinions.

Multivariate Regression Models: Estimating the Impact of Support Personnel on Nonconsensual Opinion Writing

Included in Table 7.4 are three multiple regression equations which estimate the number of dissenting, concurring, and separate opinions written by the justices in each term during the 1935-1995 period. The equations presented in Table 7.4 are designed to estimate the independent effect of changes in the number of support personnel employed by the Court on the three measures of nonconsensual opinion writing.

The data presented in Table 7.4 support the findings presented in Chapter 6. Equation 7D indicates that the number of support personnel is not related to the statistically significant increase in the frequency of written dissents. When the highly collinear Rehnquist dummy variable is removed from the model, the support personnel variable is statistically significant at the modest 0.10 level. Further, even when the Rehnquist control variable is removed from the model, the regression coefficient on the support personnel variable is 0.166, a result suggesting that the connection between support personnel and dissents is so weak as to lack substantive significance.

Equation 7D supports the finding that partisan composition, caseload, and changes in the occupant of the chief justice's seat are linked to the production of dissenting opinions. Further, Equation 7D supports the finding that when compared to the Warren Court, the presence of Chief Justices Hughes, Burger, and Rehnquist are more closely linked to the production of written dissents than Chief Justices Stone and Vinson. Most important, Equation 7D confirms the proposition that the presence of Chief Justice Rehnquist is strongly related to the number of dissents issued by the justices. The Durbin-Watson test statistic of 1.887 indicates that the model is not compromised by the presence of autocorrelation.

Contrary to the hypotheses, Equation 7E indicates that the support personnel variable is negatively associated with the frequency of written

Table 7.4. Multiple Regression Equations: Estimating the Impact of Support Personnel on the Frequency of Nonconsensual Opinion Writing When Controlling for Caseload and Docket Composition

Indep. Var.	Equation 7D (Dissents)	Equation 7E (Concurrences)	Equation 7F (Separate Opinions)
constant 77.758***		15.789	19.443
Supp. Pers.	-3.26E-02	-0.188***	0.166***
Part. Comp.	-7.674**	4.604	-5.933*
Hughes	-64.236***	-37.381***	-5.745
Stone	-6.763	-31.859***	14.318
Vinson	18.006	-23.757**	10.609
Burger	27.666***	24.692***	21.196***
Rehnquist	23.196*	55.151***	--------
Turnover	-0.117	-2.658	-3.421
Inexperience	-1.135	-0.207	-5.912E-02
C. Lib.	0.160	0.108	3.464E-02
Caseload	0.336***	-.198**	5.912E-02
F	21.449***	15.100***	20.383***
Adj. R Squ.	0.792	0.724	0.767 (0.708)****
Std. Err.	12.9375	9.9835	10.4967
Durbin d	1.887	1.641	1.107
N	61	61	61

*** p<.01; ** p< .05; *p<.10 **** Adjusted R squared statistic produced when the support personnel variable is removed from the equation.

concurrences. This result, however, is an artifact of a multicollinear relationship with the Rehnquist dummy variable. Removal of the Rehnquist variable produces a regression coefficient on the support personnel variable of 0.5389. This coefficient is not statistically significant. Thus, I find that the number of support personnel is not related to the frequency of written concurrences. This result differs from the findings presented in Table 4.3 and Table 6.3 found in Chapters 4 and 6, respectively. Moreover, Equation 7E indicates that the support personnel variable is not statistically significant when the civil liberties and caseload variables are added to the regression equations presented in Table 6.3. Caseload is related to the statistically significant increase in written concurrences. This finding suggests that as caseload increases and the justice encounter additional opportunities to draft concurrences, staff support becomes less important to the justices' opinion writing calculus.

In Equation 7E, the Hughes, Stone, Vinson, Burger, and Rehnquist dummy variables are statistically significant. These findings support propositions linking the production of concurring opinions to changes in the chief justice seat. Consistent with the data presented in Table 5.2, a regression coefficient of 55.151 on the Rehnquist dummy variable indicates that relative to Chief Justice Warren the Rehnquist Court produced more written concurrences than were written during the service of any previous chief justice.

In addition, the partisan composition variable is not related to the statistically significant increase in the number of concurring opinions written in the 1935-1995 period. Also, Equation 7E suggests that the caseload variable is inversely related to the statistically significant increase in the production of concurring opinions. Although unexpected, this result supports my growing suspicion that concurrences are linked to workload in a complex way, but are less influenced by partisan or ideological conflict. An adjusted R squared statistic of 0.724 indicates that the linear combination of variables presented in Equation 7E accounts for 72.4 percent of the variance in the number of concurring opinions written in each term. The Durbin-Watson test statistic of 1.641 is in the "zone of indecision." This indicates that no conclusive decision can be made with regard to the presence or absence of autocorrelation.

Equation 7F reveals that after the addition of the civil liberties and caseload variables to the regression models presented in Table 6.4, the support personnel variable is still related in a statistically significant fashion to the separate opinions variable. The highly collinear Rehnquist dummy variable is absent in Equation 7F. The support personnel variable remains statistically significant when the Rehnquist variable is entered. A coefficient of 0.116 (or 0.335 when the Rehnquist variable is entered in the equation) suggests that the support personnel variable is linked to historical increases in the frequency with which the Court disposes of cases via a separate opinion. However, this finding must be taken cautiously. The highly collinear relationship between the support personnel variable and the Rehnquist dummy variable means that the independent effect of the support personnel variable cannot be determined with absolute certainty.

The adjusted R square statistic of 0.767 indicates that the variables in Equation 7F account for 76.7 of the variance in the number of separate opinions issued in each term. Removing the support personnel variable from the equation produces an adjusted R squared statistic of 0.708. This indicates that the presence of the support personnel variable in the model adds 5.9 percent to the explained variance in the number of separate opinions produced by the Court in each term. The Durbin-Watson test statistic of 1.107 is exactly 0.001, below the lower limit of the "zone of indecision." Thus, I find that this equation is potentially effected by the presence of positive autocorrelation. Moreover, the presence of autocorrelation means that no definitive conclusion can be made with regard to the connection between support personnel and the production of separate opinions.[20]

What are the implications of the regression equations presented in

---

[20]Including among the predictors a lagged version of the dependent variable produced an equation in which only the Burger dummy and lagged variables are statistically significant. For reasons discussed earlier, including an autoregressive term in this model is atheoretical, introduces a variable that is correlated with the error term, and produces a regression coefficient that is overestimated.

Table 7.4? The presence of the collinear chief justice dummy variable means that all conclusions about the relationship between support personnel and nonconsensual opinion writing must be taken cautiously. The support personnel variable is not related in a statistically significant way to the frequency of written concurrences. Although the number of support personnel are related in a statistically significant way to the frequency of written dissents, the relationship lacks substantial associational properties. Thus, I find no support for hypotheses H2a, H2b, H2c, H2d, H2e, and H2f with respect to the connection between support personnel and concurring opinions. I find statistical but insufficient associational support for hypotheses H2a, H2b, H2c, H2d, H2e, and H2f with respect to the connection between support personnel and the frequency of written dissents. This finding confirms the basic finding in Chapter 6 that support personnel do not substantially impact the frequency of written dissents and concurrences. Equation 7F suggests, however, that these hypotheses are supported in that the number of support personnel employed by the Court is related to the statistically significant increase in the production of separate opinions.

The statistics presented in Table 7.4 support my earlier finding that the partisan composition variable is related in a statistically significant way to the production of written dissents. In addition, Equation 7F provides evidence that partisan composition may be linked in an important way to the frequency with which cases are disposed of by separate opinions. Finally, Table 7.3 supports my earlier finding regarding the importance of the Chief Justice Burger dummy variable as a key factor in all types of nonconsensual opinion writing.

The Comparative Importance of Law Clerks, Support Personnel and Competing Explanations of Nonconsensual Opinion Writing

What do the data presented in Tables 7.3 and 7.4 suggest about the importance of law clerks and support personnel relative to competing explanations of nonconsensual opinion writing? What do these data reveal about each type of nonconsensual opinion writing? Relative to the support personnel, law clerks are more closely linked to the production of each type of nonconsensual opinion. In fact, there is no evidence in Table 7.4 that support personnel are linked to the statistically significant increases in written dissents and concurrences in the 1935-1995 period. Support personnel are only weakly related to the production of separate opinions. One explanation for this result is that unlike the support personnel, law clerks are more proximate to the justices' decisions to draft these specific types of nonconsensual opinions; the law clerks enjoy the frequent, in-chambers contact with the justices that facilitates their desires to exploit ideological tensions on the Court. This explanation comports with Lazarus's observation that the law clerks successfully influence the justices' decisions to draft additional opinions. He writes: "Some clerks certainly encourage these independent writings. After all, every opinion represents another opportunity for a clerk (through his or her justice) to make an impression on the law and to achieve a sliver of immortality as the ghostwriter for portions of the *U.S. Reports*."[21]

The data presented in Tables 7.3 and 7.4 also suggest that dissents, concurrences, and separate opinions are, at least in some respects, discrete phenomena, differently influenced by the extent of partisan conflict on the Court. Tables 7.3 and 7.4 suggest that partisanship is related to the production of written dissents but is not linked to the writing of concurrences. This finding may reflect the fact that concurrences are by definition those writings that stem from basic agreement among justices with regard to the outcome of cases, but express what is often only a subtle disagreement as to the jurisprudential basis for that outcome. In short, concurrences are not artifacts of ideological or partisan conflict. By contrast, dissents reflect enduring, deeply-held ideological schisms that motivate the justices to publicly expose points of disagreement in the Court. Furthermore, Table 7.4 suggests that partisanship is modestly linked to the production of separate opinions. Thus, partisanship may trigger the broad patterns of disagreement that trigger dissent behavior and, relatedly, produce the fragmented opinion coalitions that lead to

---

[21] Edward Lazarus, *Closed Chambers: The First Eyewitness Account of the Epic Struggles Inside the Supreme Court* (New York: Times Books, 1998), pp. 271-272.

announcing decisions by separate opinions.

What, then, do Tables 7.3 and 7.4 suggest about the relative impact of law clerks, partisan conflict, caseload, and leadership changes on the writing of nonconsensual opinions? Based on the magnitude of the regression coefficients, changes in leadership appear to have the largest impact on the Court's production of dissents and concurrences. Similarly, the presence of Chief Justice Burger is most strongly associated with the production of separate opinions. However, as I explain in Chapter 6, because successive chief justices arrived at the Court during periods of increasing dissensus, the regression models probably overstate the actual impact of leadership changes on the writing of nonconsensual opinions. Thus, the exact importance of leadership changes is difficult to ascertain.

The relative importance of other factors is somewhat easier to relate. Based on the size of the regression coefficients reported in Tables 7.3 and 7.4, changes in the size of the majority party coalition on the Court exert a larger immediate impact on the Court than small increases in the numbers of law clerks or small increases in the size of the caseload. For example, Equation 7A estimates that a one-justice decrease in the size of the majority party coalition, like that which occurred in 1991, produces an increase of 7 dissenting opinions. However, according to Equation 7A, the addition of two law clerks in 1991 triggers the production of fewer than two additional written dissents. Yet, as I explained earlier, large increases in the number of law clerks employed by the Court, such as that which occurred between 1957 and 1976, account for notable changes in the numbers of written dissents.

A similar pattern characterizes the relative importance of increases in the size of the Court's caseload. As Equations 7A and 7B indicate, each additional case that is treated by signed opinion is associated with the production of an additional 0.354 dissents and 0.217 concurrences. Thus, small changes in caseload are of little immediate importance to the justices' decisions to write nonconsensual opinions. However, large changes in caseload do assist in explaining the production of written dissents. For example, in 1960 the Court disposed of 125 cases by signed opinion. In that year, the Court produced 94 dissents. In 1983, the justices disposed of 174 cases by signed opinion and drafted 106 dissents.

Equation 7A estimates that an increase of 49 cases will yield an additional 17 written dissents. Although this coefficient overestimates the increase in written dissents (12 additional dissents were produced in 1983), Equation 7A suggests that large increases in caseload are linked to notable changes in opinion writing behavior. Moreover, increases of 20 or more cases in the size of the Court's caseload occurred frequently in the 1935-1995 period (See Appendix A). Equations 7A and 7D estimate that the addition of 20 cases to the Court's caseload is associated with the production of nearly 7 additional dissents. Equations 7B and 7E estimate that an additional 20 cases yields approximately 4 additional concurrences per term. Thus, in instances of large increases in the size of the Court's caseload, such changes may be associated with a change in opinion writing behavior similar in magnitude to that resulting from a one-justice increase or decrease in the size of the Court's majority party coalition. Absent a large change in caseload, however, changes in partisan composition are markedly more important for patterns of nonconsensual opinion writing.

The relative importance of these factors is best summarized in the following way: discounting the effect of changes in leadership, a cautious interpretation of the regression equations suggests that shifts in partisan composition have the largest immediate impact on the production of dissenting opinions. In short, dissents are phenomena driven primarily by partisan or ideological conflict. Although frequent, only large changes in caseload, say 20 or more opinions, account for a change in dissents similar to that produced by an incremental change in the size of the Court's majority party coalition. Because partisan composition is not related to increases in the frequency of written concurrences, caseload changes are more closely associated with the production of concurrences than partisan conflict. Whereas dissents are artifacts of partisan conflict, concurrence writing may stem from increases in workload and a consequent decrease in the amount of time to seek consensus. Increases in the numbers of law clerks account for little of the year-to year change in the production of written dissents and concurrences. Only an increase of 8 to 10 law clerks yields the change in dissents and concurrences produced by an a one-justice decrease in the size of the majority party coalition. Also, because the numbers of law clerks changed little from one term to the next - the largest single increase in the numbers of law clerks occurred in 1970 (an increase of seven clerks from 1969). These changes are comparatively less important than partisan composition and workload factors with respect to changes in nonconsensual opinion writing activity from one term to the next. In short, the "law clerk effect" obtains in the long-term trend toward an increasingly large Supreme Court work group.

Conclusions

After adding the civil liberties and caseload variables to the regression analysis, I cautiously conclude, in light of the presence of collinear variables, that the increasing presence of law clerks on the Court is related to the increasing numbers of dissenting, concurring, and separate opinions written during the 1935-1995 period. I find that the number of support personnel are not significantly related to the frequency of written dissents and concurrences. However, I conclude that the increasing numbers of support personnel employed by the Court are related in a statistically significant way to the disposition of cases by separate opinion. These findings support my general argument that the law clerks comprise a unique institutional entity that produces a distinct, measurable impact on the behavior of the Supreme Court. In short, I tentatively conclude that the law clerks influence the Court's production of nonconsensual opinions. The regression models presented in this chapter support the proposition that increases in the size of the Court work group are linked to the ultimate behavior of the Court.

Although no conclusion can be made with regard to the presence or absence of autocorrelation in several of the regression models, these tentative findings are supported by the strong theoretical foundations presented in earlier chapters. Additionally, these findings are consistent with the assertions of O'Brien and Posner regarding the impact of law clerks on the production of nonconsensual opinions.[22]

---

[22]O'Brien, *Storm Center*, p. 170; Posner, *The Federal Courts: Challenge and Reform,* p. 357.

A second finding is equally compelling. The data presented in this chapter support the proposition that nonconsensual opinion writing is a multi-causal phenomenon. The increasing presence of law clerks on the Court is but one among several factors that are related to the historical decline in the consensus norm. While I find that net changes in the percentage of docket space allocated to civil liberties cases in each term are not related to historical increases in nonconsensual opinion writing, I find that one previously unexamined measure of caseload is an important factor in predicting changes in the frequency of written dissents and concurrences. Increases in the numbers of cases disposed of by signed opinion are related to statistically significant increases in the frequency of nonconsensual opinion writing. Moreover, it may be that an increasing workload lowers the threshold point at which the justices suspend a search for consensus in favor of drafting additional opinions. This conclusion is consistent with the notion that increases in the demands on an institution give shape to the task environment and, ultimately, effect the qualitative features of the organization's output. These findings should encourage a reconsideration of previous models of dissensus that account only for changes in the number of case filings.[23]

Contrary to Haynie's analysis, I find that the degree of ideological tension between justices, as measured by the size of the majority party coalition on the Court, is an important predictor of the frequency of written dissents.[24] Moreover, this finding is consistent with the recognition by many public law scholars of the primacy of attitudinal factors in models of Supreme Court decision making activities. The disparity in results between my study and that presented by Haynie may be attributable to one or more factors: First, Haynie examined a larger number of observations on her dependent variables; and second, Haynie's study examines nonconsensual opinion writing during the 1800-1990 terms. Thus, Haynie's study includes opinion writing measures during the 1800-1940 terms, a 140 year period marked by relatively low levels of nonconsensual

---

[23]Walker, Epstein, and Dixon, p. 367-8; Haynie, p. 1165.

[24]Haynie, p. 1166.

opinion writing and, relatedly, little variation on the dependent variable.[25] Including this 140 year period means that 74 percent of the observations in her study reflect little variation in the phenomena to be explained. This approach may have suppressed the statistical importance of competing explanations of dissensus. Second, Haynie presumably employed different control measures. Her decision to exclude measures of work group size and to define caseload as the number of case filings represents two notable differences from the analysis I present; these approaches may have failed to reveal important interactions between partisanship, the number of law clerks, and an alternative measure of caseload. Third, Haynie employs a different estimation technique. Haynie uses Box-Jenkins times series methods to obtain a "white noise" time series in which the effects of serial correlation are reduced, aiding the efficient estimation of a linear regression model. In short, my decision to use an ordinary least squares regression technique despite the presence of "noise" in the time series means that conclusions about covariational relationships must be made cautiously, if not tentatively.

Additionally, I find support for the proposition that changes in the occupant of the chief justice's seat are related in a statistically significant way to changing patterns of nonconsensual behavior. This finding supports the broader theoretical perspective that small group processes impact the decisions of individual justices.

In sum, I find that the historical decline in the consensus norm is attributable to a combination of factors; partisan or ideological tension, leadership, caseload, and changes in the numbers of law clerks working for the justices are linked to the gradual, persistent trend toward individual expression on the Supreme Court.

---

[25]Haynie, pp. 1159, 1160-61.

CHAPTER 8

Conclusions

In this book, I test the general proposition that increases in the numbers of law clerks and support personnel are related in a statistically significant way to historical increases in the production of dissenting, concurring, and separate opinions. This hypothesis is also a test of a reformulated version of the small group hypothesis of Supreme Court behavior - interaction among justices and their law clerks is related to the writing of additional opinions. This hypothesis reflects the basic proposition that the law clerks provide the opinion writing resources necessary for the production of increasing numbers of dissenting, concurring, and separate opinions. Relatedly, this hypothesis reflects the possibility that the increasing presence of law clerks and support personnel on the Court has altered the Court's task environment in a way that diminishes the effectiveness of consensus-building interaction among justices. In short, I present a theory linking an increasingly autonomous law clerk institution to the frequency with which the justices write opinions expressing a view different from that of the Court majority or plurality. Moreover, I proposed that increasing numbers of law clerks and support personnel make the drafting of additional opinions possible, thereby altering the justices' willingness to engage in the time-consuming search for the type of consensus that yields institutional opinions.

To test this basic proposition, I employed three quantitative methods. In Chapter 4, I presented graphical data and descriptive statistics indicating that the increasing numbers of law clerks and support personnel assigned to the Court during the 1935-1995 period parallels the historical growth in the numbers of dissenting, concurring, and separate opinions produced by the Court. Also in Chapter 4, I calculated Pearson correlation coefficients that indicate linear, statistically significant relationships between the law clerk and support personnel variables and five measures of nonconsensual opinion writing. Thus, the data presented in Chapter 4 support the general proposition that increases in the numbers of law clerks and support personnel are related in a statistically significant way to the historical increases in the frequency of nonconsensual opinion writing.

In Chapters 6 and 7, I present several multiple regression equations to estimate the independent effect of law clerks and support personnel on changes in the frequency of dissenting, concurring, and separate opinion writing while controlling for changes in ideological or partisan composition of the Court, changes in the degree of turnover and inexperience on the Court, changes in the composition of the docket of cases granted plenary review, changes in the occupant of the chief justice's seat, and changes in the size of the Court's yearly caseload. Estimation of these multiple regression equations reveals that nonconsensual opnion writing is not singularly driven by the presence of law clerks and support personnel, but is a multi-causal phenomenon, linked to institutional structures, personnel changes, ideological factors, and the size of the Court's caseload. These conclusions challenge the assertion of Caldeira and Zorn that changes in the Court's leadership is the only factor which "...accounts for the explosion of conflict under Stone and its persistence from 1941 to the present."[1]   In addition, my findings encourage a reconsideration of the workload and ideological factors rejected by Walker, Epstein, and Dixon and Haynie.[2]

From an analysis of descriptive data, Pearson correlation coefficients, and multivariate regression models, I find support for the proposition that the number of law clerks employed by the Court is related to the numbers of dissenting, concurring, and separate opinions written by the Court in each term. Yet, the presence of multicollinear relationships in the regression models means that conclusions about the independent

---

[1]Gregory Caldeira and Christopher J.W. Zorn, "Of Time and Consensual Norms in the United States Supreme Court," *American Journal of Political Science*, 42 (1998): 875.

[2]Thomas G. Walker, Lee Epstein, and William J. Dixon, "On the Mysterious Demise of Consensual Norms in the United States Supreme Court," *Journal of Politics*, 50 (1988):366-368, 374-375; Stacia Haynie, "Leadership and Consensus on the U.S. Supreme Court," *Journal of Politics*, 54 (1992): 1166.

relationship between law clerks and nonconsensual opinion writing must be taken cautiously. Estimation of more parsimonious models that contain fewer independent variables may produce regression coefficients with smaller variances, making estimates of the impact of law clerks more precise. Yet, reductions in the number of predictors would be made at the expense of not testing important, multi-causal explanations of opinion production. While imperfect, the regression models presented in Chapters 6 and 7 reveal that historical increases in nonconsensual behavior on the Court are phenomena driven by complex interactions among several factors. However, relative to the number of observations on the dependent variable, the large number of explanatory variables frustrates the precise estimation of the comparative impact of factors on historical changes in nonconsensual opinion writing.

While it is difficult to estimate the independent effect of law clerks on the historical decline in the consensus norm, I suspect that the increasing presence of law clerks on the Court has in some way altered the justices' tolerance for consensus seeking behavior. Furthermore, I conclude that the increasing presence of law clerks has lowered the threshold point at which the justices give up the search for agreement and choose to draft a dissenting or concurring opinion. The law clerks ability to cause the justices to forgo consensus building efforts contributes to the frequency with which the justices dispose of a case by an opinion reflecting the disposition of fewer than a majority of justices. Thus, I find some support for the idea that justice-law clerk interactions comprise a "small group" which measurably influences the Court's opinion writing behavior.

The number of support personnel employed by the Court is not related in a statistically significant way to the number of concurring opinions written by the Court. Although the number of support personnel employed by the Court is related in a statistically significant way to the number of dissenting opinions written by the justices, the association between the support personnel variable and dissent writing is too low to make positive substantive conclusions. I find some support, however, for the proposition that the number of support personnel employed by the Court is related in a statistically significant way to the number of separate opinions written by the justices in each term. Thus, I tentatively conclude that the number of support personnel on the Court is linked to broad patterns of disagreement that frustrate the building of stable majority opinion coalitions.

I find that nonconsensual opinion writing behavior is a multi-causal phenomenon. Contrary to the findings of Haynie, I find that changes in the partisan composition of Court are related in a statistically significant way to the production of dissenting and separate opinions. This means that underlying partisan or ideological tensions among justices are independently linked to the decline in consensual norms on the Court. Moreover, scholars should reconsider the model presented by Haynie and her finding that partisan composition does not significantly influence the frequency of written dissents.[3] The equations presented in Chapter 7 confirm Haynie's finding that changes in the partisan composition on the Court are not related in a statistically significant way to the production of concurring opinions.[4]

I also reveal that changes in one measure of caseload are related in a statistically significant way to the production of dissenting and concurring opinions. Further, changes in the number of cases disposed of by signed opinion in each term are linked to the broad trends in opinion writing activity. This means that as the number of opportunities for disagreement increases, the justices produce increasing numbers of dissenting and concurring opinions. Also, as the justices encounter increasing numbers of cases that must be disposed of by signed opinions, the justices increasingly opt for individual expressions that, in instances of dissents, reflect a lack of consensus on case outcomes, or, in instances of concurrences, reflect a lack of consensus on the jurisprudential foundations upon which a case is decided. This finding indicates that future tests of the connection between workload and the decline in the consensus norm should explore aspects of caseload other than the number of case filings per term. The Walker, Epstein, and Dixon study, as well as the study by Haynie examine only the effects of case filings, neglecting

---

[3]Haynie, p. 1166.

[4]Ibid., p. 1165.

other dimensions of the Court's workload.[5]

Similar to previous studies, I find that changes in the occupant of the chief justice's seat are related in a statistically significant way to the historical increase in the frequency of written dissents and concurrences.[6] This means that changes in the Court's leadership are linked to the business of deciding cases and drafting written opinions. This finding supports the notion that changes in the Court's "small group" environment impact the justices' willingness and ability to achieve consensus. However, I present in Chapter 6 evidence that the "chief justice" effect should not be overstated. In short, I present findings that should encourage judicial scholars to rethink the chief justice hypothesis.

Caldeira and Zorn find ". . . the extent to which consensual norms have restrained judicial behavior has varied considerably under different chief justices."[7] However, in Chapter 6, I present data indicating that nonconsensual behavior increased in frequency during the tenure of each justice since 1941, including that of William H. Rehnquist. Although the Rehnquist Court averaged fewer dissents and separate opinions per signed opinion than the Burger Court, the Rehnquist justices issued an average number of concurrences per signed opinion that was higher than any period in the Court's history. Moreover, the Rehnquist Court represents a special case; the frequency of two types of nonconsensual behavior declined but the justices were, with respect to written concurrences, among the most conflict-prone in Supreme Court history. Thus, during the 1935-1995 period, Supreme Court justices became increasingly nonconsensual regardless of the occupant of the chief justice's seat. Even if each chief justice had some influence on the Court's observance of consensual norms, that influence did not alter the historical trend in nonconsensual opinion writing. The proposition that different chief justices have significantly influenced the Court's observance of consensual norms should be

---

[5]Walker, Epstein, and Dixon, p. 368; Haynie, p. 1165.

[6]Walker, Epstein, and Dixon, p. 384, Haynie, p. 1164-65; Caldeira and Zorn, p. 900.

[7]Caldeira and Zorn, p. 900.

reconsidered.   Judicial scholars should take account of the fact that changes in the occupant of the chief justice's seat have occurred amidst a persistent, upward trend in the frequency of nonconsensual opinion writing.   The supposed importance of the "chief justice effect" on nonconsensual opinion writing is, at least in part, potentially artificial considering the long term trends in the data.

Finally, the theoretical and empirical modeling conducted in this book reveal a connection between the increasing numbers of law clerks on the Court and the historical increase in nonconsensual opinion writing.   The analysis of quantitative opinion writing data tentatively indicates that the law clerks have some effect on the justices' decisions to draft dissenting, concurring, and separate opinions.   Although taken cautiously, these findings gain currency when informed by the theoretical model that identifies the law clerks as professionalized, autonomous elements of the Supreme Court work group.   Most important, this model characterizes the law clerks as goal-oriented actors who provide the resources vital to the fulfilment of the justices' principal goal of deciding cases and drafting written opinions pursuant to their individual policy objectives.

Observations on the Declining Consensus Norm: Does Dissensus Matter?

I have presented empirical evidence that several factors are related to the historical increases in nonconsensual opinion writing. One question remains, however: Does it matter that the justices have become increasingly nonconsensual in their opinion writing activities? The historical changes in nonconsensual opinion writing is an important subject of study for two reasons.   First, the willingness and ability of Supreme Court justices to engage in dissent behavior is interpreted by several scholars as a referent of the health of the Court as a deliberative, policymaking institution.   Second, changes in opinion writing practices on the Court indicate that some underlying change has taken place with regard to how conflict about case outcomes is expressed.   For these reasons, questions of why and to what effect the justices have become increasingly nonconsensual is of broad, general importance.

The proliferation of nonconsensual opinions is an indicator that important changes have taken place in how the Court conducts the business of deciding cases. It is important that conflict among justices has increasingly found its way out of the conference room and onto the pages of the case reporters. As Igor Kirman points out, "[t]he delivery of non-institutional opinions is an important insight into ways in which conflict is handled."[8]   Thus, historical alterations in opinion writing practices reveal that some important change has occurred in the internal habits of this key policymaking institution.

This change has meant that the justices' disagreement over substantive issues are increasingly written into the corpus of statutory and constitutional law. Arguably, more, rather than fewer, written opinions signals a fragmentation in the substantive law enunciated by the Court. Fragmentation in the opinion writing process may engender a move away from legal certainty. Indeed, the interpretability of the Supreme Court's pronouncements are diminished by either opinions which reflect unstable majorities (separate opinions) or those individual expressions which define dissents and concurrences. Ruth Bader Ginsburg observes that "dissent harms consistency, predictability, clarity, and stability when the Court fails to act as a collegial body."[9] Further, if clarity of meaning is a virtue for judicial decisions, those decisions accompanied by multiple opinions are more prone to misunderstanding and misapplication than decisions announced by a single opinion produced by a majority of justices or a unanimous Court.   Richard Posner seems to recognize that some legal questions require an unambiguous resolution not supplied by multiple opinions. He writes:

> It might be one of those questions where it is more important that the law be settled than that it be got just right. In such a case a

---

[8]Igor Kirman, "Standing Apart to Be Apart: The Precedential Value of Supreme Court Opinions," *Columbia Law Review* 95 (1995): 2096-97.

[9]Ruth Bader Ginsburg, "Speaking in a Judicial Voice," *New York University Law Review* 67 (1992): 1191.

dissent will communicate a sense of the law's instability that is misleading; [in fact] the decision is as solid a precedent as if it had been unanimous.[10]

Fragmented opinion writing may trigger a related yet slightly different problem. As Igor Kirman remarks, fragmented opinions frequently produce "interpretive tensions" which are sometimes realized as "instances in which lower courts have given authoritative effect to the view of a single justice."[11] Moreover, these judicial scholars articulate the principle that the proliferation of nonconsensual opinions is of great moment for those who must interpret and apply the Court's decisions. If the proliferation of noninstitutional opinions militates against a goal of legal certainty, the identification of those factors which drive the fragmentation of Supreme Court decisions is of equal importance.

Conversely, increasing numbers of nonconsensual opinions may reflect the health of the Court's deliberative processes. Further, the proliferation of written dissents and concurrences may inform the public of the relative stability of existing doctrines. Although concerned about the disorienting effect of fragmented opinion writing practices, Posner also argues that squelching dissent behavior may actually cause uncertainty. He explains:

> Dissenting, and even concurring, opinions have played so important a role in the development of the law that it would be a great error to suppress them. It would also make the law less rather than more certain, by concealing from the bar important clues to the law of the future."[12]

Similarly, Chief Justice Hughes explains that a nonconsensual opinion may serve the broader purpose of making good law. He states that "a

---

[10]Richard A. Posner, *Federal Courts: Challenge and Reform*, p. 357.

[11]Igor Kirman, p. 2085.

[12]Posner, *Federal Courts: Challenge and Reform*, p. 356-7.

dissent in a court of last resort is an appeal to the brooding spirit of the law, to the intelligence of a future day, when a later decision may possibly correct the error onto which the dissenting judge believes the court to have betrayed."[13]

Fragmentation in the opinion writing process may also indicate that the Court has provided the sort of measured deliberation owed to issues of substantial moment. More rather than fewer opinions may signal a comprehensive discourse on legal questions which come before the Court. Kevin Stack observes that "dissent is necessary to expose the deliberative character of the Court's decision making."[14] Professor Stack goes on to argue that dissent actually promotes the quality of the deliberation.[15] Further, Justice William J. Brennan notes that "[d]issent prevents the process from becoming rigid or stale. And each time the Court revisits an issue, the justices are forced by dissent to reconsider the fundamental questions and to re-think the result."[16]

Arguably, the legitimacy of the institution is enhanced by a comprehensive airing of competing positions on questions of federal and constitutional law. Former Chief Justice Charles Evans Hughes agrees. He writes:

> But unanimity which is merely formal, which is recorded at the
> expense of strong, conflicting views, is not desirable in a court of
> last resort, whatever may be the effect on public opinion at
> the time. This is so because what must ultimately sustain the

---

[13]Charles Evans Hughes, *The Supreme Court of the United States* (New York: Columbia University Press, 1928), p. 68.

[14]Kevin M. Stack, "The Practice of Dissent in the Supreme Court," *Yale Law Journal* 105 (1996): 2246.

[15]Ibid., p. 2257.

[16]William J. Brennan, Jr., "In Defense of Dissents," *Hastings Law Journal* 37 (1986): 436, as quoted in Meredith Kolsky, "Justice William J. Brennan and the History of Supreme Court Dissent," *Georgetown Law Journal* 83 (1995): 2083.

court in public confidence is the character and independence of the judges. They are not there simply to decide cases, but to decide them as they think they should be decided, and while it may be regrettable that they cannot always agree, it is better that their independence should be maintained and recognized than unanimity should be gained through its sacrifice.[17]

Finally, historical changes in the patterns of opinion writing behavior are important to the extent that it is a referent of an institution that has changed much since 1935. The dramatic increase in nonconsensual opinion writing is important because it reveals the existence of nine justices whose behavior is driven by multiple influences. In this regard, the words of former Supreme Court law clerk Edward Lazarus are instructive. He writes:

> Today I carry with me a very different image of the Court. It is of an institution broken into unyielding factions that have largely given up on meaningful exchange of their respective views or, for that matter, a meaningful explication or defense of their own views. It is of justices who in many important cases resort to transparently deceitful and hypocritical arguments and factual distortions as they discard judicial and consistent interpretation in favor of bottom line results. This is a Court so badly splintered, yet so intent on lawmaking, that shifting 5-4 majorities, or even mere pluralities, rewrite whole swaths of constitutional law on the authority of a single, often idiosyncratic vote. It is also a Court where Justices yield great and extensive power to immature, ideologically driven clerks,
> who in turn use that power to manipulate their bosses and the institution they ostensibly serve.[18]

---

[17]Charles Evans Hughes, pp. 67-8.

[18]Edward Lazarus, *Closed Chambers: The First Eyewitness Account of the Epic Struggles Inside the Supreme Court* (New York: Times Books, 1998), p. 6.

Research Implications

Future studies of the historical decline in the consensus norm should seek a compromise between the competing goals of building multi-causal explanations of nonconsensual opinion writing and arriving at parsimonious explanations of this important phenomenon. Pooled-cross sectional analyses of the opinion writing behavior of individual justices may be an effective answer to the need to increase the number of observations, ease the effects of multicollinearity, and retain a multi-causal approach. This book provides some clues as to how this may be done.

Although this book models aggregate opinion writing activity, it indirectly characterizes the factors underlying the opinion writing behavior of individual justices. Indeed, increases in the total number of dissents and concurrences written in each term reflects the individual justice's willingness to draft an additional opinion rather than join a colleague's dissent or concurrence. It is therefore important to model the impact of changes in the number of law clerks on dissent and concurrence joining behavior. It is important that judicial scholars attempt to model the impact of changes in the number of law clerks on the Court for the decision making activities of individual justices. This requires that each observation in the study is the behavior of the individual justice; either the justices decide to join a colleague's dissent or concurrence or they choose to author an additional opinion.

Studies of the opinion writing behavior of individual justices may also confirm the multi-causal explanation of opinion production. Studies of the opinion writing practices of individual justices may aid in explaining what are likely complex patterns of interaction among predicative variables. Furthermore, a pooled-cross sectional design may better explain how individual justices utilize their law clerks under different caseload levels, ideological climates, and leadership styles.

The data presented in Chapters 6 and 7 suggest that judicial scholars should carefully consider that the choice of measures of caseload and ideological conflict informs the testing of a multi-causal model of opinion writing. In short, future studies might examine in greater detail the connection between the number of cases disposed of by signed opinion, the degree of ideological heterogeneity, the size of majority party coalitions on the Court, and instances of nonconsensual opinion writing. Most important, the measures of caseload and ideological conflict I employ leave unexamined the specific ways in which these factors interact to influence the justices' decisions to write additional opinions.

Future studies should also employ interrupted times series models to estimate the impact of sudden increases in the number of law clerks on the Court's opinion writing practices; scholars might treat the Court's 1946 and 1969 terms as key interruptions in the gradual increase in the number of law clerks on the Court. Furthermore, use of time-series regression methods will likely facilitate more efficient estimation of a model less compromised by the "noise" of serial correlation and more accurate in terms of point estimates.

Finally, evidence of the impact of law clerks on the justice's opinion writing behaviors suggests a need to reconsider the usefulness of "small group" perspectives on Supreme Court behavior. Moreover, future studies should employ qualitative methods to model the role of law clerks in structuring conflict between justices. Such investigations might aim to model the interaction between a justice's willingness to engage in nonconsensual behavior, the advocacy positions assumed by the law clerks, and historical changes in the effectiveness of consensus building strategies. In short, future studies should analyze from a "small group" perspective the impact of the structural changes in the Court's task environment brought about by the rise of a law clerk institution on the Court's adoption of a culture of dissensus.

Bibliography

Abraham, Henry J. 1993. *The Judicial Process: An Introductory Analysis of the Courts of the United States, England, and France.* Sixth Edition. New York: Oxford University Press.

Administrative Office of the United States Courts. *Cases Filed, Disposed of, and Remaining on the Dockets in the Supreme Court of the United States.* Successive terms, 1935-1995. Washington, D.C.: AOUSC Statistics Division.

Baier, Paul R. 1973. "Law Clerks: Profile of an Institution." *Vanderbilt Law Review* 26:1125-77.

Barnard, Chester. 1968. *The Functions of the Executive.* Cambridge: Harvard University Press.

Baum, Lawrence. 1997. *The Puzzle of Judicial Behavior.* Ann Harbor: The University of Michigan Press.

Beiser, Edward N. 1974. "The Rhode Island Supreme Court: A Well Integrated Political System." *Law and Society Review* 8:167-96.

Bennet, Robert W. 1991. "A Dissent on Dissent." *Judicature* 74:255-261

Berelson, Bernard R., Paul S. Lazarsfeld, and William N. McPhee. 1954. *Voting.* Chicago: University of Chicago Press.

Berry, William D. 1993. *Understanding Regression Assumptions.* London: Sage Publications.

Bickel, Alexander. 1958. "The Court: An Independent Analysis" *New York Times*, April 27, section 6 (Magazine).

_____. 1973. *The Caseload of the Supreme Court And What, If Anything, To Do About It.* Washington, D.C.: The American Enterprise Institute For Public Policy Research.

Blau, Peter M. and W. Richard Scott. 1962. *Formal Organization.* San Francisco: Chandler Publishing Co.

Blaustein, Albert P. and Roy M. Mersky. 1978. *The First One-Hundred Justices: Statistical Studies of the United States Supreme Court.* Hamden, CT: Archon Books.

Bowen, Terry. 1995. "Consensual Norms and the Freshman Effect on t he United States Supreme Court." *Social Science Quarterly* 76:222-31.

Boyum, Keith O. and Lynn Mather, eds. 1983. *Empirical Theories About Courts*. New York: Longman Press.

Brace, Paul and Melinda Gann Hall. 1990. "Neo-Institutionalism and Dissent in State Supreme Courts." *Journal of Politics* 52:44-70.

Brace, Paul and Melinda Gann Hall. 1993. "Integrated Models of Judicial Dissent." *Journal of Politics* 55:914-35.

Brennan, William J. "In Defense of Dissents." *Hastings Law Journal* 37:427-438.

Brenner, Saul. 1982. "Fluidity on the Supreme Court, 1956-1967." *American Journal of Political Science* 26:388-90.

_____. 1997. "Error Correction on the U.S. Supreme Court: A View From the Clerks' Memos." *The Journal of Social Science* 34:1-9.

Brenner, Saul and Timothy Hagle. 1996. "Opinion Writing and the Acclimation Effect." *Political Behavior* 18:235-61.

Brenner, Saul and Jan Palmer. 1990. "The Law Clerks' Recommendations and Chief Justice Vinson's Vote on Certiorari." *American Politics Quarterly* 18:68-80.

Brisbin, Richard. 1997. *Justice Antonin Scalia and the Conservative Revival*. Baltimore: The Johns Hopkins University Press.

Caldeira, Gregory A. and Christopher J.W. Zorn. 1998. "Of Time and Consensual Norms in the United States Supreme Court." *American Journal of Political Science* 42:874-902.

Campbell, Angus, et al. 1960. *The American Voter*. New York: Wiley.

Canon, Bradley C. and Dean Jaros. 1970. "External Variables, Institutional Structure, and Dissent in State Supreme Courts." *Polity* 4:185-200.

Casper Gerhard and Richard Posner. 1976. Chicago: *The Workload of the United States Supreme Court*. Chicago: American Bar Foundation.

Chen, Jim. 1994. "The Mystery and Mastery of Judicial Power." *Missouri Law Review* 59:286.

Clark, Tom. 1959. "Internal Operations of the United States Supreme
Court." *Journal of the American Judicature Society* 43:45-48.

Clayton, Cornell W. and Howard Gillman, eds. 1999. *Supreme Court
Decision Making: New Institutionalist Approaches.* Chicago:
University of Chicago Press.

Cooper, Phillip J. 1995. *Battles on the Bench: Conflict Inside the
Supreme Court.* Lawrence, KS: University Press of Kansas.

Cushman, Clare, ed. 1995. *The Supreme Court Justices: Illustrated
Biographies, 1789-1995.* 2d edition. Washington, D.C.:
Congressional Quarterly.

Danelski, David. 1960. "The Influence of the Chief Justice in the
Decision Process" in *Courts, Judges, and Politics*, edited by C.
Hermann Pritchett. New York: Random House.

_____. 1964. *A Supreme Court Justice is Appointed.* New York:
MacMillan Publishers.

_____. 1986. "Causes and Consequences of Conflict and Its
Resolution in the Supreme Court" in *Judicial Conflict and
Consensus*, edited by Sheldon Goldman and Charles Lamb.
Lexington: University of Kentucky Press.

Distlear, Corey and Lawrence Baum. 2000. Selection of Law Clerks
and Polarization in the U.S. Supreme Court." *The Journal of
Politics* 63:871

Donahue, Sean. 1995. "Behind the Pillars: Remarks on the Law
Clerks." *The Long Term View: Massachusetts School of Law* 3:77-
84.

Downs, Anthony.1967. *Inside Bureaucracy.* Prospect Heights, IL:
Waveland Press.

Ducat, Craig. 1995. *Constitutional Interpretation.* St. Paul: West
Publishing.

Eisenstein, James and Herbery Jacob. 1977. *Felony Justice: An
Organizational Analysis of Criminal Courts.* Boston: Little, Brown
and Company.

Epstein, Lee, Jeffrey Segal, Harold Spaeth, and Thomas G. Walker.
1996. *The Supreme Court Compendium.* Washington, D.C.:
Congressional Quarterly, Inc.

_____. 1997. *The Supreme Court Compendium.* Washington,
D.C.: Congressional Quarterly, Inc.

Etzioni, Amitai. 1969. *The Semi-Professionals and Their Organization:
Teachers, Nurses, and Social Workers.* Ann Harbor, MI: Books on
Demand.

Fox, Harrison W. and Susan Webb Hammond. 1977. *Congressional
Staffs: The Invisible Force in American Lawmaking.* New York:
The Free Press.

Frank, John P. 1958. *The Marble Palace: The Supreme Court in
American Life.* New York: Alfred A. Knopf.

Freund. Paul A. 1972. *Report of the Study Group on the Caseload of
the Supreme Court.* Washington, D.C.: Federal Judicial Center.

Freund, Paul A. 1972. *The Supreme Court of the United States: Its
Business, Purposes, and Performance.* Gloucester, MA: World
Publishing Co.

Gadbois, George H. 1987. "The Institutionalization of the Supreme
Court of India." in *Comparative Judicial Systems: Challenging
Frontiers in Conceptual and Empirical Analysis,* edited by. John
R. Schmidhauser. London: Butterworths.

Gibson, James L. 1983. "From Simplicity to Complexity: The
Development of Theory in the Study of Judicial Behavior."
Political Behavior 5:7-49.

Gerber, Scott D. and Keeok Park. 1997. "The Quixotic Search for
Consensus on the United States Supreme Court: A Cross-Judicial
Empirical Analysis of the Rehnquist Court Justices." *American
Political Science Review* 91:390-408.

Gillman, Howard. 1996. "The New Institutionalism: Part I." *Law and
the Courts* Winter:6-11.

Ginsburg, Ruth Bader. 1992. "Speaking in a Judicial Voice." *New York
University Law Review* 67:1185-1209.

Glick, Henry R. 1986. "Dissent in State Supreme Courts: Patterns and
Correlates of Conflict" in *Judicial Conflict and Consensus:
Behavioral Studies of American Appellate Courts.* ed. Sheldon
Goldman and Charles Lamb. Lexington: The University Press of
Kentucky.

Goldman, Sheldon and Charles Lamb, ed. 1986. *Judicial Conflict and Consensus*. Lexington: University of Kentucky Press

Gortner, Harold F., Julianne Mahler, and Jeane Bell Nicholson. 1987. *Organizational Theory: A Public Perspective*. Chicago: The Dorsey Press.

Grambihler, Kenneth L. 1993. A Longitudinal Analysis of the Freshman Effect Hypothesis of United States Supreme Court Justices (1953-1988) terms. Ph.D. diss., Southern Illinois University.

Grambihler, Kenneth Lee and Albert P. Melone. 1998. "Initial Behavior of Newly Appointed Supreme Court Justices," *Illinois Political Science Review* 4:63-71.

Greene, Johnathon S. 1996. "Supreme Insights: Inside the Most Prestigious Judicial Clerkship of All." *Student Lawyer* 24:27-31.

Greenstein, Fred I. and Nelson W. Polsby, eds. 1975. *The Handbook of Political Science, Volume 5: Government Institutions and Processes*. Reading, MA: Addison-Wellesley.

Grumm, John G. 1971. "The Effects of Legislative Structure on Legislative Performance" in *State and Urban Politics*, edited by Richard I. Hofferbert and Ira Sharkansky. Boston: Little, Brown.

Gujarati, Damodar. 1995. *Basic Econometrics*. Third Edition. New York: McGraw-Hill, Inc.

Hall, Kermit, ed. 1992. *The Oxford Companion to the Supreme Court of the United States*. New York: Oxford University Press.

Hall, Melinda Gann and Paul Brace. 1992. "Toward an Integrated Model of Judicial Voting Behavior." *American Politics Quarterly* 20:147-69.

_____. 1989. "Order in the Courts: A Neoinstitutional Approach to Judicial Consensus." *Western Political Quarterly* 42:391-407.

Hall, Peter A. and C.R. Taylor. 1996. "Political Science and the Three New Institutionalism." *Political Studies* 44:936-57.

Hall, Richard H. 1968. "Professionalization and Bureaucratization." *American Sociological Review* 33:92-104.

Hare, Paul A., Edgar F. Borgatta, and Robert F. Bales 1965. *Small Groups: Studies in Social Interaction*. New York: Alfred Knopf.

Haynie, Stacia. 1992. "Leadership and Consensus on the U.S. Supreme Court." *Journal of Politics* 54:1158-69.

Heck, Edward V. and Melinda Gann Hall. 1981. "Bloc Voting and the Freshman Justice Revisited." *Journal of Politics* 43:853-860.

Holmes, Oliver Wendell, Jr. 1991. *The Common Law.* New York: Dover Publications, Inc.

Howard, J. Woodford. 1968. "On the Fluidity of Judicial Choice." *American Political Science Review* 62:43-56.

Hughes, Charles Evans. 1928. *The Supreme Court of the United States.* New York: Columbia University Press.

Huntington, Samuel. 1968. *Political Order in Changing Societies.* New Haven: Yale University Press.

Jacob, Hebert. 1983. "Court as Organizations" in *Empirical Theories About Courts*, edited by Keith O. Boyum and Lynn Mather. New York: Longman Press.

Kirman, Igor. 1995. "Standing Apart to Be Apart: The Precedential Value of Supreme Court Opinions." *Columbia Law Review* 95:2083-2119.

Kofmehls, Kenneth. 1977. *Professional Staff in Congress.* West Lafayette, IN: Purdue University Press.

Kolsky, Meredith. 1995. "Justice William Johnson and the History of Supreme Court Dissent." *Georgetown Law Journal* 83:2069-98.

Lazarus, Edward. 1998. *Closed Chambers: The Justices, Clerks and Political Agendas that Control the Supreme Court.* New York: Times Books.

—————————. 1998. *Closed Chambers: The First Eyewitness Account of the Epic Battles Inside the Supreme Court.* New York: Times Books.

Lesinski and Stockmeyer. 1973. "Prehearing Research and Screening in the Michigan Court of Appeals: One Court's Method for Increasing Judicial Productivity." *Vanderbilt Law Review* 26:1239-40.

Malbin, Michael W. 1979. *Unelected Representatives: Congressional Staff and the Future of Representative Government.* New York: Basic Books, Inc.

Maltzman, Forest and Paul J. Wahlbeck. 1996. "May it Please the Chief? Opinion Assignments in the Rehnquist Court." *American Journal of Political Science* 40:421-43.

Maltzman, Forrest, James F. Spriggs, and Paul J. Wahlbeck. 2000. *Crafting Law on the Supreme Court: The Collegial Game.* Cambridge, UK: Cambridge University Press.

March, James G. and Johan P. Olsen. 1984. "The New Institutionalism: Organizations in Political Life." *American Political Science Review* 78:734-49.

Mason, Alpheaus T. 1956. *Harlan Fiske Stone: Pillar of the Law.* New York: Viking Press.

Meier, Kenneth J. 1993. *Politics and the Bureaucracy: Politics and Policymaking in the Fourth Branch of Government.* Pacific Grove, CA: Brookes-Cole Publishers.

Melone, Albert P. 1990. "Revisiting the Freshman Effect Hypothesis: The First Two Terms of the Justice Anthony Kennedy." *Judicature* 74:6-13.

Mintzberg, Henry. 1979. *The Structuring of Organizations.* Englewood Cliffs, NJ: Prentice-Hall Publishers.

Mosher, Frederick. 1968. *Democracy and the Public Service.* New York: Oxford University Press.

_____. 1986. "The Professional State." in *Bureaucratic Power in National Policymaking,* Francis Rourke, ed. Boston: Little, Brown.

Murphy, Walter F. 1964. *The Elements of Judicial Strategy.* Chicago: The University of Chicago Press.

Murphy, Walter F. and Joseph Tanenhaus. 1972. *The Study of Public Law.* New York: Random House.

Newland, Chester A. 1961. "Personal Assistants to Supreme Court Justices: The Law Clerks." *Oregon Law Review* 40:299-317.

Nisbit, Robert. 1959. "Comment." *American Sociological Review* 24:1139-53.

Oakley, John Bilyeu and Robert S. Thompson. 1980. *Law Clerks and the Judicial Process: Perceptions of the Qualities and Functions of Law Clerks in American Courts.* Berkeley: University of California Press.

O'Brien, David M. 1990. *Storm Center: The Supreme Court in American Politics.* New York: W.W. Norton and Company.

_____. 1996. Storm Center: *The Supreme Court in American Politics.* New York: W.W. Norton and Company.

O'Connor, Karen and John R, Hermann. 1995. "The Law Clerk Connection. Appearances Before the Supreme Court By Former Law Clerks." *Judicature* 78:247-49.

Ostrum, Charles W. 1978. *Time Series Analysis: Regression Techniques.* Beverly Hills: Sage Publications, Inc.

Pacelle, Richard L. 1991. *The Transformation of the Supreme Court's Agenda.* Boulder, CO: Westview Press, Inc.

Paddock, Lisa. 1996. *Facts About the Supreme Court of the United States.* New York: H.W. Wilson Company.

Palmer, Jan and Saul Brenner. 1995. "The Law Clerks' Recommendations and the Conference Votes On-The-Merits." *The Justice System Journal* 18:185-97.

Parsons, Talcott. 1960. *Structure and Processes in Modern Societies.* New York: The Free Press.

Perry, H.W. 1992. "Certiorari, Writ of" in *The Oxford Companion to the Supreme Court of the United States,* edited by Kermit Hall. New York: Oxford University Press.

Polsby, Nelson. 1975. "Legislatures" in *The Handbook of Political Science, Volume 5: Government Institutions and Processes,* edited by Fred I. Greenstein and Nelson W. Polsby. Reading, MA: Addison-Wellesley.

Polsby, Nelson. 1987. "The Institutionalization of the U.S. House of Representatives" in *Congress: Structure and Policy,* edited by Mathew McCubbins and Terry Sullivan. Cambridge: Cambridge University Press.

Posner, Richard A. 1985. *The Federal Courts: Crisis and Reform.* Cambridge: Harvard University Press.

_____. 1996. *Federal Courts: Challenge and Reform.* Cambridge: Harvard University Press.

Pritchett, C. Herman. 1948. *The Roosevelt Court: A Study in Judicial Politics and Values.* 1937-1947. New York: MacMillan Publishers.

_____. 1969. "The Development of Judicial Research." in *Frontiers of Judicial Research*, edited by Joel B. Grossman and Joseph Tanenhaus. New York, John Wiley and Sons.

Provine, Doris. 1980. *Case Selection on the United States Supreme Court*. Chicago: University of Chicago Press.

Raelin, Joseph. 1991. *The Clash of Cultures: Managers Managing Professionals*. Cambridge: Harvard Business School Press.

Rehnquist, William H. 1957. "Who Writes the Opinions of the Supreme Court?" *U.S. News and World Report*, December 13, 74-5.

Rehnquist, William H. 1958. "Another View: Clerks Might 'Influence' Some Actions" *U.S. News and World Report*, February 21, 116.

_____. 1987. *The Supreme Court: How It Was, How It Is*. New York: William Morrow and Company.

Report of the Study Group on the Caseload of the Supreme Court. 1972. Washington, D.C.: Federal Judicial Center.

Riker, William H. 1980. "Implications from the Disequalibrium of Majority Rule for the Study of Institutions." *American Political Science Review* 74:444-45.

Ritzer, George. 1992. *Sociological Theory*. New York: McGraw-Hill, Inc.

Romzek, Barbara S. and Jennifer Utter. 1997. "Congressional Legislative Staff: Political Professionals or Clerks." *American Journal of Political Science* 41:1251-79.

Rostow, Eugene. 1967. "The Supreme Court as a Legal Institution." in *Perspectives on the Court*, edited by Max Freedman, William N. Beaney, and Eugene v. Rostow, Evanston: Northwestern University Press.

Rubin, Alvin B. and Laura B. Bartell. 1989. *The Law Clerk Handbook: A Handbook for Law Clerks to Federal Judges*. Washington, D.C.: Federal Judicial Center.

Rubin, Thea F. and Albert P. Melone. 1988. "Justice Antonin Scalia: A First Year Freshman Effect?" *Judicature* 72:98-102.

Rundquist, Paul S. Judy Schneider, and Frederick Pauls. *Congressional Legislative Staff: An Analysis of their Roles, Functions, and Impacts*, CRS Report to Congress. Library of Congress, Washington, D.C.

Salisbury, Robert H. and Kenneth A. Shepsle. 1981. "U.S. Congressmen as Enterprise." *Legislative Studies Quarterly* 6:559-76.

Schmidhauser, John R. 1973. "An Explanation of the Institutionalization of Legislatures and Judiciaries," in *Legislatures in Comparative Perspective*, edited by Allan Kornberg. New York: Oxford University Press.

Schubert, Glendon. 1965. *The Judicial Mind.* Evanston, IL: Northwestern University Press.

Schubert, Glendon and David Danelski, eds. 1969. *Comparative Judicial Behavior:Cross-Institutional Studies in Political Decision-Making in the East and West.* New York: Oxford University Press.

Schwartz, Bernard. 1983. *Super Chief: Earl Warren and His Supreme Court.* New York: New York University Press.

_____. 1993. *A History of the United States Supreme Court.* New York: Oxford University Press.

_____. 1996. *Decision: How the Supreme Court Decides Cases.* New York: Oxford University Press. New York: Oxford University Press.

_____. 1990. *The Ascent of Pragmatism: The Burger Court in Action.* Reading, MA: Addison-Wesley Publishing Co., Inc.

Schwartz, Bernard and Stephen Lesher. 1993. *Inside the Warren Court.* Garden City, NY: Doubleday and Company.

Segal, Jeffrey A. and Albert D. Cover. "Ideological Values and the Values of U.S. Supreme Court Justices." *American Political Science Review* 83:557-65.

Segal, Jeffery A., Lee Epstein, Charles Cameron, and Harold Spaeth. 1995. "Ideological Values and the Votes of Supreme Court Justices Revisited." *Journal of Politics* 57:812-23.

Segal, Jeffery A. and Harold J. Spaeth. 1993. *The Supreme Court and the Attitudinal Model.* New York: Cambridge University Press.

Selznick, Philip. 1948. "Foundations of the Theory of Organization." *American Sociological Review* 13:25-35.

_____. 1949. *The TVA and the Grass Roots: A Study of Politics and Organization.* Berkeley: The University of California Press.

Sharkansky, Ira. 1982. *Public Administration: Agendas, Policies, and Politics.* San Francisco: W.H. Freeman and Co.

Sheb, John A. and Lee W. Ailshie. 1985. "Justice Sandra Day O'Connor and the Freshman Effect." *Judicature* 69:9-12.

Shepsle, Kenneth and Barry R. Weingast. 1987. "The Institutional Foundations of Committee Power." *American Political Science Review* 81:85-104.

_____. 1994. "Positive Theories of Congressional Institutions." *Legislative Studies Quarterly* 19:149-79.

Simon, Herbert A. 1957. *Administrative Behavior: A Study in Decision Making Processes in Administrative Organization.* New York: The Free Press.

Smith, Rogers M. 1988. "Political Jurisprudence, the 'New Institutionalism,' and the Future of Public Law." *American Political Science Review* 82:89-108.

Snyder, Eloise. 1958. "The Supreme Court as a Small Group." *Social Forces* 36:232-38.

Songer, Donald R. 1982. "Consensual and Nonconsesnual Decisions in Unanimous Opinions of the U.S. Courts of Appeals." *American Political Science Review* 26:225-39.

Sprague, John. 1968. *Voting Patterns of the United States Supreme Court: Cases in Federalism.* Indianapolis: Bobbs-Merrill, Inc.

Squire, Peverill. 1992. "Legislative Professionalism and Membership Diversity in State Legislatures." *Legislative Studies Quarterly* 17:69-79.

Stack, Kevin M. 1996. "The Practice of Dissent in the Supreme Court." *Yale Law Journal* 105:2235-2259.

Stephens, Otis H. and John M. Sheb. 1999. *American Constitutional Law.* Belmont, CA: West/Wadsworth.

Stevens, John Paul. 1992. "Some Thoughts on Judicial Restraint" in Elliot Slotnick, ed. *Judicial Politics: Readings from Judicature.* Washington, D.C.: The American Judicature Society.

Stewart, Joseph and Edward Heck. 1985. "Caseloads and
    Controversies: A Different Perspective on the Overburdened U.S.
    Supreme Court." *Justice System Journal* 12:370-83.

Ulmer, S. Sidney. 1965. "Toward a Theory of Subgroup Formation in
    the United States Supreme Court." *Journal of Politics* 27:133-154.

Urofsky, Melvin I., ed. 1987. *The Douglas Letters: Selections from the
    Private Papers of Justice William O. Douglas.* Bethessda, MD:
    Adler and Adler Publishers, Inc.

U.S. House. 1974. Committee on Appropriations. *Hearings Before a
    Subcommittee of the Committee on Appropriations*, 94th Cong., 1st
    sess., 433. [Government Document Y4.Ap6/1:St2/976/pt.1]

U.S Senate. 1969. Committee on Appropriations. *Hearings Before a
    Subcommittee on Appropriations, State, Justice, Commerce, the
    Judiciary, and Related Agencies*, 90th Cong., 2d sess., 159.
    [Government Document Y4.Ap6/2:St2/976 pt.1]

Wahlbeck, Paul J., James F. Spriggs, and Forest Maltzman. 1996.
    "Marshalling the Court: Bargaining and Accommodation on the
    U.S. Supreme Court." Annual Meeting of the Western Political
    Science Association, San Francisco, March 14-16.

_____. 1999. "The Politics of Dissents and Concurrences on
    the U.S. Supreme Court." *American Politics Quarterly* 27:488.

Wald, Patricia M. 1990. "Selecting Law Clerks." *Michigan Law Review*
    89:152-163.

Walker, Thomas G., Lee Epstein, and William Dixon. 1988. "On the
    Mysterious Demise of Consensual Norms on the United States
    Supreme Court." *Journal of Politics* 50:361-89.

Wasby, Stephen L. 1988. *The Supreme Court in the Federal Judicial
    System.* Chicago: Nelson-Hall Publishers.

Weiden, David. 1998. "Conflicts and Cues: The Institutionalization of
    the Supreme Court Law Clerk and the Court's Agenda." Annual
    Meeting of the Midwest Political Science Association, Chicago, IL,
    April 23-26.

Wilkinson, J. Harvie. 1974. *Serving Justice: A Supreme Court Law
    Clerk's View.* New York: Charterhouse Publishers.

Wald, Patricia M. "Selecting Law Clerks." *Michigan Law Review*
89:154.

Wolin, Sheldon. 1960. *Politics and Vision*. Boston: Little, Brown.

Wood, Sandra L. 1998. "Bargaining on the Burger Court: Of Memos,
Changes and endorsements." Annual Meeting of the Midwest
Political Science Association, Chicago, IL, May 23-25.

Wood, Sandra L., Linda Camp Keith, Drew Lanier, and Oyo Ogundele.
1998. "'Acclimation Effect' on the U.S. Supreme Court: A
Replication." *American Journal of Political Science* 42:690-697.

Appendix A

Observations on Variables Used in Testing General Hypotheses H1 and H2

Year	Diss.	Conc.	S. Opin.	Op. For Ct	Tot. Opin.
1935	20	4	1	145	170
1936	17	2	2	149	170
1937	27	6	2	145	180
1938	29	5	12	136	182
1939	18	3	4	136	161
1940	25	4	6	158	193
1941	53	17	2	150	222
1942	59	22	11	140	232
1943	65	15	9	128	217
1944	64	26	13	157	260
1945	64	34	6	135	239
1946	78	29	3	142	252
1947	70	31	4	110	215
1948	90	32	4	114	240
1949	54	10	5	87	256
1950	54	32	4	91	181
1951	68	17	3	83	171
1952	90	24	5	104	223
1953	54	12	1	65	132
1954	45	14	1	78	138
1955	52	19	4	82	157
1956	62	24	0	100	186
1957	74	20	5	104	203
1958	56	28	11	99	194
1959	80	18	27	97	222
1960	94	33	16	110	253
1961	62	32	12	85	191
1962	65	33	11	110	219
1963	68	34	13	111	226
1964	58	45	14	91	208

Year	Diss.	Conc	S. Opin.	Opin. for Ct	Total Opin
1965	57	32	15	97	201
1966	74	30	14	100	218
1967	79	65	15	110	269
1968	77	48	19	99	243
1969	73	49	17	88	227
1970	91	63	28	109	291
1971	125	63	11	129	328
1972	140	46	31	140	357
1973	125	40	23	140	328
1974	88	34	26	123	271
1975	98	51	36	133	318
1976	117	47	66	126	356
1977	97	38	77	130	342
1978	90	44	56	130	320
1979	122	36	67	132	357
1980	92	35	68	123	318
1981	111	32	62	141	346
1982	114	27	69	164	374
1983	106	26	67	166	365
1984	101	30	50	151	332
1985	136	33	70	159	398
1986	127	65	20	153	365
1987	75	59	18	147	299
1988	98	73	9	149	329
1989	86	72	21	136	315
1990	78	45	15	127	265
1991	74	75	17	119	285
1992	65	59	17	116	257
1993	55	76	11	90	232
1994	52	50	8	87	197
1995	63	50	7	68	188

Year	Tot. Noncons Opin.	Clerks	Supp. Pers.	Ideology
1935	25	3	54.5	---
1936	21	5	156.9	---
1937	35	6	160.5	---
1938	46	10	172.8	---
1939	25	5	173.8	---
1940	35	6	176.8	---
1941	72	11	177.8	---
1942	92	6	179	---
1943	89	8	172.7	---
1944	103	6	144.5	---
1945	104	8	144.1	---
1946	110	9	133.4	.46
1947	105	13	142	.46
1948	126	14	151	.46
1949	69	16	157	.41
1950	90	15	159	.41
1951	88	16	162	.41
1952	119	18	162	.41
1953	67	18	163	.41
1954	60	18	163	.37
1955	75	17	162	.37
1956	86	18	162	.43
1957	99	17	163	.45
1958	95	19	163	.34
1959	125	18	164	.34
1960	143	18	164	.34
1961	106	19	166	.34
1962	109	21	168	.33
1963	115	19	168	.33
1964	117	16	168	.33
1965	104	20	189	.37
1966	118	17	189	.37
1967	159	21	190	.33
1968	114	18	190	.33

Year	Tot. Noncons. Opin.	Clerks	Supp. Pers.	Ideology.
1969	139	23	191	.59
1970	182	30	204	.69
1971	199	30	220	.78
1972	217	31	227	.78
1973	188	30	238	.78
1974	148	30	243	.78
1975	185	31	254	.78
1976	230	37	274	.78
1977	212	35	297	.78
1978	190	32	304	.78
1979	225	32	325	.78
1980	195	32	325	.78
1981	205	34	325	.74
1982	210	32	316	.74
1983	199	34	320	.74
1984	181	33	322	.74
1985	239	33	317	.74
1986	212	33	318	.77
1987	152	36	319	.68
1988	180	35	319	.68
1989	179	35	319	.68
1990	138	36	329	.38
1991	166	38	338	.48
1992	141	38	340	.48
1993	142	39	341	.53
1994	110	39	345	.60
1995	120	38	345	.60

Year	Py Comp.	Hughes	Stone	Vinson.	Warr.	Burger	Rehnq.
1935	5	1	0	0	0	0	0
1936	5	1	0	0	0	0	0
1937	6	1	0	0	0	0	0
1938	5*	1	0	0	0	0	0
1939	6	1	0	0	0	0	0
1940	6	1	0	0	0	0	0
1941	8	0	1	0	0	0	0
1942	8	0	1	0	0	0	0
1943	8	0	1	0	0	0	0
1944	8	0	1	0	0	0	0
1945	8	0	1	0	0	0	0
1946	8	0	0	1	0	0	0
1947	8	0	0	1	0	0	0
1948	8	0	0	1	0	0	0
1949	8	0	0	1	0	0	0
1950	8	0	0	1	0	0	0
1951	8	0	0	1	0	0	0
1952	8	0	0	1	0	0	0
1953	7	0	0	0	1	0	0
1954	6	0	0	0	1	0	0
1955	6	0	0	0	1	0	0
1956	6	0	0	0	1	0	0
1957	5	0	0	0	1	0	0
1958	5	0	0	0	1	0	0
1959	5	0	0	0	1	0	0
1960	5	0	0	0	1	0	0
1961	5	0	0	0	1	0	0
1962	6	0	0	0	1	0	0
1963	6	0	0	0	1	0	0
1964	6	0	0	0	1	0	0
1965	5	0	0	0	1	0	0
1966	5	0	0	0	1	0	0
1967	6	0	0	0	1	0	0
1968	6	0	0	0	1	0	0

Appendix A

Year	Py Comp.	Hughes	Stone	Vinson	Warren	Burger	Rehnq
1969	6	0	0	0	0	1	0
1970	5	0	0	0	0	1	0
1971	5	0	0	0	0	1	0
1972	5	0	0	0	0	1	0
1973	5	0	0	0	0	1	0
1974	5	0	0	0	0	1	0
1975	5	0	0	0	0	1	0
1976	5	0	0	0	0	1	0
1977	5	0	0	0	0	1	0
1978	5	0	0	0	0	1	0
1979	5	0	0	0	0	1	0
1980	5	0	0	0	0	1	0
1981	5	0	0	0	0	1	0
1982	5	0	0	0	0	1	0
1983	5	0	0	0	0	1	0
1984	5	0	0	0	0	1	0
1985	5	0	0	0	0	1	0
1986	5	0	0	0	0	0	1
1987	6	0	0	0	0	0	1
1988	6	0	0	0	0	0	1
1989	6	0	0	0	0	0	1
1990	7	0	0	0	0	0	1
1991	8	0	0	0	0	0	1
1992	8	0	0	0	0	0	1
1993	8	0	0	0	0	0	1
1994	7	0	0	0	0	0	1
1995	7	0	0	0	0	0	1

Year	Turn.	Inex.	Civil Lib. Cases	C. Lib Change	Caseload	Case Filings
1935	0	0	5.8	---	187	1092
1936	0	0	6.8	1.0	180	1052
1937	1	1	10.3	3.5	180	1091
1938	1	2	8.7	-1.6	174	1020
1939	1	4	9.0	0.3	151	1078
1940	1	4	9.1	0.1	195	1109
1941	2	5	13.3	4.2	175	1302
1942	0	3	20.7	7.4	196	1118
1943	1	4	14.3	-6.4	154	1118
1944	0	1	11.2	-3.1	199	1393
1945	1	2	15.5	4.3	170	1460
1946	1	2	17.8	2.3	190	1678
1947	0	2	31.3	13.5	143	1470
1948	0	1	24.6	-6.7	147	1605
1949	2	2	26.1	1.5	108	1448
1950	0	2	24.0	-2.1	114	1335
1951	0	2	36.7	12.7	96	1368
1952	0	0	28.9	-7.8	122	1437
1953	1	1	28.0	-0.9	84	1463
1954	1	1	24.4	-0.36	86	1566
1955	1	2	23.9	-0.5	103	1856
1956	1	1	28.2	4.3	112	2052
1957	2	3	40.4	12.2	125	2008
1958	1	2	33.4	-7.0	116	2062
1959	0	3	30.3	-3.1	110	2178
1960	0	1	49.2	18.9	125	2313
1961	0	1	34.0	-15.2	100	2585
1962	1	2	35.8	1.8	129	2824
1963	1	2	44.1	83	123	2779
1964	0	2	42.2	1.9	103	2662
1965	1	1	38.6	3.6	120	3284
1966	0	1	48.8	10.2	132	3356
1967	1	2	58.4	9.6	156	3686

Year	Turn	Inex.	Civil Lib. Cases	C. Lib. Change	Caseload	CaseFilings
1968	0	1	61.1	2.7	116	3918
1969	1	1	51.8	-9.3	105	4202
1970	1	1	60.3	8.5	137	4212
1971	0	2	66.1	5.8	140	4533
1972	2	2	54.8	-11.3	159	4640
1973	0	2	58.9	4.1	161	5079
1974	0	3	51.3	-7.6	144	4668
1975	1	3	51.1	-.20	160	4761
1976	0	1	60.4	9.3	154	4730
1977	0	1	50.7	-9.7	153	4704
1978	0	1	55.3	4.6	153	4731
1979	0	0	51	-4.3	143	4781
1980	0	0	44.1	-6.9	144	5144
1981	1	1	49.6	5.5	170	5311
1982	0	1	48.2	-1.4	174	5079
1983	0	1	58.8	10.6	174	5100
1984	0	0	55.6	-3.2	159	5006
1985	0	0	64.8	9.2	161	5158
1986	1	0	55.1	-9.7	164	5134
1987	0	1	51.4	-3.7	151	5268
1988	1	2	60.5	9.1	156	5657
1989	0	1	55.9	-4.6	143	5746
1990	1	2	49.2	-6.7	121	6516
1991	1	3	46.1	-3.1	120	6770
1992	0	2	53.1	7.0	111	7245
1993	1	2	50.0	-3.1	93	7786
1994	1	2	46.1	-3.9	91	8100
1995	0	2	52.2	6.1	87	7565

* Although he identified himself as an Independent, Paddock identifies Felix Frankfurter as a Democrat. This characterization is consistent with Segal and Cover's decision to assign Frankfurter an ideological value of 0.33 (see Appendix B). Cushing explains that prior to coming to the Court Frankfurter was associated with liberal causes such as the legal defense of

communists, the NAACP, and the American Civil Liberties Union. Cushing also notes that Frankfurter was active in labor movements aimed at securing minimum wage and maximum hour legislation. See Clare Cushman, ed., *The Supreme Court Justices: Illustrated Biographies*, 1789-1995. 2d edition. (Washington, D.C.: Congressional Quarterly, Inc.), p. 387-388.

Appendix B

Calculation of the Ideological Heterogeneity Score

The following are the ideology values assigned to the justices by Segal and Cover.[19] The numbers in parentheses are the ideological heterogeneity scores I calculated using Segal and Cover's ideology values. Recall from the discussion in Chapter 5 that the ideological heterogeneity score for each term is equal to the standard deviation of ideological values for the justices serving in each term.

The ideological values calculated by Segal and Cover reflect the results of content analysis of newspaper editorials written during the period between each justice's nomination and the final confirmation vote of the Senate. The authors employed three coders to content analyze editorials in two newspapers with a liberal stance (the *New York Times* and the *Washington Post*) and two newspapers with a more conservative stance (the Chicago Tribune and the Los Angeles Times).[20] The coders identified the frequency of statements that indicated the nominee held liberal, moderate, or conservative views. Liberal statements include those indicating the nominee's support for the rights of women, criminal defendants, racial minorities, and the interests of individuals in First Amendment cases. Statements were regarded as conservative if indicating that the nominee held a view opposite to those values in the liberal category. An editorial statement was considered to have reflected a nominee's moderate stance if explicit references were made to the nominees moderate views.[21] Inter-coder reliability was determined using a 25% random sample of the data collected via content analysis and calculation of the *pi* statistic as an index of reliability. For the *pi* statistic

---

[19]Jeffrey A. Segal and Albert D. Cover, "Ideological Values and Votes of U.S. Supreme Court Justices," *American Political Science Review* 83 (1989):

[20]Segal and Cover, "Ideological Values and Votes," p. 559.

[21]Ibid., p. 559.

the authors report a result of 0.72 (significant at .001 level).[22]

Segal and Cover determined each justice's ideology score according to the following formula:

Justice Ideology = (liberal - conservative statements) / (liberal + moderate + conservative statements)

In short, each justice's ideology score is some number ranging from - 1.0 for justices regarded as unanimously conservative to +1.0 for justices regarded as unanimously liberal. A score of 0.0 is calculated for those justice regarded as moderate.

Segal and Cover use these ideology values to test the attitudinal model. In response to the criticism that the attitudinal model suffers from a circularity problem, namely that the model uses votes in previous cases to predict votes in subsequent cases, the authors employ ideology scores in an effort to devise a measure of attitudes based on data unrelated to votes. Further, Segal and Cover use the ideological scores to predict subsequent voting behavior. Segal and Cover report a correlation between the ideological scores of the justices and their votes in civil liberties and cases during the 1953-1987 period of 0.80.[23] Using the Segal and Cover ideology scores, Segal and Spaeth calculated a correlation between the justice's ideology and votes of 0.79. [24]

Ideology Scores and Ideological Heterogeneity Scores

1946	(.46)
Vinson	.50
Black	.75

---

[22]Ibid., p. 559.

[23]Ibid., p. 559.

[24]Jeffrey A. Segal and Harold J. Spaeth, *The Supreme Court and the Attitudinal Model*, (Cambridge: Cambridge University Press, 1993), p. 228.

Reed	.45
Frankfurter	.33
Douglas	.46
Murphy	1.0
Jackson	1.0
Rutledge	1.0
Burton	-0.44

1947   (0.46)
Membership is identical to 1946.

1948   (0.46)
Membership is identical to 1946.

1949   (0.41)

Vinson	.50
Black	.75
Reed	.45
Frankfurter	.33
Douglas	.46
Jackson	1.0
Burton	-0.44
Clark	0.0
Minton	0.44

1950   (0.41)
Membership is identical to 1949.

1951   (0.41)
Membership is identical to 1949.

1952   (0.41)
Membership is identical to 1949.

1953	(0.41)
Warren	.50
Black	.75
Reed	.45
Frankfurter	.33
Douglas	.46
Jackson	1.0
Burton	-0.44
Clark	0.0
Minton	.44

1954	(0.37)
Warren	.50
Black	.75
Reed	.45
Frankfurter	.33
Douglas	.46
Jackson	Died, October 1945
Burton	-0.44
Clark	0.0
Minton	.44

(Harlan was seated on March 28, 1955 and served only in the final three months of the 1954 term. He is therefore excluded from calculations for the 1954 term. Note, however, that inclusion of Harlan does not change the value of the ideological heterogeneity score. Including Harlan produces an ideological heterogeneity score of 0.3740. Excluding Harlan produces a score of 0.3679. When rounded to two decimal places both scores equal 0.37.)

1955	(0.37)

Membership identical to 1954

1956	(0.43)
Warren	.50
Black	.75

Reed	.45 (Retired, February 1957)
Frankfurter	.33
Douglas	.46
Burton	-.44
Clark	0.0
Minton	Retired, October, 1956
Harlan	.75
Brennan	1.00 (Seated, October 1956)

1957	(0.45)
Warren	.50
Black	.75
Frankfurter	.33
Douglas	.46
Burton	-.44
Clark	0.0
Harlan	.75
Brennan	1.00
Whittaker	0.0

1958	(0.34)
Warren	.50
Black	.75
Frankfurter	.33
Douglas	.46
Clark	0.0
Harlan	.75
Brennan	1.00
Whittaker	0.0
Stewart	.50 (Recess appointment, October 1958)

1959   (0.34)
Membership identical to 1958.

1960   (0.34)
Membership identical to 1958.

1961   (0.34)
Ideological heterogeneity values is identical to 1960. Whittaker retired in April 1962 and is included in the calculation of the heterogeneity score for the 1961 term. White replaced Whittaker in April 1962 and is not included in the calculations for the 1961 term.

1962   (0.33)
Warren   .50
Black   .75
Douglas   .46
Clark   0.0
Harlan   .75
Brennan   1.00
Stewart   .50
White   0.0
Goldberg   .50 (Seated, October 1962)
(Frankfurter retired August, 1962)

1963   (0.33)
Membership identical to 1962.

1964   (0.33)
Membership identical to 1962.

1965   (0.37)
Warren   .50
Black   .75
Douglas   .46
Clark   0.0
Harlan   .75
Brennan   1.00
Stewart   .50
White   0.0
Fortas   1.0

<u>1966</u>   (0.37)
Membership identical to 1965

<u>1967</u>	(0.33)
Warren	.50
Black	.75
Douglas	.46
Harlan	.75
Brennan	1.00
Stewart	.50
White	0.0
Fortas	1.0
Marshall	1.0

(Clark retired June 1967)

<u>1968</u>   (0.33)
Membership identical to 1967.

<u>1969</u>	(0.59)
Burger	-.77
Black	.75
Douglas	.46
Harlan	.75
Brennan	1.00
Stewart	.50
White	0.0
Marshall	1.0

(Thornberry, Haynsworth and Carswell were nominated by Nixon to replace Fortas. None were confirmed to serve in the 1969 term)

(Blackmun seated June 1970)

<u>1970</u>	(0.69)
Burger	-.77
Black	.75
Douglas	.46

Harlan	.75
Brennan	1.00
Stewart	.50
White	0.0
Marshall	1.0
Blackmun	-.77

1971	(0.78)
Burger	-.77
Douglas	.46
Brennan	1.00
Stewart	.50
White	0.0
Marshall	1.0
Blackmun	-.77
Powell	-.67 (Seated, January 7, 1972)
Rehnquist	-.91 (Seated, January 7, 1972)

(Harlan retired September 1971
(Black retired September 1971)

1972	(0.78)

Membership identical to 1971.

1973	(0.78)

Membership identical to 1971.

1974	(0.78)

Membership identical to 1971.

1975	((0.78)
Burger	-.77
Brennan	1.0
Stewart	.50
White	0.0
Marshall	1.0
Blackmun	-.77

Powell   -.67
Rehnquist   -.91
Stevens   -.50 (Seated December 19, 1975)
(Douglas retired November 1975)

<u>1976</u>   (0.78)
Membership identical to 1975.

<u>1977</u>   (0.78)
Membership identical to 1975.

<u>1978</u>   (0.78)
Membership identical to 1975

<u>1979</u>   (0.78)
Membership identical to 1975

<u>1980</u>   (0.78)
Membership identical to 1975

<u>1981</u>   (0.74)
Burger   -.77
Brennan   1.0
White   0.0
Marshall   1.0
Blackmun   -.77
Powell   -.67
Rehnquist   -.91
Stevens   -.50
O'Connor   -.17 (Seated, September 1981)
(Stewart retired June 1981)

<u>1982</u>   (0.74)
Membership is identical to 1981.

<u>1983</u>   (0.74)
Membership is identical to 1981.

<u>1984</u>   (0.74)
Membership is identical to 1981.

<u>1985</u>   (0.74)
Membership is identical to 1981.

<u>1986</u>	(0.77)
Rehnquist	-.91
Brennan	1.0
White	0.0
Marshall	1.0
Blackmun	-.77
Powell	-.67
Stevens	-.50
O'Connor	-.17
Scalia	-1.0

<u>1987</u>	(0.68)
Rehnquist	-.91
Brennan	1.0
White	0.0
Marshall	1.0
Blackmun	-.77
Stevens	-.50
O'Connor	-.17
Scalia	-1.0
Kennedy	-.27 (Seated, February 18, 1988)

(Powell retired June 1987)

<u>1988</u>   (0.68)
Membership identical to 1987.

<u>1989</u>   (0.68)
Membership identical to 1987.

<u>1990</u>   (0.38)
Rehnquist   -.91
White   0.0
Marshall   1.0
Blackmun   -.77
Stevens   -.50
O'Connnor   -.17
Scalia   -1.0
Kennedy   -.27
Souter   -.34

<u>1991</u>   (0.48)
Rehnquist   -.91
White   0.0
Blackmun   -.77
Stevens   -.50
O'Connnor   -.17
Scalia   -1.0
Kennedy   -.27
Souter   -.34
Thomas   -.68 (Seated, November 1991)
(Marshall retired October 1991)

<u>1992</u>   (0.48)
Membership identical to 1991.

<u>1993</u>   (0.53)
Rehnquist   -.91
Blackmun   -.77
Stevens   -.50
O'Connnor   -.17
Scalia   -1.0
Kennedy   -.27

Souter	-.34
Thomas	-.68
Ginsburg	.36

1994	(0.60)
Rehnquist	-.91
Stevens	-.50
O'Connnor	-.17
Scalia	-1.0
Kennedy	-.27
Souter	-.34
Thomas	-.68
Ginsburg	.36
Breyer	-.05

1995	(0.60)

Membership identical to 1994.

Index

Princeton University Library

32101 055285181

PRINCETON UNIVERSITY LIBRARY

This book is due on the latest date
stamped below. Please return or renew
by this date.

JUN 15 2006

JUN 15 2006

APR 10 2011